A Dictionary of
South African History

A Dictionary of South African History

Christopher Saunders
& Nicholas Southey

David Philip
Cape Town & Johannesburg

Published 1998 in southern Africa by David Philip Publishers (Pty) Ltd, 208 Werdmuller Centre, Newry Street, Claremont 7708 South Africa

This work will be published in hardback by Scarecrow Press in the United States in 1999 as *A Historical Dictionary of South Africa.*

© 1998 Christopher Saunders and Nicholas Southey

ISBN 0 86486 414 0

Cover design Abdul Amien

Printed in South Africa by Creda Press, Eliot Avenue, Epping, Cape Town

contents

preface

This dictionary is a substantially revised, rewritten and updated version of my *Historical Dictionary of South Africa*, which was first published in hardback in the United States in the 1980s. I am delighted that a South African publisher has agreed to bring out this new edition for the South African market. In preparing it I have had the help of Nicholas Southey of the University of South Africa, who has revised many of the old entries and written some of the new ones. I have added brief bibliographical references.

Asterisks indicate other relevant entries, but have been used sparingly. Inevitably, the choice of what to include is our own, but we hope that the text will prove a useful guide to some of the more significant events, personalities and processes in South African history, and will stimulate further reading.

My thanks to David Worth and Richard Mendelsohn for scanning material from the first edition for me. Robert Shell and Mohamed Adhikari kindly looked through a draft of the revised text. Pam made sure my mind was not entirely focused on the past when I was working on this project.

Christopher Saunders
Cape Town
April 1998

abbreviations

AG	Administrator-General (South West Africa/Namibia)
AMEC	African Methodist Episcopal Church
ANC	African National Congress
APLA	Azanian People's Liberation Army
AWB	Afrikaner Weerstandsbeweging (Afrikaner Resistance Movement)
BC	Black Consciousness
BPC	Black People's Convention
CA	Constitutional Assembly
C-in-C	Commander-in-Chief
CCB	Civil Co-operation Bureau
CI	Christian Institute
CODESA	Convention for a Democratic South Africa
COSAG	Concerned South Africans Group
COSATU	Congress of South African Trade Unions
CLPP	Coloured Labour Preference Policy
CRC	Coloured Persons Representative Council
CP	Conservative Party; Communist Party
DP	Democratic Party
DRC	Dutch Reformed Church
GNU	Government of National Unity
HNP	Herenigde Nasionale Party; Herstigte Nasionale Party
ICU	Industrial and Commercial Workers' Union
IFP	Inkatha Freedom Party
KTC	Kakaza Trading Centre (Crossroads, Cape Town)
LMS	London Missionary Society
MDM	Mass Democratic Movement
MK	Umkhonto weSizwe
MP	member of parliament
MPLA	Popular Movement for the Liberation of Angola
NGK	Nederduitse Gereformeerde Kerk
NP	National Party
NRC	Natives Representative Council
NSMS	National Security Management System
NUSAS	National Union of South African Students
OFS	Orange Free State
PAC	Pan Africanist Congress of Azania
PEBCO	Progressive Federal Party
RDP	Reconstruction and Development Programme
SA	South Africa
SAAF	South African Air Force
SACP	South African Communist Party
SADC	Southern African Development Community

SADF	South African Defence Force
SANNC	South African Native National Congress
SAP	South African Police
SAR	South African Republic
SSC	State Security Council
SWAPO	South West African People's Organization
SASCO	South African Students' Organization
TEC	Transitional Executive Council
TRC	Truth and Reconciliation Commission
TUCSA	Trade Union Congress of South Africa
UDF	United Democratic Front
UN	United Nations
UNITA	National Union for the Total Independence of Angola
UP	United Party
VAT	value-added tax
VOC	Verenigde Oost-Indische Compagnie

chronology

2.5 – 3 million years BP	Beginning of Early Stone Age
1 – 3 million years BP	*Australopithecus africanus* lives in southern Africa
90,000 – 1 million years BP	*Homo erectus* lives in southern Africa, mastering the use of fire and shaping stone implements
30,000 – 100,000 years BP	Middle Stone Age; *Homo sapiens* lives in southern Africa
26,000 BP	Earliest dated rock art
20,000 BP	Late Stone Age begins
15,000 BP	San hunter-gatherers widely distributed in southern Africa
2200 BP	Some San in northern Botswana acquire domestic livestock and move south, becoming known as Khoikhoi hunter-herders
3rd century	Iron-using cultivators establish themselves south of the Limpopo River; beginning of Early Iron Age
6th century	Lydenburg Heads indicate ritual practices among Early Iron Age people
7th century	Early Iron Age sites stretch along south-eastern coast as far south as Mpame in Transkei
10th century	Beginnings of Late Iron Age and more concentrated settlement on the highveld interior
1250–1400	Mapungubwe the dominant power in the Limpopo River valley
1300–1500	Sotho–Tswana speakers settle widely across highveld interior; Nguni-speakers settle along south-eastern coast and in the Drakensberg; Khoisan established as dominant society in the southern and south-western Cape
1488	Portuguese navigator Bartolomeu Dias rounds the Cape, opening sea route from Europe to the East
1497	Portuguese fleet under Vasco da Gama sails along South African coast on its way to India; first detailed information on the indigenous inhabitants transmitted to Europe
1510	Portuguese viceroy Almeida killed in skirmish with Khoikhoi in Table Bay
1590s	Dutch and English ships begin to put in regularly in Table Bay and trade with Khoikhoi
1652	(6 April) Dutch East India Company (VOC) refreshment station founded on the shores of Table Bay by Jan van Riebeeck

1657	First free burghers exempted from VOC service to farm along the banks of the Liesbeek River
1658	First party of slaves arrive at Cape
1659	First Dutch–Khoikhoi war
1673–1677	Second Dutch–Khoikhoi war
1679	Land granted to white farmers in Stellenbosch district
1688	Arrival of Huguenots from France
c.1690s	Trekboer movement begins into the Cape interior
1702	Whites travelling east from the Cape first meet Bantu-speaking Africans near Somerset East
1713	Smallpox epidemic decimates Khoikhoi
1717	VOC decides not to grant further freehold land, only loan farms
1745	District of Swellendam established
c.1775	Death of Phalo; Xhosa divided between Gcaleka and Rharhabe
1775	Upper Fish and Bushmans rivers declared Cape's eastern border
1778	Fish River proclaimed Cape's eastern border
1779	First Cape–Xhosa frontier war
1786	Graaff-Reinet district established
1793	H.C.D. Maynier appointed landdrost of Graaff-Reinet; second Cape–Xhosa war
1795	First British occupation of the Cape; Maynier driven out of Graaff-Reinet
1799–1802	Khoisan rebellion in Cape eastern districts
1803–1806	Cape under Batavian regime
1806	(January) Second British occupation
1808	Abolition of slave trade
1809	Caledon code to regulate Khoisan labour
1811–1812	War to expel Xhosa from Zuurveld
1812	Apprenticeship ordinance
1814	Netherlands cedes Cape to Britain
c.1817	Ndwandwe under Zwide defeat Mthethwa; Dingiswayo killed
1817	Cape Governor Somerset's alliance with Ngqika

*c.*1818	Dingiswayo of the Mthethwa defeated by Zwide of the Ndwandwe
1818	Battle of Amalinde; Ndlambe defeats Ngqika
1819	Cape–Xhosa war; Somerset demands the 'ceded territory'
*c.*1819	Shaka's Zulu defeat the Ndwandwe at Gqokoli Hill
1820	Almost 5000 British settlers arrive in Algoa Bay
*c.*1822	Ngwane crosses Drakensberg and enters Caledon River valley
*c.*1823	Mzilikazi moves north of the Vaal River
1823	(June) Griqua and Tlhaping defeat the Kololo at Battle of Dithakong; slave conditions at the Cape ameliorated
1824	Cape traders settle at Port Natal
*c.*1824	Moshoeshoe moves to Thaba Bosiu
1825	Slave revolt in Worcester district
1827	Cape Charter of Justice
1828	Ngwane defeated by the British and Thembu at Battle of Mbholompo; Ordinance 50; death of Shaka
1829	Establishment of the Kat River Settlement
1833	French missionaries join Moshoeshoe
1834	First legislative council at the Cape; (December) slaves emancipated; beginning of four-year 'apprenticeship'; war on Cape eastern frontier
1835	Hintsa, Xhosa paramount, held captive by British army and murdered when he tries to escape; beginning of Great Trek; Mfengu move into Cape Colony, D'Urban's annexation of Queen Adelaide Province
1836	Battle of Vegkop; Voortrekkers defeat Mzilikazi's Ndebele
1836	Queen Adelaide Province is given up
1837	Ndebele leave Transvaal; Voortrekkers enter Natal under Piet Retief
1838	The 'apprenticeship' of ex-slaves ends; the Zulu ruler Dingane massacres Retief's party; the establishment of the Republic of Natalia; the Battle of Blood River; Potgieter founds Potchefstroom
1840	Mpande and the Voortrekkers overthrow Dingane
1841	Cape Masters and Servants Ordinance; the Natal Volksraad resolves to move 'surplus' Africans south of Natal
1843	British annexation of Natal; Napier signs treaties with Adam Kok and Moshoeshoe; the Napier line defines Moshoeshoe's territory

1844	Potgieter founds Ohrigstad
1845	Shepstone appointed Diplomatic Agent in Natal
1846–1847	War of the Axe on the Cape frontier
1847	Annexation of British Kaffraria
1848	Annexation of Transorangia (the Orange River Sovereignty)
1849	Founding of Lydenburg
1850–1853	War of Mlanjeni on the Cape frontier; Kat River Settlement rebellion
1852	Sand River Convention
1853	Grant of representative government to the Cape
1854	Bloemfontein Convention; creation of the Orange Free State; first meeting of the Cape parliament; Boer commandos lay siege to Ndebele community who took refuge in a cave under Makopane
1856	Cape Masters and Servants Act; representative government granted to Natal; Zulu civil war
1856–1857	Xhosa cattle-killing; famine follows mass slaughter of cattle and burning of crops
1858	First Free State–Sotho war
1860	First indentured Indian labourers arrive in Natal
1861	Griqua leave Philippolis to cross Drakensberg
1864	Brand elected President of the Orange Free State
1865	Death of Mswati of Swaziland
1865–1866	Second Free State–Sotho war
1866	British Kaffraria joined to Cape Colony
1867	Boers abandon Schoemansdal; discovery of diamonds in Griqualand West
1868	High Commissioner Wodehouse annexes Basutoland
1869	Treaty of Aliwal North sets Basutoland's boundaries; diamond digging begins at what is to become Kimberley
1870	Death of Moshoeshoe; diamond rush
1871	British annexation of Griqualand West
1872	Cape granted responsible government; death of Mpande; pass laws on diamond fields
1873	Langalibalele revolt in Natal

1874	Lord Carnarvon becomes Secretary of State for Colonies
1875	Formation of Die Genootskap van Regte Afrikaners in Paarl to campaign for recognition of Afrikaans; Carnarvon proposes confederation
1876	War between the South African Republic and the Pedi; Carnarvon's conference on confederation in London
1877	Frere appointed Governor and High Commissioner
1877	Shepstone proclaims British annexation of the Transvaal; the South Africa Act provides for confederation
1877–1878	Cape–Xhosa frontier war
1878	Resignation of Lord Carnarvon as Secretary of State for Colonies
1879	Anglo-Zulu war; battles of Isandlwana and Ulundi; British army moves to conquer Pedi; defeat of Sekhukhune, Pedi ruler
1880	Transkeian rebellion; Gun War in Basutoland; Britain abandons attempt to bring about a confederation; annexation of Griqualand West to Cape Colony
1880–1881	Transvaal war of independence
1881	Defeat of British forces at Majuba; Pretoria Convention grants Transvaal limited self-rule
1882	Imbumba yama Nyama formed in eastern Cape
1883	Kruger elected State President of the Transvaal
1884	Britain assumes direct rule of Basutoland; London Convention; *Imvo Zabantsundu* started by Jabavu
1885	Annexation of Bechuanaland
1886	Discovery of main gold reef on Witwatersrand on the farm Langlaagte; founding of Johannesburg
1887	British annexation of Zululand; King Dinuzulu deported; Cape Parliamentary Voters Registration Act declares that Africans who own land communally do not qualify for the franchise
1888	De Beers Consolidated Mines controls all diamond mining in Kimberley; Brand succeeded by Reitz as President of the Orange Free State
1890	Cecil Rhodes becomes Prime Minister of Cape
1892	Cape Franchise and Ballot Act raises property qualifications for franchise; Ethiopian Church founded; railway reaches Johannesburg
1893	Natal granted responsible government; Mohandas Gandhi arrives in South Africa
1894	Passage of Glen Grey Act at Cape; Cape annexation of Pondoland; Natal

Indian Congress founded

1895   British Bechuanaland added to Cape; (December) Jameson crosses border of Transvaal with an armed force

1896   (January) the fiasco of the Jameson Raid causes Rhodes's resignation as Prime Minister; Steyn elected President of the Orange Free State; Ethiopian church joins African Methodist Episcopal Church

1896   Indians in Natal disqualified from voting and a limit set on future immigration of Indians

1896–1897 Rinderpest epidemic spreads through southern Africa

1897   Annexation of Zululand to Natal; Alfred Milner appointed High Commissioner; Enoch Sontonga writes 'Nkosi Sikelel' iAfrika'

1899   Bloemfontein conference between Milner and Kruger fails; (October) Transvaal and Orange Free State declare war on Britain

1900   (January) battle of Spion Kop; (February) surrender of Cronje at Paardeberg, relief of Ladysmith; (March) capture of Bloemfontein; (May) relief of Mafeking; annexation of Orange Free State, renamed Orange River Colony; Roberts captures Johannesburg; (June) Roberts captures Pretoria; (October) Kruger sails for France; formal proclamation of annexation of Transvaal; (November) Kitchener succeeds Roberts as Commander-in-Chief in South Africa.

1901   (January) Smuts captures Modderfontein; massacre of Africans; (February) De Wet's 'invasion' of Cape Colony; abortive Middelburg peace talks between Kitchener and Botha; (March) Cape Town's Africans moved forcibly to Uitvlugt (Ndabeni); (August) Kitchener's proclamation of banishment for captured Boer leaders

1901–1902 Tens of thousands of Boers and Africans die in concentration camps

1902   (March) Death of Rhodes; (April) Boer peace delegates meet at Pretoria; (May) meeting of Boer delegates at Vereeniging; (31 May) surrender terms signed in Pretoria

1904–1907 Importation of Chinese labour to the gold mines

1905   South African Native Affairs Commission reports; strike of Chinese labourers at the North Randfontein mine; School Boards Act segregates Cape schools; Africans permitted to buy land in Transvaal; much of Zululand given to white farmers; poll tax introduced in Natal

1906   Bambatha Rebellion in Natal crushed brutally; passive resistance in Transvaal by Indians

1907   Transvaal and Orange River Colony granted responsible government; white miners' strike on Witwatersrand

1908–1909 National Convention meets to consider terms of unification

1909 South Africa Bill passed by British parliament; Indian passive resistance in Transvaal; (white) Labour Party founded

1910 (31 May) Union of South Africa comes into being; Louis Botha becomes first Prime Minister

1911 Mines and Works Act provides for mine job reservation

1912 (January) South African Native National Congress (SANNC) formed, with Dube first president; South African Races Congress formed under Jabavu; (December) Hertzog ousted from Botha's cabinet

1913 (June) Natives Land Act: Africans not allowed to own or rent land outside designated reserves (7% of land); sharecropping illegal; white miners strike on Witwatersrand; Indian passive resistance; African women demonstrate against passes in Free State

1914 Strike by white miners; National Party (NP) founded in Bloemfontein; SANNC delegation goes to England to protest against the Natives Land Act; Gandhi returns to India; Afrikaner Rebellion

1915 South African forces occupy German South West Africa

1916 South African Native College opened; (July) Battle of Delville Wood; report of the Natives Land (Beaumont) Commission

1917 Industrial Workers of Africa founded; the birth of Anglo American Corporation

1918 Strike by African sanitation workers in Johannesburg; Afrikaner Broederbond founded; Spanish flu epidemic

1919 Industrial and Commercial Workers' Union (ICU) formed; Botha dies; Smuts becomes Prime Minister; Union parliament accepts mandate for South West Africa

1920 African mineworkers strike; African demonstrators shot in Port Elizabeth

1921 (May) 183 Israelites shot at Bulhoek, near Queenstown in the Cape; (July) formation of Communist Party (CP)

1922 (January) white miners strike; (March) Rand Revolt; Stallard Commission reports

1923 SANNC changes name to African National Congress (ANC); Natives (Urban Areas) Act provides for locations for Africans in urban areas

1924 NP and Labour pact wins election; Hertzog becomes Prime Minister; Industrial Conciliation Act provides for job reservation

1925 Wage Act; South Africa on gold standard; Afrikaans replaces Dutch as official language; Hertzog's Smithfield speech

1926	Mines and Works Amendment Act provides for colour bar in employment; Balfour Declaration defines relations with Britain; Hertzog's 'Native Bills' published; Communists expelled from ICU
1927	Nationality and Flag Act; mass ICU protests of various kinds; Immorality Act prohibits sexual relations between whites and others; Native Administration Act
1928	CP told to work for a 'native republic'; iron and steel industry established by Act of parliament
1929	NP wins 81 seats in election
1930	Seme replaces Gumede as ANC president; pass-burning campaign launched by CP; white women get the vote; Natives (Urban Areas) Amendment Act
1931	Property and literacy qualifications removed for white voters; Statute of Westminster; pass-burning campaign and violence in Durban
1932	Depression reaches its peak; report of the Carnegie Commission on Poor Whites; Report of the Native Economic Commission; South Africa leaves gold standard
1933	Severe drought; Hertzog and Smuts agree on coalition; coalition wins overwhelming victory in general election; Smuts becomes Deputy Prime Minister
1934	NP and South African Party form United Party (UP); Malan forms Purified NP; Dominion Party formed
1935	All-African Convention formed to resist disfranchisement of Africans; National Liberation League established
1936	Representation of Natives Act, passed by 169 votes to 11, removes Africans from Cape voters' roll; Natives Trust and Land Act
1938	(May) UP wins general election; (December) Great Trek centenary celebrated
1939	(4 September) Smuts defeats Hertzog in vote on South African participation in the war, and (6 September) becomes Prime Minister; pro-Nazi Ossewa-Brandwag formed
1940	(January) Hertzog and Malan form Herenigde Nasionale Party (HNP); (December) Xuma elected president of the ANC
1941	African Mine Workers' Union formed; South African troops enter Addis Ababa, Ethiopia
1942	Influx control relaxed; draft constitution for South African republic published; (June) South African division captured at Tobruk, North Africa

1943   UP wins election; ANC releases 'African Claims'; Non-European Unity Movement founded

1944   First meeting of ANC Youth League, Lembede elected president; Mpanza and followers squat in Orlando location; anti-pass campaign

1945   Consolidated Urban Areas Act tightens up influx control restrictions; end of World War II

1946   Asiatic Land Tenure and Indian Representation Bill provokes Indian passive resistance campaign; strike by 60,000 African mineworkers brutally suppressed; adjournment of the Natives Representative Council

1948   Report of the Native Laws (Fagan) Commission; (May) HNP wins general election on a platform of apartheid; suburban railway apartheid in the Cape Peninsula; death of Jan Hofmeyr

1949   Prohibition of Mixed Marriages Act; Zulu–Indian riots in Durban; (December) 'Programme of Action' adopted at ANC congress; Xuma replaced by Moroka as president of ANC

1950   (May) stayaway in Transvaal; (June) CP dissolves itself before passage of Suppression of Communism Act; (26 June) national day of protest and mourning; Immorality Act amended; Population Registration Act; Group Areas Act

1951   Beginning of attempt to remove Coloured vote; Doctors' Pact for co-operation between ANC, Natal Indian Congress and Transvaal Indian Congress; Bantu Authorities Act provides for tribal, regional and territorial authorities in reserves; Torch Commando holds rallies in support of Coloured voters

1952   (March) Separate Representation of Voters Act is declared illegal by Supreme Court; (6 April) Van Riebeeck tercentenary festival; (26 June) beginning of countrywide Defiance Campaign, which leads to mass arrests and mass protests; Abolition of Passes Act provides that all Africans must carry passes, and in terms of Section 10 of the Act none are to remain more than 72 hours in urban area without permission

1953   South African Communist Party (SACP) formed underground; (April) NP wins election; Liberal Party formed; Congress of Democrats formed; Separate Amenities Act provides for segregated public facilities; Bantu Education Act provides for inferior education for Africans; Public Safety Act provides for declaration of a state of emergency, banning of meetings; Criminal Law Amendment Act makes civil disobedience punishable by a three-year jail sentence.

1954   Federation of South African Women formed; Strijdom Prime Minister

1955   Formation of South African Congress of Trade Unions; (June) Freedom Charter adopted by Congress of the People; Sophiatown destroyed

1956   ANC conference approves Freedom Charter; (9 August) 20,000 women march to the Union Buildings, Pretoria; Treason trial of 156 begins; Senate Act enables Separate Representation of Voters Act to be passed to remove Coloureds from common voters' roll; Industrial Conciliation Act provides for job reservation

1957   Alexandra bus boycott

1957–1958 Peasant uprising in Sekhukhuneland

1958   (April) NP wins 103 of 163 seats in National Assembly election; (August) Verwoerd succeeds Strijdom as Prime Minister; Africanists walk out of Transvaal ANC conference

1959   (April) Pan Africanist Congress (PAC) formed under Sobukwe; (November) Progressive Party founded; Promotion of Bantu Self-Government Act provides for transforming reserves into independent bantustans; Extension of University Education Act extends apartheid to higher education

1960   Representation for Africans in parliament abolished; (February) 'wind of change' speech by British Prime Minister Macmillan to South African parliament; (21 March) at Sharpeville police open fire and kill 69; two killed in Langa in Cape Town; Sobukwe sentenced to three years; (26 March) Luthuli burns his pass and declares 28 March a day of mourning; (27 March) Tambo leaves country to set up exile mission; (28 March) national stayaway; (30 March) Kgosana leads 30,000 marchers to Caledon Square police station, is promised that a delegation would be received later, and crowd returns peacefully; State of Emergency declared; beginning of revolt in Pondoland; (April) Unlawful Organizations Act passed; (8 April) ANC and PAC banned; attempted assassination of Verwoerd; (June) 11 killed when police open fire in Pondoland; end of State of Emergency; (October) white referendum on whether South Africa should become a republic: 52.3% of white voters in favour

1961   (March) Verwoerd withdraws South Africa's application to remain in the Commonwealth; (March) Treason trial ends with acquittal; (March) All-In conference, Pietermaritzburg, addressed by Mandela; (May) Luthuli awarded Nobel Peace Prize; (31 May) South Africa leaves the Commonwealth when it becomes a republic; Vorster appointed Minister of Justice and Police; ANC adopts armed struggle, Umkhonto weSizwe (MK) formed, with Mandela as chief of staff; (October) NP wins election; (16 December) launch of armed struggle with beginning of MK's sabotage campaign

1962   (January–June) Mandela visits African and European countries to gain support for armed struggle; (August) Mandela arrested near Howick, Natal; (November) Mandela sentenced to five years' imprisonment; (November) Paarl uprising; United Nations General Assembly votes for economic and diplomatic sanctions against South Africa; Sabotage Act provides for harsh penalties for sabotage; house arrest introduced and the state's banning powers extended

1963 (March) Leballo of PAC announces that a general uprising is imminent; his office in Maseru is raided and membership lists are seized; (May) General Law Amendment Act provides for detention for up to 90 days, and for further detention of persons convicted of political offences (the Sobukwe clause); foundation of Christian Institute by Beyers Naudé; (July) arrest of Umkhonto (MK) High Command at Lilliesleaf farm, Rivonia; (October) Rivonia trial begins; (December) Transkei self-government

1964 Armscor established; (11 June) eight Rivonia accused sentenced to life imprisonment; (July) John Harris of African Resistance Movement sets off bomb in Johannesburg railway station; numerous sabotage and other political trials

1965 Detention without trial for 180 days introduced; Bram Fischer goes underground, is recaptured after ten months

1966 (August) First clash between SWAPO guerrillas and South African police in Ovamboland; General Law Amendment Act provides for detention of suspected 'terrorists' for up to 14 days; (6 September) Tsafendas stabs Verwoerd to death in House of Assembly; Vorster becomes Prime Minister; District Six is proclaimed white area; (October) South Africa's mandate for Namibia is revoked by the UN General Assembly

1967 Terrorism Act provides for indefinite detention without trial on authority of policemen; Wankie campaign by MK, and South African police enter Rhodesia; death of Luthuli; formation of University Christian Movement; diplomatic relations established with Malawi

1968 English cricket tour is cancelled because of the D'Oliveira affair; Prohibition of Political Interference Act prohibits non-racial political parties and Progressive Party becomes all-white; Liberal Party dissolves itself; Coloured representatives in parliament abolished; PAC forms armed wing, APLA

1969 Bureau of State Security created, accountable to the Prime Minister; ANC holds first conference since banning, at Morogoro, Tanzania, where it adopts programme entitled 'Strategy and Tactics' and opens membership to whites; South African Students' Organization formed by Biko; Albert Hertzog forms Herstigte Nasionale Party (HNP)

1970 Bantu Homelands Citizenship Act; NP wins election and no HNP candidates are returned; Mulder of NP says that aim of policy is that there should be no black South African citizens

1971 International Court of Justice rules that South Africa's occupation of Namibia is illegal

1972 Black People's Convention formed; establishment of State Security Council; Africans in urban areas brought under Bantu Affairs

Administration Boards

1973 (January–March) strikes by 61,000 black workers in Durban–Pinetown area; re-emergence of independent trade unionism; formation of Afrikaner Weerstandsbeweging (AWB); South African Defence Force (SADF) takes over from police in northern Namibia

1974 Affected Organizations Act provides for declaration of organizations which are not able to solicit foreign funds; (April) coup in Lisbon, Portugal

1975 (August) SADF invades Angola; (November) SADF troops close to Luanda encounter resistance from Cubans; television introduced; Inkatha movement formed; Breytenbach sentenced to nine years for 'terrorism'

1976 (March) South African forces withdraw from Angola; Theron Commission report released; (16 June) police open fire on march of school children to Orlando West secondary school, and widespread resistance follows in which hundreds are killed and others stream into exile; (October) Transkei declared 'independent'; MK resumes operations inside South Africa; SWAPO and ANC begin to open military bases in Angola

1976–1977 Continuous protest; over 700 deaths by police; many detentions, stayaways, school boycotts, etc.

1977 Demolition of Cape Town squatter camps; (June) shooting in central Johannesburg leads to arrest of two MK cadres; (September) Steve Biko murdered in detention; (October) 17 organizations and three newspapers banned; (November) United Nations imposes compulsory arms embargo against South Africa; 'independence' of Bophuthatswana; disintegration of UP

1978 (April) South Africa accepts Western plan for transition to independence in Namibia; (4 May) Cassinga massacre in Angola: over 600 killed when SADF attacks SWAPO camp; Information (Muldergate) scandal breaks; (September) Vorster resigns and P.W. Botha becomes Prime Minister; UN Security Council passes resolution 435 for transition to independence in Namibia; Robert Sobukwe dies; at Sobukwe's Graaff- Reinet funeral Buthelezi is attacked by youths

1979 (April) Reprieve for Crossroads squatters; formation of Federation of South African Trade Unions; formation of civics in Port Elizabeth (PEBCO), Soweto and Cape Town, of the Congress of South African Students for high-school students, and of the Azanian Students' Organization; (August) P.W. Botha visits Soweto; (September) Van Zyl Slabbert becomes leader of the opposition; 'independence' of Venda bantustan; Industrial Conciliation Act embodies recommendations of Wiehahn Commission, including the official recognition of black trade unions; meeting between ANC and Inkatha in London ends in acrimony; Solomon Mahlangu executed

1980 Gold price soars, creating economic boom; (January) Silverton bank siege in which MK operatives take hostages, followed by shoot-out; Release Mandela campaign launched; school and consumer boycotts; (June) Sasol refinery and Sasol plants at Secunda and Sasolburg bombed by MK; Senate abolished, replaced with multi-racial President's Council of nominated members to discuss new constitution

1981   (January) 14 killed in SADF raid on Matola outside Maputo, including commander of attack on Sasol; (January) abortive UN conference at Geneva on Namibia; (August) Operation Protea launched against SWAPO in Angola; (November) Griffiths Mxenge killed by Vlakplaas hit squad; (December) Ciskei declared 'independent'; MK attack on main military base at Voortrekkerhoogte

1982   February) Trade unionist Neil Aggett dies in detention at John Vorster Square; (March) right-wing NP members of parliament, under leadership of Treurnicht, ousted and form Conservative Party (CP); gold price drops and country enters recession; (July) NP federal congress approves proposals for new constitution providing for a strong executive president and tricameral parliament; (August) Ruth First assassinated by parcel bomb in Maputo; (9 December) SADF raid on Maseru and 42 killed; (December) Koeberg nuclear plant sabotaged by MK, causing millions of rands in damage

1983   (20 May) Car-bomb outside SAAF building in Church Street, Pretoria, kills 19; (23 May) retaliatory attack on Maputo kills six, five of whom are Mozambican civilians; (June) inauguration of National Forum at Hammanskraal, near Pretoria; (August) launch of United Democratic Front (UDF) at Mitchell's Plain; (November) in a referendum two-thirds of white voters approve the new constitution, providing for a tricameral parliament, with separate houses for whites, Coloureds and Indians, a distinction between general and own affairs, and a strong executive President; at a meeting at Howick in Natal, the Labour Party decides to participate in the new parliament

1984   (January) South African troops withdraw from Angola after Operation Askari; (February) Lusaka agreement with Angola providing for Joint Military Commission to monitor South African troop withdrawal; (16 March) Nkomati Accord signed by Botha and Samora Machel; (May) the Administrator-General (AG) of South West Africa and Namibian parties meet in Lusaka; after mutiny of MK soldiers in Pango camp, Angola, the mutineers are sent to detention camp Quatro and seven are executed; (June) Botha's tour of Europe; (July) Cape Verde talks between the AG and Nujoma of SWAPO; (3 September) fire-bombing of black policeman's home in Sharpeville begins township revolt in Vaal Triangle, which soon spreads to East Rand, Soweto and other areas; the SADF is sent into townships, but the revolt spreads from the Vaal Triangle to other parts of the country; (3 September) Botha inaugurated as first executive State President and the first tricameral parliament is opened; Bishop Tutu awarded Nobel Peace Prize

1985   (February) Mandela's daughter reads a statement from him in Soweto in which he refuses conditional freedom and says he will return; (March) on anniversary of Sharpeville and Langa massacres, police open fire on a march near Uitenhage; (June) 13 killed in SADF raid against suspected ANC houses in Gaborone, Botswana; (June) at Kabwe, Zambia, the ANC holds its second consultative conference, which calls for the intensification of the armed struggle, and says civilians may be caught in crossfire; security police murder the Cradock Four; (20 July) partial State of Emergency in 36 magisterial districts; vast powers given to police and Minister of Law and Order; (August) killing of UDF's Victoria Mxenge sparks protest in Durban and many die; (August) P.W. Botha's failure to make concessions in his 'Rubicon' speech in the Durban City Hall leads to crisis of confidence; planned march to Pollsmoor prison to demand the release of Mandela is stopped by police; (September) the *Kairos Document* supports struggle against injustice; Anglo American head leads delegation to meet ANC in Zambia; (November) Minister of Justice Kobie Coetsee meets Nelson Mandela at Volks Hospital, Cape Town; (December) formation of Congress of South African Trade Unions in Durban; (December) nine killed in SADF raid on Lesotho

1986   (February) Van Zyl Slabbert resigns from parliament; (March) end of partial State of Emergency; (May) SADF raid on Botswana, Zambia and Zimbabwe results in collapse of the Eminent Persons Group mission; (May–June) destruction of satellite squatter camps and then KTC camp on Cape Flats by *witdoeke* vigilantes, aided by police; (June) nation-wide State of Emergency declared in terms of Public Safety Act; regulations prevent publication of information concerning police conduct or 'unrest incidents'; the security forces are indemnified for unlawful acts carried out in 'good faith'; many thousands are detained; Mixed Marriages Act, section 16 of Immorality Act, and Prohibition of Political Interference Act repealed; pass laws and influx control abolished; (August) Johannesburg headquarters of the South African Council of Churches destroyed by a bomb, later revealed to have been planted by the police; NP federal congress approves the idea of participation of all in government to highest levels; (September) the US Congress passes the Comprehensive Anti-Apartheid Act, overriding President Reagan's veto; (19 October) death of all people on a plane carrying President Machel of Mozambique, which crashes just within South African territory; a camp in Caprivi is established for training 200 Inkatha members (Operation Marion)

1987   (January) 12 people die in an attack on a house in KwaMakhutha in Natal; (February) the government approves the Mossgas oil-from-gas project; (May) the CP replaces the PFP as the official opposition in parliament; (June) the State of Emergency is renewed; (July) 61 Afrikaners meet ANC representatives in Dakar, Senegal; (September) in a prisoner-of-war exchange in Maputo, the SADF's Wynand du Toit is exchanged; (October) Stella Sigcau becomes prime minister of Transkei; (November) Govan Mbeki is released unconditionally and confirms his allegiance to the ANC and the SACP

1988   (January) ANC declares 1988 the year of united action for people's power; (February) Bophuthatswana president Lucas Mangope is ousted in a coup, and restored to power by the SADF; 18 organizations, including the UDF and COSATU, are restricted; (July) widespread celebrations of Mandela's 70th birthday; (July) Ellis Park bomb kills two in Johannesburg; (August) the End Conscription Campaign is effectively banned; (October) all races in municipalities go to polls in local government elections for the first time; (November) former policeman Barend Strydom kills many blacks in shooting spree in the centre of Pretoria; Natal police captain Brian Mitchell organizes massacre at Trust Feed

1989   (18 January) P.W. Botha suffers mild stroke; (2 February) he announces his resignation as leader of the NP; F.W. de Klerk elected as NP leader; (4 February) Democratic Party formed; (16 February) UDF distances itself from Winnie Mandela; hunger strike achieves release of political detainees; (5 July) meeting between P.W. Botha and Mandela at Tuynhuis in Cape Town; (12 July) Mandela's statement affirming desire to contribute to a climate that will promote peace; (August) Tambo suffers stroke; (August) Harare Declaration outlines ANC's conditions for negotiations; defiance campaign for desegregation of hospitals, beaches and public transport; (14 August) P.W. Botha resigns; (15 August) F.W. de Klerk sworn in as Acting State President; (6 September) white election; nation-wide protests are met with police violence especially in western Cape; De Klerk interprets election result as mandate for reform; meeting between members of National Intelligence Service and ANC in Switzerland; (20 September) De Klerk is sworn in as State President; (October) peaceful march in Cape Town by 30,000; National Security Management System dismantled; (15 October) eight long-term political prisoners, including Walter Sisulu, are released on the eve of a Commonwealth heads of government meeting in Kuala Lumpur; convicted murderer Nofomela confesses to hit-squad activity and is supported by former police captain Dirk Coetzee; (29 October) Soweto rally in support of ANC addressed by Sisulu; (November) Namibian elections; Berlin wall falls; bathing beaches open to all; last SADF troops in Namibia return to South Africa; (13 December) De Klerk meets Mandela for the first time

1990   (2 February) De Klerk speech opening parliament legalises ANC, SACP and other opposition parties, lifts restrictions on listed people; he announces that Mandela is to be released unconditionally; (11 February) Mandela walks through gates of Victor Verster prison a free man; (March) Ciskei government is overthrown in military coup; preliminary talks between government and ANC; Sebokeng killings by police, and ANC calls off talks; (21 March) Namibian independence; (April) resumption of talks about talks; (April) Venda government overthrown in military coup; (4–5 May) ANC and government meet at Groote Schuur, Cape Town, and agree on a framework for the release of political prisoners, indemnity for exiles and commitment to end violence; (June) the State of Emergency is lifted except in Natal; Separate Amenities Act is repealed; Mandela visits the United States; (July) ANC–COSATU stayaway in protest against violence in Natal; arrests of ANC and SACP members in connection with Operation Vula; ANC–Inkatha clashes spread from Natal to Reef and hundreds are killed; beginnings of train violence; relaunch of SACP; (8 August) at a Pretoria meeting with the government the ANC suspends the armed struggle; (August–September) escalation of violence on Reef and in Natal; (September) De Klerk visits Washington; (October) State of Emergency lifted in Natal; (November) attempted coup in Transkei does not succeed; (November) Harms Commission reports and absolves security police at Vlakplaas of hit-squad activities, but uncovers a covert SADF unit known as the Civil Co-Operation Bureau; (December) ANC consultative conference held in Johannesburg

1991   (1 February) De Klerk announces that the pillars of apartheid are to be repealed; (12 February) D.F. Malan Minute is signed by government and ANC: (April) ANC demands dismissal of Ministers Vlok and Malan, dismantling of hit squads, suspension of police implicated in massacres, the transformation of hostels into family units, and the establishment of an independent commission of inquiry into the violence; (June) repeal of Natives Land Act, Separate Amenities Act, Group Areas Act, and Population Registration Act; the Further Abolition of Racially-Based Measures Act removes racial distinctions in other laws; (July) at ANC congress in Durban, Mandela is elected president of the ANC; (July) Inkathagate scandal reveals government funding of Inkatha and of anti-SWAPO parties in Namibia; (August) clash at Ventersdorp where the AWB is dispersed by police outside a hall in which De Klerk spoke; (September) the National Peace Accord is signed by the ANC, the government, the IFP and others; the introduction of value-added tax leads to massive protests against the levying of the tax on basic foods and services; (October) South Africa signs the nuclear non-proliferation treaty; a commission of inquiry is established under Justice Richard Goldstone to investigate public violence and intimidation; (November) agreement to start talks; (20 December) 19 parties attend Convention for a Democratic South Africa (CODESA) at the World Trade Centre in Kempton Park; two-day meeting ends with agreement on a Declaration of Intent by 17 parties

1992   (17 March) A whites-only referendum gives De Klerk a mandate to continue negotiations: 68.6% of voters approve of continuing the reform process, which aimed at a new constitution through negotiations; (April) former police captain Brian Mitchell and others are sentenced for Trust Feed massacre in 1988; (15 May) CODESA 2 deadlocks; (16 June) ANC begins mass action campaign to force government to speed up reform process; (17 June) Inkatha supporters from KwaMadala hostel kill 43 in Boipatong massacre near Vanderbijlpark and provoke an international outcry; (19 June) Mandela accuses the government of complicity in the massacre and suspends talks; (July) rolling mass action is launched to topple anti-ANC bantustan leaders; South Africa is to attend the Olympics for the first time since 1960; (August) a COSATU-sponsored stayaway involves more than 4 million workers; (7 September) 28 die in massacre at Bisho, when unarmed ANC supporters march to oust Gqozo and Ciskei troops open fire; (September) Record of Understanding reached between ANC and government to break deadlock in negotiations, includes agreement to release further political prisoners, fence and patrol hostels, and prohibit carrying and display of dangerous weapons; (October) amnesty legislation passed; political prisoners released; formation of Concerned South Africans Group (COSAG); (November) the ANC agrees to power-sharing after Joe Slovo proposes 'sunset' clauses; Goldstone uncovers campaign by Directorate of Covert Collection to discredit the ANC; (December) De Klerk suspends or retires 23 senior SADF officers for involvement in illegal activities; year of severe drought and economic depression

1993   (January) European Economic Community announces that sanctions will be lifted; (March) Multi-Party Negotiating Forum planning conference attended by 26 parties, now including the CP and PAC; government delegation meets PAC in Botswana to negotiate a suspension of its armed struggle; De Klerk announces that six nuclear weapons built in the 1980s have been dismantled; (April) negotiations resume at the World Trade Centre; (10 April) Chris Hani, secretary general of the SACP and former MK chief of staff, is assassinated; (May) 200 PAC members are arrested in a country-wide pre-dawn swoop; (June) decision to agree on an election date leads to IFP and CP walk-out, and they form Freedom Alliance; (25 June) armed right-wingers break through gates and enter World Trade Centre, occupying the building and causing damage; (3 July) election set for 27 April; (25 July) eleven churchgoers shot dead in Kenilworth, Cape Town, a crime for which APLA members are later found guilty; (August): much violence on East Rand; Amy Biehl is killed in Guguletu, Cape Town; report of Motsuenyane Commission into alleged human rights abuses against ANC detainees; (October) announcement that Mandela and De Klerk have jointly been awarded the Nobel Peace Prize; (October) UN lifts sanctions except for arms and oil embargoes; Janusz Waluz and Clive Derby-Lewis are given death sentences for the murder of Hani; SADF raid on APLA house in Umtata; (18 November) agreement reached at World Trade Centre on an interim constitution providing for a non-racial, multi-party democracy with justiciable Bill of Rights and nine provinces; (December) APLA attack on tavern in Observatory, Cape Town, kills four; parliament approves legislation to establish a Transitional Executive Council (TEC), with seven sub-councils, an Independent Electoral Commission and an Independent Broadcasting Authority; TEC installed; (18 December) parliament approves interim constitution; government and ANC involved in talks with Freedom Alliance concerning its participation in the election

1994   (March) Rioting in Bophuthatswana, and TEC then ousts Mangope and brings the bantustan under Pretoria's control; (28 March) battle of Shell House, when IFP marchers attack ANC headquarters in downtown Johannesburg, and over 50 are killed; (31 March) State of Emergency declared in KwaZulu; General Viljoen of the Freedom Front agrees to participate in the election; (19 April) Buthelezi agrees to call off election boycott and allow IFP to be included on ballots; (26–29 April) first democratic election; (27 April) interim constitution takes effect, providing for re-incorporation of Transkei, Ciskei, Bophuthatswana and Venda into South Africa; (2 May) Mandela proclaims that South Africa is free at last; (10 May) Mandela is inaugurated President at the Union Buildings, Pretoria; (24 May) the Constitutional Assembly begins work on a final constitution; South Africa rejoins the Commonwealth after 33 years; it also joins the Non-Aligned Movement; (16 June) the United Nations lifts its embargo on arms sales to South Africa; (24 June) South Africa reclaims its seat in the UN General Assembly; launch of Reconstruction and Development Programme and Masakhane ('let us build together') campaign to end rent and bond boycotts

1995   (January) Death of Joe Slovo; (June) Constitutional Court in first judgment rules the death penalty to be unconstitutional; (July) passage of National Unity and Reconciliation Act, providing for establishment of Truth and Reconciliation Commission (TRC); (November) draft of the final constitution is released; (December) TRC appointed by President Mandela

1996   (February) Bafana Bafana, the national soccer team, wins Africa Cup of Nations; (March) beginning of trial of General Magnus Malan and others; (April) TRC begins to hear accounts of human rights abuses from victims; (8 May) final constitution sent to Constitutional Court for certification; National Party announces it is to leave the Government of National Unity at end of June; (July) RDP redeployed to line ministries; agreement in principle on Armscor dispute between South Africa and the United States; Bantu Holomisa sacked as Deputy Minister of Environmental Affairs; Sarafina 2 anti-Aids play fiasco; (September) Constitutional Court refers constitution back to Constitutional Assembly; Nelson Mandela becomes chairperson of Southern African Development Community; (October) Malan and others found not guilty; De Kock convicted and sentenced for atrocities as commander of Vlakplaas; TRC begins to hear from perpetrators and issues its first subpoenas; (November) Labour Relations Act comes into effect; (10 December) final constitution signed by Mandela at Sharpeville; extension of amnesty date to 10 May 1994; Bishop Stanley Mogoba elected president of PAC

1997   (January) Proposed arms deal with Syria put on hold; (4 February) final constitution brought into effect; National Council of Provinces inaugurated; (March) Cape Town chosen as one of short-listed cities for 2004 Olympic Games; TRC revelations concerning apartheid murders continue; De Klerk accused of participating in decision to set up a third force in the mid-1980s; (May) South Africa mediates in the Zairean crisis; Winnie Madikizela-Mandela re-elected president of the ANC Women's League; last amnesty applications presented to TRC; extensive mismanagement in the Independent Broadcasting Authority confirmed; (Sept.) De Klerk resigns as NP leader and from parliament; Cape Town not chosen for 2004

Olympic Games; Mathole Motshekga elected Gauteng ANC chairman and successor to Tokyo Sexwale; United Democratic Movement led by Roelf Meyer and Bantu Holomisa founded; (November) Winnie Madikizela-Mandela testifies to TRC at the end of a nine-day hearing on the activities of the Mandela United Football Club in the late 1980s and denies charges of murder levelled against her; Western Cape constitution approved by Constitutional Court; (December) in Ottawa, Foreign Minister Alfred Nzo signs the convention banning landmines; commercial farming sector hit by a further spate of murders of white farmers; P.W. Botha refuses to attend TRC hearing despite subpoena; 50th annual congress of ANC at Mafikeng in North-West Province: Mandela hands over presidency of ANC to Thabo Mbeki; Jacob Zuma chosen as ANC deputy president

1998   (January) Full diplomatic relations established with Beijing; (March) US President Bill Clinton's state visit; centenary of the Kruger National Park celebrated

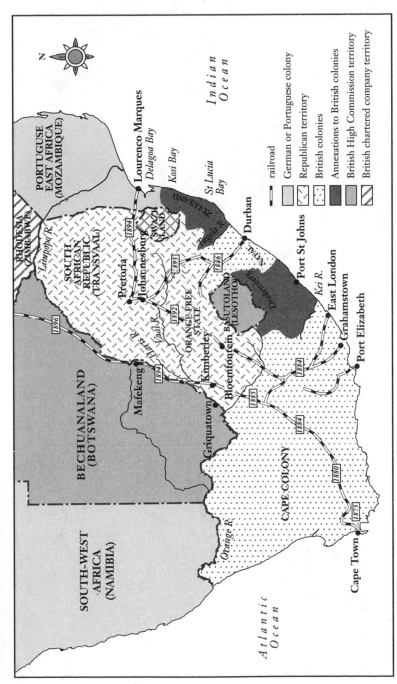

Southern Africa in the 1890s

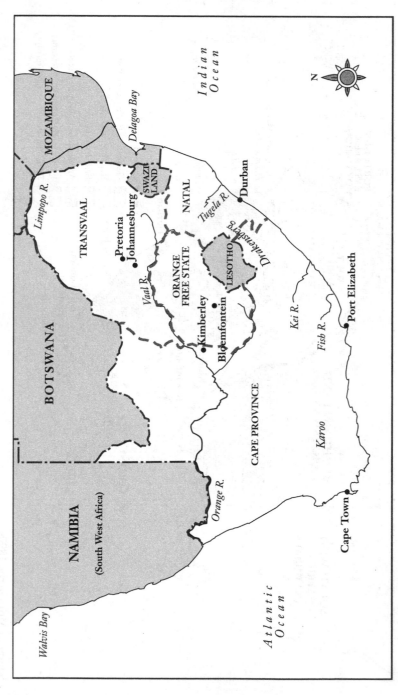

Provinces of South Africa 1910–1994

Bantustans

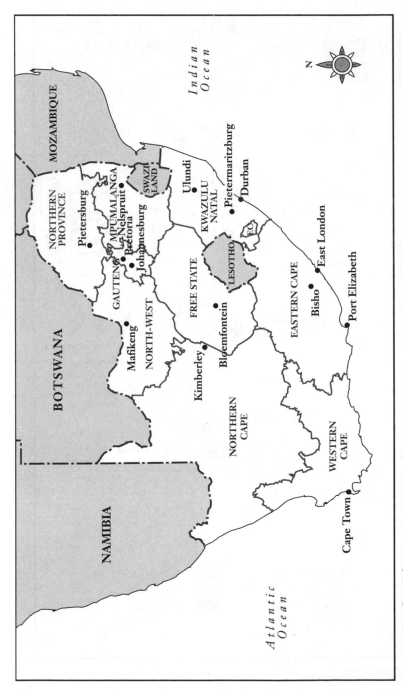

Provinces in the mid-1990s

A Dictionary of
South African History

a

....

ABDURAHMAN, Abdullah (1872–1940). The most important Coloured political leader of the early 20th century, he served as president of the African People's Organization* from 1905 to his death. The grandson of freed slaves,* he trained as a medical doctor in Glasgow, Scotland, before returning to Cape Town to practise medicine and participate in political life. The first Coloured person to serve on the Cape Town City Council (1904–1940) and on the Cape Provincial Council (1914–1940), he was much criticised in the late 1930s by a new, more militant generation of Coloured activists. [G. Lewis, *Between the Wire and the Wall* (Cape Town, 1987)]

AFRICAN METHODIST EPISCOPAL CHURCH (AMEC). In 1896 the Ethiopian Church, the first important African independent church,* founded by Mangena Mokone in Pretoria in 1892, decided to become part of the AMEC, the leading African American church. Bishop Henry Turner of the AMEC made a highly successful six-week visit to South Africa in 1898 and by the end of that year the AMEC in South Africa boasted over 10,000 adherents in 73 congregations. From the late 1890s the American church constituted the major link between black South Africans and African Americans. A number of black South Africans were educated at the AMEC's Wilberforce Institute in the United States, and the AMEC sent a succession of ministers to South Africa. For its South African members, the AMEC symbolized freedom from white control in a segregated society. It did not, however, engage politically, and tended to remain aloof from other independent churches. [J. Chirenje, *Ethiopianism and Afro-Americans in South Africa* (Baton Rouge, 1987); J. Campbell, *Songs of Zion* (New York, 1995)]

AFRICAN NATIONAL CONGRESS (ANC). Founded in January 1912 in Bloemfontein as the South African Native National Congress (SANNC), the ANC (a name adopted in 1923) is today the oldest national political organization in the country. For almost 50 years it worked within the law against racial discrimination, and in 1956 it committed itself to a South Africa which 'belongs to all'. Banned in 1960, it was forced for three decades underground and into exile. From exile, it conducted an armed struggle for liberation. In its exile years it opened its membership to whites and other non-Africans. Unbanned in 1990, it entered formal negotiations with the government; and gradually dropped the socialist policies it had earlier espoused. The negotiations eventually produced the compromise settlement which allowed the ANC to take power as a result of the election of April 1994.

The successor to a number of provincial African congresses formed by Africans in the aftermath of the South African War,* the SANNC was a response to the establishment of the Union* of South Africa in 1910. The initiative for its formation came largely from a group of young overseas-trained lawyers, of whom the most important was Pixley Seme.* In its early years the ANC was an extremely moderate organization, which believed in petitioning the government and acting 'respon-

1

sibly' as a pressure group for the promotion of African interests. Its first main concern was the Natives Land Bill, and protest delegations were sent to Cape Town and London, in vain. Another delegation was sent to Versailles and London in the aftermath of World War I. For a brief period the Transvaal section of Congress adopted a militant stance and in the late 1920s a new president, Josiah Gumede, tried to persuade the organization to challenge the pass system more directly, but he was voted out in 1930. In the western Cape the ANC split, and an 'Independent ANC' briefly adopted a more militant line, but by the mid-1930s the ANC had reached a low point in its fortunes.

It was in the 1940s, under the presidency of A.B. Xuma,* that there began the transformation of the ANC into a mass movement. This was in large part under the influence of the ANC Youth League,* formed by Fort Hare* graduates in 1944. In the aftermath of the victory of the National Party in 1948 and its adoption of apartheid policies, the Youth League was able to get the ANC to adopt a Programme of Action in 1949, which called for new methods of struggle, including boycotts, strikes and civil disobedience. In 1952 the ANC launched a Defiance Campaign,* which helped swell its membership from 20,000 to 100,000. It then took the lead in the Congress Alliance* and the movement for a Freedom Charter. Drawn up in 1955, and adopted by the ANC the following year, the Charter committed the organization to a multi-racial, social democratic future for South Africa. Those of an Africanist persuasion within the organization rejected this, and in 1958 broke away. By the end of the 1950s it was clear that little had been achieved by the ANC's attempts to resist the implementation of apartheid, attempts which had included protest campaigns against Bantu Education,* passes* for women and the destruction of Sophiatown.

Instead, apartheid had intensified. A major turning-point for the ANC came in April 1960, when it was banned in the aftermath of the Sharpeville massacre.* In October that year its president, Albert Luthuli,* went to Oslo to collect the Nobel Peace Prize, which was awarded for the non-violent struggle he had led, but Nelson Mandela* and others, working closely with members of the South African Communist Party (SACP),* decided to adopt the strategy of armed struggle and launched Umkhonto weSizwe (MK).* This was announced publicly on 16 December 1961, and a campaign of sabotage began. The ANC suffered a massive blow when its key internal leaders were arrested, and given life sentences in the Rivonia trial* in 1964. In exile, the organization was led by Oliver Tambo,* who established its headquarters in Lusaka, Zambia, and worked to win international support. A consultative conference held at Morogoro, Tanzania, in 1969 adopted a new programme, 'Strategy and Tactics of the ANC', admitted non-Africans to membership for the first time, and created a Revolutionary Council, which strengthened the influence of the SACP within the exile movement. Meanwhile, the ANC's armed wing, MK, had sent detachments into Rhodesia in 1967 and 1968, en route to South Africa, but they were soon routed. Although the ANC played no significant role in the Soweto uprising,* most of those who fled the country as a result of that revolt joined the ANC in exile, and many of them returned to the country as members of MK. From the late 1970s, MK was increasingly active in mounting attacks on targets in South Africa, including the Sasol oil refinery, the Koeberg nuclear power plant, and the defence force base at Voortrekkerhoogte. A car-bomb attack on the headquarters of the South African Air Force in Pretoria in 1983 killed 19 people.

Support for the banned organization escalated in the townships. Many of those who were supporters of Black Consciousness* when sent to Robben Island* came to join the ANC because of the remarkable moral influence of Mandela and his colleagues on the Island. Though the ANC could not organize effectively within the country, it gained great influence within the United Democratic Front* from 1983, and from late 1985 its legitimacy among whites in South Africa and in the international community grew dramatically. It began to be seen as a possible alternative government. At its conference in Kabwe, Zambia, in June 1985, the ANC both opened its top structures to non-Africans and accepted that the armed struggle should be intensified and that the risk of civilians being caught in the crossfire should no longer impede such intensification.

The imprisoned Mandela, icon of the struggle, was widely seen as the key to its resolution. From 1985 he began to enter into 'talks about talks' with the government. The exile leadership started to explore ideas about a future South Africa with delegations from South Africa in Dakar (Senegal), the United Kingdom and elsewhere. Though the ANC–SACP alliance was broadened to include the newly established Congress of South African Trade Unions (COSATU),* the ANC's adherence to socialist rhetoric began to be modified, and as it moved to power after 1990, it slowly abandoned talk of nationalization and became increasingly pragmatic in outlook.

When F.W. de Klerk* unbanned the ANC and the SACP in 1990, he probably hoped that the ANC or the alliance would split, but neither happened. The released Mandela soon took over the leadership from an ailing Tambo. The ANC began formal talks with the government in May 1990, agreed to suspend its armed struggle in August that year, and in December 1991 entered formal multi-party negotiations with the government and other parties on a new constitution to provide for a democratic order. It is generally agreed that in these negotiations the ANC, whose chief negotiator was Cyril Ramaphosa,* outmanoeuvred the National Party, and got the better of the compromise deal providing for the establishment of a new democratic order.

Under Mandela's inspirational leadership, the ANC successfully held together a number of different constituencies: those who had gone into exile, those who had been on Robben Island, and those who had worked in the United Democratic Front and the Mass Democratic Movement.* The alliance with COSATU and the SACP held firm, and in the first democratic election in April 1994 the ANC won 62.6% of the votes, just short of the two-thirds which would have allowed it to write the final constitution on its own. From May it governed as the majority party in the Government of National Unity.* After the withdrawal of the National Party from that government in 1996, some political commentators began to talk of a one-party dominant system, as there was no effective alternative to the ANC on the political scene.

Once in power, the ANC championed a Reconstruction and Development Programme* but by 1997 this had effectively been replaced by a Growth,

Employment and Redistribution (GEAR) strategy which emphasized the need for fiscal discipline and measures to encourage foreign investment to promote economic growth; this meant cutbacks in social spending. COSATU was critical of GEAR and other policies of the ANC-led government, but did not break away. The popular Bantu Holomisa was expelled from the organization for indiscipline, and Winnie Madikizela-Mandela proved difficult to handle, but the party emerged from its 50th congress, held at Mafikeng in December 1997, seemingly as strong as ever, with Thabo Mbeki,* its new president, committed to do what he could to increase delivery of what had been promised to the electorate: houses, running water, electricity and, above all, jobs. [P. Walshe, *The Rise of African Nationalism in South Africa* (London, 1970); T. Karis and G. Carter/G. Gerhart, eds., *From Protest to Challenge* (5 vols., 1972–97); S.M. Davis, *Apartheid's Rebels* (New Haven, 1987); F. Meli, *South Africa Belongs to Us* (London, 1988); H. Holland, *The Struggle* (London, 1989); H. Barrell, *MK* (London, 1990); S. Ellis, *Comrades Against Apartheid* (London, 1992); N. Mandela, *Long Walk to Freedom* (London, 1994)]

AFRICAN NATIONAL CONGRESS YOUTH LEAGUE. The Youth League was founded in 1944 to represent the interests of younger, more militant members of the African National Congress. It probably had most influence on the parent organization in its first decade of life. Its early leaders, many educated at Fort Hare,* included Anton Lembede* (its first president), Oliver Tambo,* Nelson Mandela,* and Walter Sisulu.* In the early 1990s the Youth League gained a new lease of life under the presidency of Peter Mokaba, then a fiery politician. [R. Edgar and L. Msumza, eds., *Freedom in Our Lifetime* (Athens, Ohio, 1996)]

AFRICAN PEOPLE'S ORGANIZATION (APO). Founded in 1902 as the African Political Organization, it was the leading Coloured political formation in the first three decades of the 20th century. Seeking equality for its members with whites, it represented mostly the Coloured elite and was closely identified with Abdullah Abdurahman* and the newspaper he edited, the *APO*. In the late 1930s the importance of the APO declined as a more radical generation challenged its conservatism. [G. Lewis, *Between the Wire and the Wall* (Cape Town, 1987)]

AFRICAN RESISTANCE MOVEMENT. See LIBERAL PARTY

AFRIKAANS. A language which evolved from the Dutch spoken by the first white settlers at the Cape. From the late 17th century, the form of Dutch spoken at the Cape developed differences in pronunciation and accidence and, to a lesser extent, in syntax and vocabulary, from that of Holland. Settlers who arrived speaking German and French soon converted to Dutch. The process of creolization was influenced by the languages spoken by slaves, Khoikhoi and people of mixed descent, as well as by Malay and Portuguese. While the Dutch of Holland remained the language of officialdom, the new creolized form, often known as Cape Dutch or belittled as 'kitchen Dutch', developed into a separate language by the 19th century.

The first book published in Afrikaans appeared in 1856, but it was not until the 1870s that the language was used as a vehicle for cultural expression, in opposition to British imperialism. S.J. du Toit (1847–1911), a clergyman of the Dutch Reformed Church who lived in Paarl, near Cape Town, produced a journal, *Die Afrikaanse Patriot* (1876), a concise grammar (1876) and a history (1877), all of which aided the growth of Afrikaans as a written as well as a spoken language.

A second phase of the Afrikaans language movement began after the South African War,* partly as a response to the attempts of Sir Alfred Milner* to anglicize the white Afrikaans-speakers of the Transvaal. Newspapers and periodicals published in Afrikaans began to appear more regularly. One of the central figures in the language movement, J.D. du Toit (1877–1953), son of S.J. du Toit, wrote poetry under the name 'Totius'. Other prominent poets and writers early in the century included Eugène Marais, C. Louis Leipoldt and Jan F. Celliers. In 1909 an Academy was founded to promote the language and its scientific study, and in the early 1920s the influential Cape Town newspaper, *De Burger*, and the journal of the Dutch Reformed Church, *De Kerkbode*, both changed from Dutch to Afrikaans. In 1925, Afrikaans was recognized as one of the two official languages of the Union of South Africa.

Usage of Afrikaans among whites was aggressively promoted from the late 1920s, mainly by the Afrikaner Broederbond* and the (Purified) National Party,* both instruments of Afrikaner nationalism.* An Afrikaans translation of the Bible was published early in the 1930s; the language was strongly encouraged in white schools; and bodies such as the Federasie van Afrikaanse Kultuurvereniginge (Federation of Afrikaans Cultural Organizations) and the Afrikaanse Taal en Kultuurvereniging (Afrikaans Language and Cultural Organization) were established. The work of the poet N.P. van Wyk Louw (1906–1970) helped give the language standing as a literary medium.

Though the majority of those called Coloureds continued to use the language, from 1948 it became closely associated with apartheid and Afrikaner domination. White Afrikaans-speakers took control of the civil service, ousting English-speakers, and Afrikaans became the language of the apartheid government. A large Taalmonument (language monument) was erected in Paarl in 1976, the year in which the Soweto uprising* was sparked by the insistence of the authorities that Africans be taught in high school through the medium of Afrikaans. A strongly dissident literary tradition had begun in the 1960s, associated with such writers and poets as Etienne Leroux, Ingrid Jonker, André Brink and Breyten Breytenbach. As work by Brink and Breytenbach became available in other languages, they gained international reputations. Breytenbach went so far as to reject the language for a time because of its association with apartheid. No significant pro-apartheid literature emerged in Afrikaans.

With the collapse of apartheid, Afrikaans, as the first language of only five million of the country's people, lost status and became one of eleven official languages. Some white Afrikaners sought constitutional protection for the language in the new political dispensation, while others, having rejected Coloureds in the apartheid era, now re-discovered kinship with them on the basis of a shared language. [J.C. Kannemeyer, *A History of Afrikaans Literature* (Pietermaritzburg, 1993); J. Cope, *The Adversary Within* (Cape Town, 1982)]

5

AFRIKANER, Jonker (c.1790–1861). Leader of the Afrikaners, an Oorlam* group founded by his grandfather, Klaas Afrikaner, and built up by his father, Jager Afrikaner (d. 1823). Jonker Afrikaner exercised wide power on the Cape northern frontier in the 1820s and 1830s. From his base on an island in the Orange River he subjugated Khoisan people in the region in return for arms and ammunition from whites, but at times also assisted Khoisan to resist Cape colonial encroachment on their hunting grounds. In the 1840s he moved a long way north of the Orange, into what is now Namibia, and there carried out extensive and brutal raids on the Herero people, plundering large herds of cattle and destroying numerous villages. [B. Lau, *Southern and Central Namibia in Jonker Afrikaner's Time* (Windhoek, 1987)]

AFRIKANER BOND (League of Afrikaners). The first and most important political party in the Cape before Union,* the Bond was established in 1880 to further the interests of Afrikaner white farmers in the south- western Cape. Under Jan Hendrik Hofmeyr,* it entered an alliance with Cecil Rhodes* and gained some black support, including that of the influential John Tengo Jabavu.* With the advent of Union,* the Bond was dissolved in 1911. [T.R.H.Davenport, *The Afrikaner Bond* (Cape Town, 1966)]

AFRIKANER BROEDERBOND (League of Afrikaner Brothers). For a long time a highly influential secret society which promoted the interests of Afrikaner nationalism. Formed in 1919 to spearhead the movement for an Afrikaner republic, it worked to secure Afrikaner control in government, the economy and culture, and did much to promote the cause of the National Party. Beginning in the 1960s, a series of revelations about its membership began to erode its power, but most influential male Afrikaners continued to be members. By the mid-1980s it was, under Professor Pieter de Lange, ahead of the government of the day in promoting the idea of moving away from apartheid. In the new order after 1990, it came to accept that its ranks should be opened to Afrikaans-speaking males who were not white, but by then its influence was negligible. [I. Wilkins and H. Strydom, *The Super-Afrikaners* (Johannesburg, 1978); J. Serfontein, *Brotherhood of Power* (London, 1979); C. Bloomberg, *Christian-Nationalism and the Rise of the Afrikaner Broederbond* (Bloomington, 1989)]

AFRIKANER NATIONALISM. From the time of the Great Trek,* whites who spoke Afrikaans as their mother tongue were deeply divided. It was not until the 1870s that a common consciousness began to develop among Afrikaners in the interior and at the Cape, formed on the basis of the idea of a distinct culture and history and in opposition to British imperialism, at the time of the British annexation of the Transvaal. A strong nationalist movement did not emerge until the early 20th century. This had the goal of winning political power in the Union* inaugurated in 1910, and creating an Afrikaner republic.*

In the process of welding different Afrikaner groups into an ethnic coalition large enough to win political power, important roles were played by the Afrikaner Broederbond,* the Nasionale Pers group of newspapers, and the financial institutions Santam and Sanlam. Afrikaner intellectuals dwelt on the second-class status of Afrikaans, and in the 1930s took advantage of the economic crisis to mobilize poor Afrikaners with the message that their future was bound up with that of the *volk* as a whole. Immense popular enthusiasm for the nationalist cause was whipped up in 1938 during the commemoration of the centenary of the Great Trek. Gustav Preller and other writers created a largely mythical history in which a united Afrikaner people, chosen by God, had been oppressed by Britain and the English in South Africa. Eventually, sufficient Afrikaner farmers and urban workers, though still a minority of the white electorate, were persuaded to vote for the National Party (NP) to enable it to form a government in 1948. It was another decade before Afrikaner nationalist control was firmly in place, and not until 1961 that the NP was able to introduce the promised republic.

Only in the early 1990s, when the prospect of losing political power loomed, did a significant section of Afrikaners seek a separate territory (a *volkstaat*) for themselves, though no realistic, specific proposal for such a territory was advanced. [T. Moodie, *The Rise of Afrikanerdom* (Berkeley, 1976); H. Adam and H. Giliomee, *The Rise and Crisis of Afrikaner Power* (Cape Town, 1983); D. O'Meara, *Volkskapitalisme* (Johannesburg, 1983); L.M. Thompson, *The Political Mythology of Apartheid* (New Haven, 1985); G. le May, *The Afrikaners* (Oxford, 1995)]

AFRIKANER REBELLION (1914). Rebellion of Afrikaners in the Orange Free State and the Transvaal, many of them poor farmers or *bywoners* who opposed the government's decision, at the beginning of World War I, to invade South West Africa and seize it from the Germans. The rebels hoped to overthrow the government of Louis Botha,* and regain their lost republican independence. When government troops quickly put down the rebellion, the rebels were treated leniently, but the execution of Jopie Fourie turned him into a martyr, and some Afrikaners never forgave Botha and Smuts* for their role in suppressing the rebellion.

AFRIKANER RESISTANCE MOVEMENT (Afrikaner Weerstandsbeweging, AWB). A neo-Nazi, proto-fascist political movement led by the charismatic Eugène Terre'Blanche, it was established in 1973 to promote the interests of the 'Afrikaner *volk*', which its members claimed were being betrayed by the National Party and Afrikaner intellectuals. The movement first came to public prominence in 1979, when Terre'Blanche and others tarred and feathered the well-known historian Professor Floors van Jaarsveld in Pretoria for challenging the orthodox notion of divine intervention at the Battle of Blood River.* When the government began to negotiate the establishment of a democratic order, the AWB threatened that it would prevent any such transition by force. On 25 June 1993 a group of AWB members stormed the World Trade Centre, where multi-party negotiations were taking place. Driving an armoured vehicle through its plate-glass doorway, they occupied and trashed the negotiating chamber, before withdrawing. In March 1994 the AWB again overplayed its hand, when its armed wing, the Ystergarde, entered Bophuthatswana,* then had to withdraw, but not before the murder of three AWB members was captured on television. Some of its members set off bombs as the democratic election began in April 1994, but the threat of serious resistance to majority rule did not materialize. Concern about the far right as a potentially de-

7

stabilizing force nevertheless helped make the new ANC-led government move cautiously in its first years in power. [J. van Rooyen, *Hard Right* (London, 1994)]

AFRIKANERS. Before the 20th century, 'Afrikaner' often meant 'native of Africa', a person who identified with, and was usually born in, South Africa rather than Europe; 'Afrikaners' (variant form 'Afrikander') could therefore be of diverse origins. In the 20th century the term became confined to whites whose home language was Afrikaans. Always the majority of whites, and for most of the 20th century politically dominant, they were by the 1990s under 7% of the total population. At the beginning of the 20th century, most were rural people, but by the mid-1990s, when white Afrikaners numbered over three million people, over 80% lived in towns and cities.

Those whites who came to be known as Afrikaners were earlier often called Boers or, in the Cape, Cape Dutch. Descendants of immigrants of mainly Dutch, German and French extraction, they had by 1800 established themselves as a distinct people who saw themselves as independent of Europe. Under British rule in the 19th century, some in the western Cape became anglicized, while others sought to maintain a separate identity through the Dutch Reformed Church* and the promotion of their language, while yet others sought to escape British rule in the Great Trek.*

The South African War* was the most significant attempt by Afrikaners in the two republics to maintain their independence from Britain. Their terrible experiences in that conflict (see CONCENTRATION CAMPS) left a legacy of great bitterness, which was channelled into an incipient Afrikaner nationalism. The political party representing this nationalism won exclusive political power in 1948. Afrikaner hegemony was strongest during the 1960s and early 1970s, after which deep divisions among Afrikaners over the best methods to preserve Afrikaner identity again became significant. In 1990 F.W. de Klerk* seized what he saw as the best moment to end apartheid so as to preserve Afrikaner identity in the long term. [R. Elphick and H. Giliomee, eds., *The Shaping of South African Society* (Cape Town, 1989); H. Adam and H. Giliomee, *The Rise and Crisis of Afrikaner Power* (Cape Town, 1983); G. le May, *The Afrikaners* (Oxford, 1995)]

AFRIKANER VOLKSFRONT (Afrikaner People's Front). General Constand Viljoen emerged from retirement in late 1993 to lead right-wing Afrikaners who believed the National Party had betrayed Afrikaner interests, but who rejected the extremism of the Afrikaner Resistance Movement.* The Volksfront that Viljoen helped establish wanted a territory (*volkstaat*) to be demarcated, within which Afrikaners could enjoy self-determination. To that end, it sought for a time to forge an electoral alliance with the Inkatha* Freedom Party and bantustan leaders. The Volksfront was divided about participation in the April 1994 election, however, and Viljoen went his own way, registering a Freedom Front* party for the election. The fiasco of failed intervention to prop up the Mangope regime in Bophuthatswana* in March 1994 gravely weakened the Volksfront movement, which thereafter bore very little independent significance. [J. van Rooyen, *Hard Right* (London, 1994)]

AIDS (Acquired Immune Deficiency Syndrome). The first instances of AIDS in South Africa were recorded in 1982, when two white males died after infection by the human immuno-deficiency virus (HIV). The majority of initial infections occurred among white homosexual and bisexual men, but by the early 1990s, as was the case in the rest of Africa, most people infected were black heterosexuals, with men and women affected in roughly equal proportions. By November 1991, there were 985 known cases of people afflicted with AIDS, of whom 385 people had died; many thousands more had been exposed to HIV, but as AIDS was not a notifiable disease, accurate statistics of infections were difficult to obtain. By November 1996, official estimates of the Department of Health, based on the number of pregnant women entering antenatal clinics of the public health service, placed the number of people infected with HIV/AIDS at 2.5 million people, 6% of the total population, and it was estimated that new infections were occurring at the rate of approximately 1500 people per day, mainly among the economically active sector of the population in the 15–29-year age group. This made the South African epidemic one of the fastest-growing in the world. Although HIV/AIDS was well established throughout the country, the worst-affected region was KwaZulu-Natal. The rapidity of its spread was attributed in part to the legacy of apartheid, as migrant labour,* the disruption of family life, illiteracy, poverty, malnutrition and inadequate primary health-care facilities contributed to infection in rural areas and overcrowded urban settlements.

Government anti-AIDS programmes were dogged by controversy: much money was wasted over the production of a play, *Sarafina 2*, and the government was criticised in 1997–1998 for backing South African-based research into the Virodene drug before it had been properly tested. [M. Crewe, *AIDS in South Africa* (London, 1992); S. Cross and A. Whiteside, eds., *Facing up to AIDS* (New York, 1993)]

ALL-AFRICAN CONVENTION (AAC). Umbrella African political movement established in 1935 to try to halt the passage of legislation removing Cape African voters from the common voters' roll. After that legislation was passed in 1936 the AAC remained in existence and for a time existed alongside, and posed a challenge to, the African National Congress. But though the AAC tried to enter alliances with Coloured and Indian organizations, and gained considerable support in the Transkei, it lacked cohesion and disintegrated as the ANC revived itself in the 1940s. [C. Higgs, *The Ghost of Equality* (Cape Town, 1997)]

AMABUTHO (plural form of Zulu word *ibutho*, meaning 'those gathered together'). Groups of men or women who, on reaching puberty, were formed into age or circumcision sets. In the 18th century, in what became northern Natal, *amabutho* had important non-military functions: they colonized new land, hunted, and provided labour for their chief. The restrictions placed by the king on the marriage of members of *amabutho* (who were typically forbidden to marry for many years after recruitment) gave him control over their labour power for that period. The transition of male *amabutho* from traditional age-sets into military units stationed at royal barracks has been seen as crucial to the process leading to the formation of the Zulu kingdom* in the early 19th century. At a time of increasing competition for scarce resources and a share in the benefits of trade with Delagoa Bay, extended military and non-military service was required. The *amabutho* system remained fundamental to the organization of the Zulu kingdom throughout its independent existence. [J. Laband, *Rope of Sand* (Johannesburg, 1995)]

ANGLICAN CHURCH. After the second British occupation of the Cape (1806), Church of England ministers were appointed to serve the spiritual needs of colonial and military officials. With the arrival of the first bishop of Cape Town, Robert Gray (1809–1872), the church began to expand. Gray organized five dioceses and created the autonomous Church of the Province of South Africa (CPSA) in 1870, but his episcopate was plagued by controversies. Above all, he clashed with the Bishop of Natal, J.W. Colenso (1814–1883), whom he accused of heresy. Colenso's supporters formed a splinter church, but the Church of the Province was recognized by the Anglican Church in England and remained by far the more important of the two institutions. The Anglican Church thereafter enjoyed slow but steady growth, nurturing mission activities and educational work in particular. After 1948, some leading Anglicans became prominent in the struggle against apartheid. The most notable of these was Desmond Tutu,* who became the first black Archbishop of Cape Town. In the 1990s over two million South Africans owed allegiance to the CPSA. [P. Hinchliff, *The Anglican Church in South Africa* (London, 1963); J. Cochrane, *Servants of Power* (Johannesburg, 1987); F. England and T. Paterson, eds., *Bounty in Bondage* (Johannesburg, 1989); M. Worsnip, *Between the Two Fires* (Pietermaritzburg, 1991)]

ANGLO-BOER WAR. See ANGLO-TRANSVAAL WAR; SOUTH AFRICAN WAR

ANGLO-TRANSVAAL WAR (1880–1881). Sometimes known as the First Anglo-Boer War or the Transvaal War of Independence, this was a short conflict in which Afrikaners in the Transvaal sought to recover the independence lost when the British annexed their country in April 1877. After the failure of protests and petitions, they took up arms in December 1880. Their strategy was to besiege British garrisons, particularly at Potchefstroom and Pretoria, and prevent British reinforcements from entering the Transvaal from Natal. The fiercest fighting took place in Natal, where the republican Afrikaners won a number of victories, most notably at Majuba in February 1881.

By the time that battle took place, Britain had decided to restore a large measure of self-rule to the Transvaal. The Convention of Pretoria of 1881 revoked Britain's annexation and provided for self-rule subject to the suzerainty of Queen Victoria. The Transvaal's foreign relations remained under British control, and the Transvaal was forbidden to alter its boundaries without British consent. A British veto over legislation dealing with Africans was, however, removed by the London Convention of 1884. [J. Lehmann, *The First Boer War* (London, 1972); D. Schreuder, *Gladstone and Kruger* (London, 1969)]

ANGLO-ZULU WAR (1879). The most important in a series of wars between white and black in southern Africa in the late 1870s. The outbreak of war followed the presentation of an ultimatum by the British High Commissioner, Sir Bartle Frere,* demanding that Cetshwayo,* the Zulu king, dismantle the Zulu military system, an order which Frere knew was impossible for Cetshwayo to accept. Frere believed that he had to deal with the Zulu 'threat' if confederation in South Africa was to be achieved.

The advance of British and colonial forces into Zululand was halted in January 1879 at Isandlwana,* where the British suffered a shock defeat. The British soon recovered from this disaster, and by July had triumphed: Ulundi, the Zulu capital, was occupied, and Cetshwayo captured and sent into exile in Cape Town. General Wolseley then imposed a settlement which divided the Zulu territory into thirteen separate units, each under a ruler appointed by the British authorities. The aim was to balance mutually antagonistic forces (many of the new rulers were hostile to the Zulu royal establishment), but the result was a bitter civil war (1883–1884), which was followed by the annexation of Zululand by the British in 1887. [J. Guy, *The Destruction of the Zulu Kingdom* (London, 1979); A. Duminy and C. Ballard, eds., *The Anglo-Zulu War* (Pietermaritzburg, 1981); J. Laband and P. Thompson, *Kingdom and Colony at War* (Pietermaritzburg, 1990); J. Laband, *Kingdom in Crisis* (Pietermaritzburg, 1992)]

ANGOLA. Under Portuguese rule, Angola was a buffer between South African-ruled Namibia and countries under African rule to the north. When the Portuguese withdrew from Angola in 1975, the South African Defence Force (SADF) moved across the Namibian border to protect the hydro-electric scheme at Ruacana built jointly with the Portuguese. Then in October that year a relatively small force of South African soldiers moved north to the outskirts of Luanda, the capital, to try to ensure that the Marxist MPLA did not become the new government, for it was known that the MPLA would give succour to the South West African People's Organization (SWAPO), which the South Africans were fighting. When the South Africans confronted Cuban forces, and the United States pulled out, the South Africans had to retreat early in 1976.

SWAPO then established bases in southern Angola, from which its guerrillas moved into northern Namibia. The SADF launched an airborne assault on what was said to be SWAPO's main military base at Cassinga in May 1978. Most people there were refugees; over 600 civilians were killed. Numerous cross-border raids followed, and from 1981 the SADF was in permanent occupation of a strip of southern Angola north of the Namibian border. The SADF increasingly found itself fighting units of the Angolan army (FAPLA), and lending support to UNITA, the main opposition to the MPLA government. By early 1984, in part under American pressure, the South African government was ready to sign an agreement with the Angolans which provided for the withdrawal of South African forces. But problems ensued in the implementation of the Lusaka Accord (February 1984), and in May 1985 a South African commando was captured in the northern Angolan enclave of Cabinda, where it was planning to blow up oil-storage tanks. South African aid for UNITA then escalated, and by early 1988 South African forces were engaged in a major battle outside the Angolan town of Cuito Cuanavale.* The stalemate in that battle helped lead to formal negotiations with the Angolans and Cubans, and an agreement which provided for the withdrawal of all South African forces from

Angola by September 1988, and the withdrawal of Cuban forces from Angola by 1991. The South African government did not pay Angola any reparations for the vast damage caused by the SADF in years of fighting in the country. [C. Crocker, *High Noon in Southern Africa* (New York, 1992); W. Minter, *Apartheid's Contras* (Johannesburg, 1994)]

ANTI-PASS CAMPAIGNS. For much of the first half of the 20th century, pass laws* were the main target of African protest, and various campaigns were mounted against the *dompas* (*dom* meaning 'stupid' in Afrikaans), which was seen as a humiliating badge of inferior status. In 1913, African women in the Orange Free State waged an extensive passive resistance campaign against a local requirement that they carry passes. Another such campaign by both men and women in the Transvaal in March 1919 achieved nothing, and the Natives (Urban Areas) Act of 1923 extended the pass system. The African National Congress (ANC) protested through petition, while the Communist Party* organized occasional pass burnings. Another anti-pass campaign took place in 1944, after a brief period in which pass controls had been relaxed. The extension of passes to African women provoked widespread protests, culminating in a march of 20,000 women on the Union Buildings in Pretoria in August 1956, organized by the Federation of South African Women. The anti-pass campaign of the Pan Africanist Congress* in March 1960 ended tragically at Sharpeville,* in the aftermath of which Albert Luthuli,* leader of the ANC, and others burnt their passes in defiance of the law. For a few weeks the pass laws were suspended, but they were then reimposed and enforced with new vigour as government efforts to prevent more Africans settling in the urban areas intensified. [T. Lodge, *Black Politics in South Africa since 1945* (Johannesburg, 1983); J. Wells, *We Now Demand* (Johannesburg, 1993)]

APARTHEID (Afrikaans, literally 'apartness'). Term often used loosely to include all forms of racial segregation. It was coined to refer to the policy adopted by the National Party (NP) in the early 1940s to extend existing segregation, to make it more comprehensive, apply it more rigorously, and broaden its application. This policy was implemented after the NP won the election in 1948, reversing tentative proposals for lessening segregation put forward under the Smuts* government.

To begin with, apartheid was applied by the NP in a rather *ad hoc*, pragmatic fashion. It chiefly involved extending various forms of segregation, which had formerly applied only to Africans, to Indians and Coloureds. In its most developed form in the 1960s it meant, on the one hand, racial discrimination in almost all areas of life, and on the other the 'grand apartheid' of the bantustan system, but beyond this it continued to lack coherence.

An early Marxist interpretation of apartheid saw it as a rational response to the breakdown of the reserve economy, and a means of keeping labour costs low when the reserves could no longer bear the cost of reproducing the labour force. Most scholars have, however, viewed apartheid as primarily a political device to preserve racial identity and secure and bolster white supremacy and white privilege. In its early years it was also a means of consolidating the position of the Afrikaner nationalist movement. By the end of the 1950s apartheid had become – in the guise of

12

'separate development' – a policy to enable white supremacy to survive in the face of an emerging African nationalism, by dividing and repressing that nationalism, and obscuring a naked white supremacist position (see BAASSKAP).

It is impossible in a few words to express the extent of the hardships suffered by the victims of apartheid: it was enormously damaging psychologically, and produced such enormities as the forced removal of over three million people in an attempt to remove from 'white South Africa' as many blacks as possible without endangering the labour supply.

Relatively minor aspects of apartheid began to be abandoned by the government in the 1970s. In stages, multi-racial sport was allowed, and certain colour-bar restrictions were eased. From the late 1970s apartheid began to be reformulated, partly as a result of strong resistance from within the country and from the international community, and in part because it was economically impractical and was creating ever more violent conflict within the country. A major step in this process was taken in 1983 when Coloureds and Indians were brought into parliament through the tricameral* system. The pass laws,* a central feature of apartheid, were abolished in 1986. But the mid-1980s saw some of the harshest repression and the most violent actions in support of apartheid, including the killing of anti-apartheid activists by members of the security forces. It was not until the early 1990s that the remaining central pillars of the policy were abandoned. Apartheid in education remained for a time after the election of the first democratic government in 1994. The ruinous legacies of apartheid would bedevil the attempt to consolidate the new democracy and create a just and prosperous society. [M. Cornevin, *Apartheid and Historical Falsification* (Paris, 1980); H. Wolpe, *Race, Class and the Apartheid State* (London, 1988); D. Posel, *The Making of Apartheid* (Oxford, 1991); P. Bonner et al., eds., *Apartheid's Genesis 1935–1962* (Johannesburg, 1993); I. Evans, *Bureaucracy and Race* (Berkeley, 1997); M. Coleman, *A Crime Against Humanity* (Cape Town, 1998)]

'APPRENTICESHIP' (*inboekeling* system, from the Dutch, meaning 'those booked in'). A system of labour widely used in the interior of South Africa in the late 18th and early 19th centuries. Khoisan boys and girls seized in raids or military campaigns were 'apprenticed' to trekboer farmers, in theory for a limited period but usually until well into adulthood. Their children were in turn bound to the masters of their parents. In 1812, a Cape proclamation sought to regularize indentured servitude by restricting the practice to persons from 8 to 18 years of age. In addition to food, clothing and shelter, apprentices were supposed to be given some form of instruction by employers, but this was rarely done.

When slaves at the Cape were emancipated in 1834, they were 'apprenticed' to their former masters for a further four years, but few received any education. Similarly, people freed from slave ships by the British navy after 1808 received little instruction; over 4000 of these 'Prize Negroes' were indentured for 14-year periods between 1808 and 1844. The practice of 'apprenticeship' was extended into the interior by the Voortrekkers* and their descendants after the late 1830s. African homesteads were raided regularly by Boers in search of 'black ivory', and thousands of children were captured. This captive labour formed an important basis of the economies of the fledgling Boer states, enriching state officials in particular. Boer leaders agreed not to practise slavery when their independence was recognized by Britain in the early 1850s, but they regarded the apprenticeship system as qualitatively different: male apprentices worked until the age of 25, could not be sold for cash (though they could be bartered for goods) and were registered (or 'booked in') by court officials to ensure regulation of the system. [N. Worden and C. Crais, eds., *Breaking the Chains* (Johannesburg, 1994); E. Eldredge and F. Morton, eds., *Slavery in South Africa* (Boulder, 1994)]

ARMS EMBARGO. A non-mandatory embargo was imposed by the United Nations* (UN) Security Council in 1963, in the aftermath of the Sharpeville massacre.* This became a mandatory embargo when on 4 November 1977, after the Soweto uprising* and the murder of Steve Biko,* the Security Council passed a resolution declaring it illegal for any member of the UN to supply South Africa with arms. Some arms continued to flow in from Eastern Europe and third-world countries, with Israel and Taiwan acting as third-party agents. In the mid-1980s the United States, which had a more restrictive policy than the UN embargo required, threatened to cut off military aid to allies suspected of breaking the international arms embargo. This induced Israel to renounce new military contracts and cut back on scientific co-operation on arms-related items.

In response to the embargo, South Africa developed its own arms industry, which grew until it not only met most local requirements but was able to export weapons to other countries. Armscor, a public armaments manufacturing corporation, was established in 1966, to promote self-sufficiency in arms, and by 1988 arms were the country's largest type of manufactured export. In 1988 a new armoured vehicle, the Rooikat, was unveiled, and work was begun on an attack helicopter, the Rooivalk. The South African-developed G5 and G6 155mm howitzers, seen in action in southern Angola in 1988, were later used in the Iran–Iraq war.

Despite the lifting of most sanctions in 1991, the arms embargo remained in place until after the installation of the first democratic government in May 1994. Even after it was lifted, Armscor had to deal with arms smuggling charges which had been brought against it, and associated companies, in the United States in November 1991. The new government argued that the charges should be dropped, because the smuggling had taken place under the former regime, but the United States administration would not lift sanctions against Armscor until it had appeared in court. After years of dispute, a settlement was reached in 1997, Armscor and the companies were fined for violating US arms export controls, and the arms embargo was finally lifted in February 1998. Under the democratic government South Africa continued to sell considerable quantities of weapons, and much about the arms trade continued to be shrouded in secrecy. [S. Landgren, *Embargo Disimplemented* (Oxford, 1989); J. McWilliams, *Armscor* (London, 1989)]

ART. South Africa's earliest paintings date back over 20,000 years to the rock art of the San,* who depicted their physical environment and spiritual experience through paintings and engravings. During the 18th and 19th centuries, European travellers and colonial officials began to sketch their surroundings and produced a significant amount of pictorial Africana. Thomas Baines* was perhaps the leading figure in this genre of art. During the 20th century, South African-born professional painters began to establish their reputations locally and internationally. Landscapists such as J.E.A. Volschenk, Hugo Naudé, Frans Oerder and Pieter Wenning contributed significantly to the development of South African art. Irma Stern and Maggie Laubser were important pioneers of Expressionist innovation from the 1920s, and from the late 1930s the post-Impressionist work of Walter Battiss and Alexis Preller, inspired by African symbols from the past, won considerable recognition. Gerard Sekoto and black artists from the townships represented a different tradition of humanistic figurative expressionism, while Sydney Kumalo and Michael Zondi were among the country's most important sculptors. [E. Berman, *Art and Artists of South Africa* (Halfway House, 1993)]

ASIANS. See CHINESE, INDIANS

AUTSHUMATO (d. 1663). Also known as Harry or Herry, he was an important intermediary between the first European settlers at the Cape and the indigenous people they found there. He led the 'Goringhaicona', a small, impoverished group of Khoikhoi outcasts who lived on the shores of Table Bay and were known to early European sailors and settlers as 'Strandlopers' (literally, 'beach walkers'). Autshumato learnt to speak English when he was taken to Java by English sailors in about 1631. After the first Dutch settlement in 1652, he developed close ties with the settlers, who were heavily reliant on his knowledge of local conditions. He managed to build considerable prestige and wealth, but fell victim to inter-clan Khoikhoi rivalry and was banished to Robben Island* after losing the trust of the settlers. [R. Elphick, *Kraal and Castle* (New Haven, 1977)]

AZANIAN PEOPLE'S LIBERATION ARMY. See PAN AFRICANIST CONGRESS

AZANIAN PEOPLE'S ORGANIZATION (AZAPO). A Black Consciousness* organization founded in 1978 to work for a socialist state to be known as Azania. Though its rhetoric was radical, its membership remained small. It rejected the compromises which the African National Congress made in the negotiations prior to the April 1994 election, and refused to participate in that election. It then fell victim to internecine quarrels, which split the organization in two.

b

BAARTMAN, Saartje (d. 1815). A Khoisan woman, she was transported from the Cape to England in 1810, at about the age of 20. Exhibited as a freak, and perceived and portrayed as the 'Hottentot Venus', she was taken in 1814 to Paris, where an animal trainer paraded her daily in a shed until her death. Her body was then dissected, and her genitals and buttocks, seen as protuberant, excessive and grotesque, were turned into scientific exhibits. She became an icon for alleged sexual and racial differences between whites and blacks in the development of 19th-century racial science. In 1996–1997 a movement led by mostly Griqua people campaigned for the return of her remains from Paris, as part of a way to claim back their past.

BAASSKAP (Afrikaans, 'boss-ship', i.e. blatant racial domination). In the late 1950s Prime Minister Strijdom* admitted that his government's policy was baasskap. H.F. Verwoerd,* his successor, realized that baasskap was morally indefensible and hoped to deflect international criticism by reformulating the policy as 'separate development'.

BADEN-POWELL, Robert (1857–1941). British soldier who became famous in the South African War* for his leadership during the seven-month Boer siege of Mafeking in the western Transvaal. It was there that he had the idea of founding the Boy Scout movement, to which he devoted his energies after he resigned from the army. [T. Jeal, Baden-Powell (London, 1989)]

BAILEY, Abe (1864–1940). Mine magnate and politician, who made a fortune on the Witwatersrand goldfields and from other investments. He worked to promote British interests in South Africa, and became a leading philanthropist.

BAINES, Thomas (1820–1875). Prominent artist, traveller and explorer, who left a priceless legacy in the thousands of paintings, drawings and sketches he completed between his arrival in Cape Town in 1842 and his death in Durban. His works mainly depicted the landscapes and peoples of southern Africa, and reveal keen powers of observation and great perception. [J. Carruthers and M. Arnold, The Life and Work of Thomas Baines (Cape Town, 1995)]

BAKER, Herbert (1862–1946). The most significant figure in South African architecture, Baker sailed to South Africa from England in 1892, became a close friend of Cecil Rhodes,* and designed numerous buildings, from modest houses to the Union Buildings, Pretoria. He left South Africa in 1912. [D. Greig, Herbert Baker in South Africa (Cape Town, 1970); M. Keath, Herbert Baker in South Africa (Cape Town, 1992)]

BALLINGER, Margaret (1894–1980). Prominent liberal politician. An immigrant to South Africa from Scotland in 1904, Margaret Hodgson was educated at Rhodes and Oxford universities, and was from 1920 a lecturer in history at the University of the Witwatersrand. She was forced to give up that post when she married William Ballinger of the Industrial and Commercial Workers' Union* in 1934. Three years later she entered parliament as Native Representative for the Cape Division, having been asked to stand by the African National Congress. A forceful critic of government policy and strong champion of African interests, she retained her seat until African representation was abolished in 1960. From 1948 to 1960 she was the leading critic of apartheid in parliament. A founder member of the Liberal Party,* she was also its first leader, but resigned in 1955 because she could no longer combine her duties as parliamentarian with the party post. She disliked the party's shift to the left from the late 1950s, but in the mid-1960s returned to party activity. In retirement she wrote *From Union to Apartheid* (1969). [F. Mouton, *Voices in the Desert* (Pretoria, 1997); P. Lewsen, *Voices of Protest* (Craighall, 1988)]

BAMBATHA REBELLION (1906–1907). The last armed revolt in South Africa organized by a traditional ruler. The main precipitant was a poll tax imposed on all adult African males in Natal at the end of 1905. In February 1906 two white police officers were killed by armed Africans in the Richmond district, martial law was proclaimed, and the militia mobilized. Bambatha (c.1865–1906), a Zulu sub-ruler in the Umvoti district, became the focus of resistance. He and his followers retreated to the Nkandla forest, where they engaged in guerrilla struggle. In June 1906 this resistance was crushed at the Mome Gorge and Bambatha was killed, but further resistance continued in northern Natal until 1907. Between 3500 and 4000 Africans were killed, and about two dozen whites. Whites mainly blamed 'Ethiopianism', but although some *amakholwa* participated in the rebellion, most remained neutral and were regarded as traitors by the rebels. The uprising led the British government and many in the Cape to believe that small vulnerable states such as Natal would inevitably be prone to panic and brutality in their treatment of Africans, and this idea helped promote the cause of unification in South Africa. [S. Marks, *Reluctant Rebellion* (Oxford, 1970)]

BANNING. Persons, meetings, organizations and publications were all banned under South African law in the apartheid era (1948–1990). There were precedents for this: in 1929 an amendment to the Riotous Assemblies Act gave the Minister of Justice the power to order any person to leave a magisterial district; this was used to restrict the movement of trade union leaders and political opponents. Very much wider powers, given to the government by the Suppression of Communism Act of 1950, were used extensively thereafter. The typical 'banning order' issued under this Act, as amended, restricted an individual to a magisterial district, required him or her to report regularly to the police, prevented anything said by the person from being quoted, excluded him or her from visiting such places as educational institutions, factories and harbours, and prevented him or her from meeting socially with more than one person at a time. A banned person was usually the subject of constant police surveillance to see whether the banning order was being strictly adhered to. If the police suspected it was not, the person was brought to court. There was no appeal to the courts against a banning order, which was usually for five years, often renewed thereafter. From 1962 banning orders sometimes meant total or partial house arrest, the banned person being prevented from leaving home. Banning sometimes meant banishment: hundreds of Africans were forced to move to remote areas, where they were then restricted. (One of these was Winnie Madikizela-Mandela.*) Major political prisoners were usually banned or banished, or both, on completion of their prison sentences. The Suppression of Communism Act also outlawed the Communist Party of South Africa* and provided for persons to be 'named' for promoting the aims of communism, which was defined extremely broadly. Such 'named' persons were then 'listed' and forbidden to attend gatherings or belong to certain organizations, and nothing they said could be quoted and nothing they wrote published. Under other legislation the African National Congress* and Pan Africanist Congress* were banned in April 1960, the Black People's Convention (see BLACK CONSCIOUSNESS) and the Christian Institute* in October 1977. The United Democratic Front* was heavily restricted in February 1988. Various left-wing and African newspapers were forced to close down. Between 1950 and 1990 some 30,000 political publications were banned under various laws. After the unbanning of political organizations on 2 February 1990, the entire system fell away. [A. Mathews, *Law, Order and Liberty in South Africa* (Cape Town, 1971); J. Dugard, *Human Rights and the South African Legal Order* (Princeton, 1978)]

BANTU EDUCATION. Educational system for Africans designed to fit them for their role in apartheid society, as H.F. Verwoerd,* architect of the Bantu Education Act (1953), conceived it: 'There is no place for [the African] in the European community above the level of certain forms of labour... It is of no avail for him to receive a training which has as its aim absorption in the European community.' In 1953, 90% of African schools were state-aided mission schools; the 1953 Act removed control of African education from the churches and provincial authorities and placed it under a separate central government department. Only the Roman Catholic Church* attempted to keep its schools going without state aid. The 1953 Act also separated the financing of education for Africans from general state expenditure and linked it to direct tax paid by Africans themselves, which meant that far less was spent on African children than on white children.

Expenditure on Bantu Education increased dramatically from the late 1960s, because of a recognition of the need for a trained African labour force; this meant that more and more African children obtained some education. Though Bantu Education was designed to isolate Africans and prevent them from receiving 'subversive' ideas, indignation at being given such inferior education became a major focus for resistance, most notably in the Soweto uprising.* In the 1980s very little education at all took place in the Bantu Education system, which was the target of almost continuous protest. The legacy of decades of inferior education would last far beyond the introduction of a single educational system in 1995. [P. Kallaway, ed., *Apartheid and Education* (Johannesburg, 1984)]

BANTU-SPEAKING PEOPLE. The Bantu language group includes hundreds of related languages spoken in most of sub-Saharan Africa. Precisely when and how these languages spread into southern Africa remains uncertain, but it is probable that the first mixed farmers and first users of iron technology, who settled south of the Limpopo River* about 1800 years ago, brought with them a Bantu language. Those who spoke such languages are thought to have spread slowly southwards and westwards. Whites first encountered Bantu-speakers in the eastern Cape in the 16th century, and in the central interior at the beginning of the 19th century. Linguists have divided Bantu-speakers into four main categories. Nguni-speakers settled in the eastern coastal region, between the Indian Ocean and the Drakensberg range, and practised pastoralism, cultivation and hunting. Settlements tended to be small, although towards the end of the 18th century the northern Nguni began a process of consolidation and state formation. The Sotho–Tswana lived on the highveld in the interior in large settlements, and engaged in mining, smelting and extensive trade, as well as herding, cultivation and hunting. Venda- and Thonga-speakers remained confined to the extreme northern and north-eastern parts of the country respectively.

When white settlement began in the mid-17th century, Bantu-speaking farmers, perhaps between one and two million in all, occupied most of the well-watered areas of the country, apart from the extreme south-western portion. Their polities, though still relatively small, were stronger and more complex than those of the Khoikhoi pastoralists, some of whom were absorbed into Bantu-speaking groups.

The term 'Bantu' replaced 'Native' in official government usage during the 1960s and 1970s, and was despised by Africans chiefly because of its association with apartheid and inferior treatment. The words 'Bantu' and 'Bantus' were grammatical absurdities. From 1977 'Bantu' was gradually replaced by 'black'. [W.D. Hammond-Tooke, *The Bantu-speaking Peoples of Southern Africa* (London, 1974) and *The Roots of Black South Africa* (Johannesburg, 1993)]

BANTUSTAN POLICY. H.F. Verwoerd,* Minister of Native Affairs and then Prime Minister, and Dr. W.M. Eiselen, his Secretary for Native Affairs, were the architects of the policy of transforming the African reserves into self-governing states, the bantustans. In 1951 Verwoerd ruled out the possibility of full independence for these states, but in 1959 this became the goal of policy. Formulated in part as a response to increasing international pressure on South Africa to give some political rights to Africans in an era of African decolonization and independence, the bantustan policy was designed to maintain and strengthen white supremacy in the greater part of the country.

There were three main phases in the evolution of the bantustan policy. The Bantu Authorities Act (1951) created a hierarchical system of authority in the reserves in which appointed chiefs and headmen played a key role. Territorial authorities were set up for each so-called ethnic group except that the Xhosa,* for historical reasons, were given separate authorities on either side of the Kei River. Chiefs who did not co-operate in the new system were deposed and replaced, while those who co-operated became more clearly identified as instruments of the state. There was considerable resistance at the popular level to the implementation of

19

Bantu Authorities, especially in Pondoland in the Transkei and in Sekhukhuneland (see PEDI) in the eastern Transvaal. In the second phase, the Promotion of Bantu Self-Government Act (1959) recognized eight 'national units' (also called 'homelands') on ethnic grounds, and provided the machinery for these territories to be led to self-government. A ninth was later created in the Transvaal for the Ndzundza Ndebele.* The Transkei,* which had the largest single block of land under African occupation, was the first to be given limited self-government in 1963.

The third phase took the bantustans from self-government to full 'independence'. Again the Transkei led the way, being given its 'independence' in October 1976, followed by Bophuthatswana* in the western Transvaal, the Ciskei* in the eastern Cape, and Venda* in the far northern Transvaal. Other bantustans, including KwaZulu,* obtained self-government but not nominal independence, for Mangosuthu Buthelezi* of KwaZulu and Cedric Phatudi, chief minister of Lebowa in the Transvaal, refused to consider 'independence' for their territories. Because the whole bantustan policy was an integral part of apartheid, none of the 'independent' bantustans received international recognition. Each was recognized only by South Africa and the other independent bantustans (though the Transkei did not recognize Ciskei, because it wanted one political unit for all Xhosa-speakers).

For the new ruling elites 'independence' brought a certain power and status, considerable investment by Pretoria, and the opportunity to rid their countries of the racial indignities of apartheid. The rulers were quick to use authoritarian methods against their opponents, and their regimes were soon notorious for corruption. The possession of a casino, forbidden in South Africa proper, was often the best-known token of 'independence'. As bantustans became 'independent', large numbers of Africans, whether they lived in them or not, were deprived of their South African citizenship and made citizens of the new states. Government spokesmen expressed the hope that if all bantustans could be led to 'independence' or absorbed by other states (KaNgwane,* for Swazis, by Swaziland, QwaQwa* by Lesotho), no Africans would have South African citizenship, or any claim to rights within South Africa.

In reality, the bantustans were rural slums, totally dependent on South Africa. Only the minute QwaQwa, on the border of Lesotho, was a single block of land. The South African government spent vast sums buying land for 'homeland consolidation'. In 1960 about a third of the African population of South Africa lived within the borders of these territories; by 1980 over 40% did, because of some adjustments of borders, a fierce influx control policy and forced removals. In 1955 the Tomlinson report found that the maximum number of people these territories could support was 2.3 million, but by 1981 three times that number were living in them, and in that year they contributed only 3% to the country's total output. Well over half their economically active men were away working as migrants* at any one time. Though Bophuthatswana was the best endowed, thanks to platinum and the Sun City hotel complex, all the bantustans could survive only on hand-outs from Pretoria. Superfluous bureaucracies were created at great expense to the South African taxpayer. In Transkei, Ciskei and Venda, military rulers took power and governed autocratically.

The reincorporation of the bantustans was a *sine qua non* for the African National

Congress (ANC), and in the run-up to the April 1994 election, ANC leaders targeted bantustan governments hostile to them, in particular Ciskei, Bophuthatswana and KwaZulu. An ANC-organized march across the Ciskei border to the capital, Bisho, on 7 September 1992, was fired upon by Ciskeian troops (see BISHO MASSACRE). With the advent of a democratic order in April 1994, all the bantustans became part of the nine provinces of the new South Africa. [J. Butler, R. Rotberg and J. Adams, *The Black Homelands of South Africa* (Berkeley, 1977); B. Rogers, *Divide and Rule* (London, 1980); Surplus People Project, *Forced Removals in South Africa*, 5 vols. (Cape Town, 1983); L. Platzky and C. Walker, *The Surplus People* (Johannesburg, 1985); B. Egero, *South Africa's Bantustans* (Uppsala, 1991)]

BARENDS, Barend (c.1770–1839). Leader of a group of people of mixed descent in the Orange River area at the end of the 18th century. He was persuaded by missionaries of the London Missionary Society* to settle at Klaarwater (later Griquatown) in 1804. Within ten years, his people had merged into those called Griqua,* a relatively stable and established community in the area which came to be called Griqualand West.

BARNARD, Lady Anne (1750–1825). Writer and socialite at the Cape between 1797 and 1802. Her journals and letters, which recorded her extensive travels at the Cape and her close contacts with British and Dutch leaders from all walks of life, provide a valuable source of information on the period of the first British occupation of the Cape. [A. Robinson, ed., *The Letters of Lady Anne Barnard* (Cape Town, 1973)]

BARNATO, Barney (1852–1897). Prominent diamond magnate, born Barnett Isaacs, into a Jewish family from the Whitechapel district in London's East End. Barnato's career epitomized the dreams of thousands who sought their fortunes from the diamond mines of Kimberley.* He arrived there penniless in 1873, and managed to build his wealth through the Kimberley Central Company, which by 1888 had succeeded in taking over all the holdings at the Kimberley mine. Barnato's company was in turn taken over by the De Beers Company of Cecil Rhodes,* at a sum of over £5 million. Barnato served as a member of the Cape Legislative Assembly. He died mysteriously at sea. [R. Lewinson, *Barney Barnato* (London, 1937); S. Jackson, *The Great Barnato* (London, 1970)]

BARRY, James (c.1795–1865). Prominent surgeon at the Cape. A personal physician to Lord Charles Somerset, the Governor from 1814 to 1826, she was later Medical Inspector for the Cape Colony and Principal Medical Officer of the army at the Cape. Barry clashed regularly with the authorities over conditions in prisons and hospitals, and gained notoriety at the time when it was divulged on her death that she had spent her life disguised as a man in order to pursue a medical career. [I. Rae, *The Strange Story of Dr James Barry* (London, 1958)]

BARRY COMMISSION (1881–1883). Cape government commission on 'Native Laws and Customs' which sat under the chairmanship of J.D. Barry (1832–1905), a judge of the Cape's Eastern Districts Court. Appointed immediately after the Transkeian rebellion of 1880, the last armed African resistance to Cape rule, the commission recommended a system of law for the conquered societies east of the Kei River. It collected a mass of valuable evidence from Theophilus Shepstone* and others, and its report helped shape Cape African policy from 'identity' – one law for all – towards differential administration for the large African population of the Transkei.

BASTARDS (Bastaards, Basters). Term used in the 18th century for the offspring of mixed unions of whites with people of colour, most commonly Khoikhoi but also, less frequently, slaves. The offspring of African–Khoikhoi or slave–Khoikhoi unions were sometimes known as Bastard-Hottentots. Children produced of extramarital liaisons between whites and people of colour were not usually regarded as white, and Bastards were not usually accepted as free burghers.* Only in a few rare cases were children born out of wedlock of white fathers and Khoikhoi mothers baptized and accorded burgher status. Most offspring of white–Khoikhoi unions were regarded by whites as 'free persons of colour', 'free' because not slaves.

Rejected by white society, Bastards often formed separate communities on or beyond the Cape's northern frontier. There many lived a precarious existence between the advancing trekboers and indigenous peoples. Most Bastards used the name with pride, viewing themselves as superior to Khoikhoi because of their 'white blood'. The term was also extended to poor whites and dispossessed Khoikhoi who spoke some Dutch and owned firearms. One group of Bastards living north of the Orange River in the early 19th century was persuaded by a missionary of the London Missionary Society to change its name to Griqua.* [R. Elphick and H. Giliomee, eds., *The Shaping of South African Society* (Cape Town, 1989); R. Ross, *Adam Kok's Griquas* (Cambridge, 1976)]

BASUTOLAND. Name given by whites to the country of the BaSotho (southern Sotho), the state created by Moshoeshoe* as annexed by the British High Commissioner, Wodehouse, in 1868. It was taken over by the Cape in 1871. The magisterial system which the Cape government then imposed provoked Sotho resistance; a small revolt in the south-west of the region in 1878 developed into more widespread rebellion in 1880, when the Cape attempted to disarm the people. After the Gun War (1880–1881) ended in stalemate, the Cape, unable to assert its authority, asked Britain to assume direct responsibility for the territory; this occurred in 1884. During the 1870s Basutoland supplied large quantities of grain to the diamond fields, but by the early 20th century it was importing food and exporting only migrant labourers. The segregationist policies of South African governments after Union precluded its incorporation into South Africa.

When it achieved its independence from Britain in 1966 under the name Lesotho, it was already suffering extreme poverty and so was almost entirely dependent on South Africa. In the late 1960s Chief Leabua Jonathan developed friendly relations with the Vorster* government, though still advancing a claim to land in the eastern Free State, but then in the 1970s switched support to the ANC. This in turn led the opposition Basutoland Congress Party to seek support from pro-apartheid elements within South Africa. In the early 1980s the South African

Defence Force twice launched raids to kill ANC cadres living in Maseru, the capital. The imposition of a trade embargo by the South African authorities forced out the government, allowing pro-South African military men to take over. With the advent of a democratic regime in South Africa in 1994, relations between the two countries became more harmonious. A giant Highlands Water scheme, designed in the mid-1980s to provide water to the Witwatersrand, was continued and helped bind the two countries even further together; the first water from the Lesotho dams built in the first phase of the scheme reached South Africa at the beginning of 1998. At the same time, tens of thousands of Sotho migrants lost jobs on South Africa's gold mines, intensifying poverty in the mountain kingdom. S. Burman, *Chiefdom Politics and Alien Laws* (London, 1981); E. Eldredge, *A South African Kingdom* (Johannesburg, 1993); J. Bardill and J. Cobbe, *Lesotho* (Boulder, 1985)]

BATAVIAN RULE OF THE CAPE (1803–1806). Following the first British occupation (1795–1803), the Cape was ruled by the Batavian regime then in power in the Netherlands. The military governor, Jan Willem Janssens (1762–1838), assisted by an astute administrator, J.A.U. de Mist (1749–1823), implemented an extensive reform of the system of government, but financial constraints prevented them from dealing with frontier issues. At the Battle of Blaauwberg, near Cape Town, in January 1806, a British force under General Sir David Baird defeated Janssens and inaugurated the second, and permanent, British occupation. Historians once judged the Batavian period an enlightened one but now stress how conservative and authoritarian it was. [R. Elphick and H. Giliomee, eds., *The Shaping of South African Society* (Cape Town, 1989)]

BECHUANALAND. Land of the Tswana, or western Sotho. Believing that the Transvaal's westward expansion was threatening the strategically and economically important Road to the North,* and fearing that the Transvaal might eventually link up with German South West Africa and cut the Road completely, Britain annexed the Tswana territory in 1885. The region south of the Molopo River, the crown colony of British Bechuanaland, was incorporated into the Cape in 1895; much of it was to form part of the Bophuthatswana bantustan in the 1970s. The large area north of the Molopo, the Bechuanaland Protectorate, remained a High Commission territory, until it acquired independence as Botswana in 1966. After independence a major diamond industry was built up with De Beers expertise, though Debswana emerged as a separate company. Seretse Khama (1921–1980), whose marriage to a white English woman had greatly upset the apartheid government of D.F. Malan,* skilfully allowed people fleeing apartheid to transit through Botswana but would not give open support to the African National Congress (ANC). In June 1985 and May 1986, however, the South African Defence Force launched raids on ANC cadres living in Gaborone, the Botswana capital. After South Africa became a democratic country, the two countries worked together in the Southern African Development Community. [A. Sillery, *Founding a Protectorate* (The Hague, 1965); T. Tlou, N. Parsons and W. Henderson, *Seretse Khama, 1921–1980* (Braamfontein, 1995)]

BEIT, Alfred (1853–1906). Prominent mining magnate. A close confidant of Cecil Rhodes,* he assisted Rhodes in the amalgamation of the diamond mines in Kimberley,* as well as with the foundation of De Beers Consolidated in 1888 and the British South Africa Company* in 1889. A pioneer in the gold-mining industry in Johannesburg, he provided capital for the sinking of deep-level shafts on the Witwatersrand. [G. Fort, *Alfred Beit* (London, 1932)]

BERLIN MISSIONARY SOCIETY. Missionary society formed in Berlin, Germany, in 1824. It began to work in southern Africa in 1834, when five missionaries of the society established a mission station called Bethany among the Korana,* on land granted by the Griqua* leader Adam Kok, in what became the Orange River Sovereignty.* The society established missions across southern Africa, and also worked among labourers on the gold mines. [P. Delius, *The Conversion* (Johannesburg, 1984); L. Zollner and J. Heese, *The Berlin Missionaries* (Pretoria, 1984)

BIKO, Stephen Bantu (Steve) (1946–1977). Founder and martyr of the Black Consciousness* movement. Born in King William's Town, he attended a Roman Catholic school in Natal, then the University of Natal Medical School. Under his inspiration, African students broke with the National Union of South African Students* and established their separate South African Students' Organization in 1969. Dropping his medical studies, the charismatic Biko emerged as an outstanding organizer and theoretician, promoting Black Consciousness through his writing, speeches and actions. From 1973 he endured banning and other forms of state harassment. In September 1977 he died after being assaulted while in police custody. The Minister of Justice suggested he had died of a hunger strike, and said his death 'left him cold'. The subsequent inquest revealed that he had suffered brain damage and other injuries, then been kept naked and chained while transported overland from Port Elizabeth to Pretoria. The magistrate who presided at the inquest failed to find any person responsible for his death. Biko's family sued the state for damages and in 1979 settled for an out-of-court payment. The policemen responsible for his death applied for amnesty from the Truth and Reconciliation Commission* in 1997.

Biko's murder provoked an outraged reaction both in South Africa and abroad. The government responded in October 1977 by banning various individuals and organizations, including the Black Consciousness bodies Biko had been involved with. The following month the United Nations* Security Council agreed to a mandatory arms embargo* against South Africa. [S. Biko, *I Write What I Like* (London, 1978); D. Woods, *Biko* (New York, 1978); B. Pityana et al., *Bounds of Possibility* (Cape Town, 1991)]

BISHO MASSACRE (7 September 1992). Tens of thousands of African National Congress supporters marched from King William's Town to Bisho, capital of the Ciskei bantustan, to push for the removal of the Ciskei military leader, Brigadier Oupa Gqozo, from power. The march was part of an ANC campaign to unseat bantustan leaders who were seen to be allies of the apartheid government and unwilling to allow free political activity in their territories. Some of the unarmed demonstrators left the agreed path of the march and Ciskei soldiers opened fire on them, killing 28 and injuring 200. This shock to the ANC helped bring it back to the negotiating table and led directly to the Record of Understanding* between the government and the ANC. [R. Kasrils, *Armed and Dangerous* (London, 1994)]

BLAAUWBERG, Battle of (1806). Fought just north of Cape Town between the Dutch defenders of the Cape and the invading British forces. The victory of the latter meant the re-establishment of British rule, which then lasted into the 20th century. See also CAPE, BRITISH OCCUPATIONS OF.

BLACK CIRCUIT. Circuit courts were introduced by the Cape Governor Sir John Cradock in 1811 in order to extend government control and justice over the frontier districts; they were partly intended to control Khoikhoi vagrancy and regularize master–servant relations. In 1812, the 'black circuit' court sat, at which a number of colonists were accused of ill-treating their Khoikhoi servants on the basis of evidence collected by the missionaries James Read and Johannes van der Kemp.* Eight farmers were convicted, causing great resentment among the frontier colonists. [R. Elphick and H. Giliomee, eds., *The Shaping of South African Society* (Cape Town, 1989)]

BLACK CONSCIOUSNESS (BC). In reaction to white racism and liberal paternalism, black intellectuals, led by Steve Biko,* decided in the late 1960s that blacks (defined as all who were discriminated against on grounds of race) must organize themselves to promote black assertion and self-esteem, as blacks in the United States were doing. Blacks were told to rid themselves of their slave mentality: 'Black man, you are on your own' was the cry, and other slogans were freely borrowed from the American Black Power movement.

From the all-black South African Students' Organization (SASO) there emerged in 1972 a Black People's Convention (BPC), an umbrella political organization, 'to unite and solidify the Black people of South Africa with a view to liberating and emancipating them from both psychological and physical oppression'. Advocates of BC viewed the struggle in colour, not class, terms; its philosophy appealed to a small educated elite, at the black universities and church seminaries, and it never won mass worker support. African critics of BC argued that Coloureds and Indians had different interests, or rejected the emphasis BC placed on race.

Various black self-help, legal aid, and community programmes were established, but from 1973 the government, which initially had tolerated the movement because it seemed to fit in with 'separate development' ideology, began to clamp down on BC. Virtually the whole leadership of SASO and BPC was banned*; in 1974 rallies in support of the Frelimo government taking power in Mozambique were broken up by the police; and in 1975 twelve BPC and SASO leaders were charged under the Terrorism Act, nine of whom were subsequently convicted.

BC contributed significantly to the ferment behind the Soweto uprising,* but in September 1977 Biko died in detention and the following month the BC organizations were banned. BC ideas lived on in the Azanian People's Organization* and the banned Pan Africanist Congress* in particular. However, many leading BC members, especially those who after the Soweto uprising were imprisoned on Robben Island* or went into exile, were persuaded of the merits of the African National Congress. [G. Gerhart, *Black Power* (Berkeley, 1979); T. Lodge, *Black Politics in South Africa since 1945* (Johannesburg, 1983); B. Pityana et al., *Bounds of Possibility* (Cape Town, 1992)]

BLACK SASH. An organization of white women, originally the Women's Defence of the Constitution League, founded in 1955 to propagate respect for the constitution at the time of the Coloured vote issue. Its members stood in silence in public places, carrying placards and wearing white dresses crossed by broad diagonal black sashes, a symbol of mourning for the government's treatment of the constitution. While such picketing continued in subsequent decades, mainly on civil rights issues, the Sash's most significant work in the 1970s and 1980s was carried out in its advice offices in urban centres, which tried to help Africans with such problems as influx control,* unemployment, contracts, housing, and pensions. [C. Michelman, *The Black Sash of South Africa* (Oxford, 1975); K. Spink, *Black Sash* (London, 1991)]

BLACK SPOTS. When whites took over land from blacks in the 19th century, small areas in the midst of white-owned land were sometimes left in African hands. These became known as 'black spots' by the apartheid regime, which took steps, especially in the 1960s and 1970s, to clear them and consolidate all such land in white hands. In the late 1980s and 1990s some of these areas were given back to their former occupants.

BLEEK, Wilhelm Heinrich Immanuel (1827–1875). German-born linguist, scholar and librarian, whose most important work was on the /Xam language of the southern San. Together with his sister-in-law, Lucy Lloyd, who transcribed San myths and ritual accounts, he compiled over 12,000 pages of /Xam texts with English translations, an unrivalled ethnographic collection. His work was continued by his daughter, Dorothea Bleek, who produced a Bushman Dictionary based on his research. [J. Deacon and T. Dowson, eds., *Voices from the Past* (Johannesburg, 1966)]

BLOEMFONTEIN. Capital of the Free State, one of South Africa's nine provinces. Founded in 1846 by Major Douglas Warden as a fort, it became the centre of the British-administered Orange River Sovereignty (1848–1854) and of the independent Boer Republic of the Orange Free State (1854–1900). After the unification of South Africa in 1910, it became the judicial capital of South Africa, housing the appellate division of the Supreme Court. In the late 1990s it put itself forward as a possible seat for parliament, were it to move from Cape Town. [K. Schoeman, *Bloemfontein* (Cape Town, 1980)]

BLOEMFONTEIN CONVENTION. Treaty of February 1854 by which the British recognized the independence of the Boers living between the Orange and Vaal rivers. It made possible the establishment of the Republic of the Orange Free State.*

BLOOD RIVER, Battle of (1838). After considerable conflict between the Voortrekkers and the Zulu king Dingane in what is now KwaZulu-Natal, a Voortrekker commando of 470 men under the leadership of Andries Pretorius (1798–1853) set out to encounter the forces of Dingane. On 16 December 1838, at Blood River, their *laager* (a circle of ox-wagons bound together to keep enemies at bay) was attacked by an army of some 10,000 Zulu soldiers. Over 3000 Zulu were killed, while only three men were wounded on the Voortrekker side. The disaster forced the Zulu to recognize Voortrekker claims to Natal, and white settlement in the region was never again seriously threatened.

Before the battle, the Voortrekkers had made a vow to commemorate the day of victory. In the 20th century, 16 December became a day of great emotional significance for Afrikaner nationalists, who used it to stress their divine mission and proclaim their faith that God would stand with them against their enemies. The day was long known as Dingaan's Day, but it was renamed the Day of the Covenant in 1952 (from 1980, renamed the Day of the Vow). It was the day chosen by Umkhonto weSizwe* to launch its armed struggle in 1961, and so acquired new significance in resistance politics. From 1995 it was celebrated as the Day of Reconciliation. [L. Thompson, *The Political Mythology of Apartheid* (New Haven, 1985)]

BOER REPUBLICS. See ORANGE FREE STATE and SOUTH AFRICAN REPUBLIC

BOERS. Afrikaans word meaning 'farmers'. In the 18th century, it referred to white farmers but in the 19th century it came to be used for Afrikaners in general, or for the white inhabitants of the Voortrekker republics, or for those who fought on the republican side in the South African War.*

The term came to have derogatory connotations when used by non-Afrikaners. When used by English-speakers, it suggested backwardness and lack of culture, and many blacks used it for any white person associated with racism and apartheid.

BOER WAR. See SOUTH AFRICAN WAR

BOESAK, Allan (1946–   ). Preacher and politician. Having grown up in poverty, and suffered under the Group Areas Act,* he studied in the Netherlands in the 1970s for a doctorate on black power and black theology. As a minister in the Coloured section (Sendingkerk) of the Dutch Reformed Church,* he asked a meeting of the World Alliance of Reformed Churches in 1982 to declare apartheid a heresy, and was elected president of that organization. A founding member of the United Democratic Front (UDF) in August 1983, he led much UDF resistance in the mid-1980s, most notably a planned march on Pollsmoor prison in August 1985. He also founded and headed a Foundation for Peace and Justice, to channel foreign money to aid those who suffered under apartheid.

When in 1990 his extramarital affair with a television producer was exposed, he left the church. In 1994 he led the African National Congress's election campaign in the Western Cape, and after the election was named as ambassador-designate to the United Nations in Geneva. But then the leading donor supporting his

Foundation, DanChurch Aid of Denmark, questioned where some of its funds had gone to, and his ambassadorship was cancelled. He left for the United States to teach and preach, but returned in March 1997 to face charges that he had misappropriated over R1 million in donor funds.

BOOMPLAATS, Battle of (1848). It took place in the north of the present Free State. Sir Harry Smith, Governor of the Cape and High Commissioner, led British forces which defeated a Voortrekker commando under Andries Pretorius, who was seeking to reverse the British annexation of the land between the Orange and Vaal rivers. The British victory confirmed the establishment of British rule north of the Orange, and those Boers who had sought to resist it retreated north of the Vaal.

BOPHUTHATSWANA. Bantustan for the Tswana which the South African government led to nominal 'independence' in 1977. It then comprised seven non-contiguous pieces of land in the central and western Transvaal and the north-western Cape, as well as Thaba Nchu in the Orange Free State. The most viable economically of all the bantustans, thanks to its platinum and chrome mines and the revenue it derived from the Sun City casino complex, it nevertheless obtained a quarter of its budget directly from Pretoria, and another 30% from the South African customs union. Half its labour force were migrants in South Africa.

The autocratic Lucas Mangope (1923–), its first chief minister and then president, was ousted by a military coup in 1988, but then was restored to power by the South African Defence Force. A white Bophuthatswanan representative played an active role in the negotiations for a democratic South Africa in the early 1990s. But the end came quickly: in March 1994 civil servants went on strike, violence erupted in Mmabatho, the capital, and Mangope, in enlisting the support of General Viljoen,* opened the door to the arrival of members of the Afrikaner Resistance Movement (AWB), whose presence further inflamed the situation. Television cameras recorded a local soldier shooting two members of the AWB as they lay wounded besides their car. Representatives of the Transitional Executive Council (TEC) informed Mangope that he had to resign. Bophuthatswana was then administered by the TEC until formally reincorporated into South Africa in April 1994. A commission of inquiry which reported in 1995 found that Mangope had been involved in massive corruption, and in 1997 a large number of charges were brought against him. [A. Jeffrey, *Conflict at the Crossroads in Bophuthatswana* (Johannesburg, 1993)]

BOTHA, Louis (1862–1919). First Prime Minister of the Union of South Africa. The son of Voortrekker parents, he spent his early life in the north-eastern Free State. He aided Dinuzulu* in the Zulu civil war of 1884, and settled in the New Republic, which was later incorporated into the Transvaal. During the South African War,* in which he rose to the rank of general, he displayed outstanding tactical and leadership abilities. After the war, he forged ahead with a political career, becoming chairman of Het Volk party in the Transvaal (1904), Prime Minister of the Transvaal (1907) and Prime Minister of the Union in 1910, a position which he held until his death in 1919. He preached reconciliation between Afrikaners and English-speaking whites, and defended the preservation of South Africa's imperial connections with Britain. Many former Afrikaner allies were alienated by this stance, and in particular by his forceful suppression of the Afrikaner Rebellion in 1914. The occupation of German South West Africa by South African forces in 1915 was regarded as one of his most significant triumphs. He attended the Paris Peace Conference in 1919 shortly before his death.

BOTHA, Pieter Willem (1916–) National Party (NP) Prime Minister and State President. A full-time NP organizer from 1936, he served in the South African parliament from 1948 to 1989. From 1966 he was Minister of Defence. His election as Prime Minister in September 1978 by the NP caucus (the parliamentary members meeting together) was a result of the Information Scandal, which divided the Transvaal members of the caucus and gave Botha, Cape leader of his party, the support of the Free State bloc. Closely associated with the military, he supported the South African army's invasion of Angola in 1975 and the great increase in military spending thereafter. After his election as Prime Minister, government rhetoric became dominated by talk of 'total onslaught' and of a total strategy to combat such a total onslaught. During his premiership vast destabilization took place of neighbouring countries, the work of covert South African forces. Though he told his electorate soon after becoming Prime Minister that they must 'adapt or die', his reformist vision did not extend much beyond the establishment of a new tricameral constitution which provided for a measure of Coloured and Indian participation in central government. This was enough to drive the far-right members to break from the NP in 1982 and establish the Conservative Party.*

Under the tricameral* constitution, Botha became the country's first executive State President in 1984, with greatly increased powers. Always authoritarian in manner, his irascibility increased as resistance grew. His 'Rubicon speech' of August 1985, which failed to deliver on expectations for change, was a disaster for the country, and in May 1986 he ended the attempt by the Commonwealth Eminent Persons Group to bring about negotiations between the government and the ANC. But he did abolish the pass laws,* permitted his officials to begin negotiations with the ANC in 1986, agreed in 1988 to allow Namibia* to move to independence, and had a cordial meeting with Nelson Mandela* in July 1989, the month before he was ousted as State President by his own cabinet. His cabinet claimed that the stroke he suffered in January that year had impaired his health, but he charged that this was merely an excuse for getting rid of him. In retirement, he settled at the Wilderness, in the Cape, and made clear that he disliked the course F.W. de Klerk took as State President. In late 1997 he was subpoenaed by the Truth and Reconcilation Commission to give evidence in public before it, but he refused to attend and was then served a summons to appear in court. [B. Pottinger, *The Imperial Presidency* (Johannesburg, 1988); R. Schrire, *Adapt or Die* (Cape Town, 1992); D. O'Meara, *Forty Lost Years* (Johannesburg, 1996)]

BOTHA, Roelof ('Pik') (1932–). Flamboyant and controversial politician who became the longest-serving Foreign Minister in the world. A lawyer by training, he joined the Department of Foreign Affairs, and became a member of South Africa's legal team in the South West Africa case at the International Court of Justice at The

Hague, then served as ambassador to the United Nations from 1974 and thereafter to the United States, until in 1977 he became Minister of Foreign Affairs, a post he retained until the new government took office in May 1994. A political survivor, he was almost dismissed by P.W. Botha in 1986 when he suggested that South Africa might one day have a black President.

A popular speaker at National Party (NP) rallies, he was regarded as being on the left of the party. He lost out in elections to the leadership of the party in 1978 and 1989, but strongly backed De Klerk in his reform initiative, was active in the negotiations of the early 1990s, and was appointed to the Government of National Unity (GNU) as Minister of Mineral and Energy Affairs in 1994. He left politics when the NP withdrew from the GNU in mid-1996.

BOTSWANA. See BECHUANALAND

BOYCOTTS. From the 1940s boycotts of various kinds were a much-used form of protest against white domination, at a time when few other legal forms of protest were possible. Between 1940 and 1945 rises in bus fares on the Witwatersrand produced a spate of bus boycotts, and further boycotts of public transport took place in the townships of Evaton in 1950 and Alexandra in 1957. The latter lasted over three months and involved over 60,000 commuters; the outcome was that employers had to subsidize the transport costs of their African workers. In 1959 the African National Congress organized a three-month consumer boycott of potatoes, in protest against the oppressive treatment by farmers of their labourers. Schools were boycotted in 1955, in response to the implementation of Bantu Education,* and school boycotts became frequent in the late 1970s and 1980s. In the 1980s numerous rent and service boycotts were mounted by township inhabitants; by 1990 R1.15 million was owed to local authorities. Such boycotts continued and grew during the transition period. After the establishment of a democratic government a Masakhane campaign was launched to persuade township residents to pay rents and service charges; after the local government elections of November 1995 this began to achieve some successes.

BRAND, Johannes Henricus (1823–1888). Cape lawyer and parliamentarian who was summoned from Cape Town to become President of the Orange Free State in 1864, an office he held until his death. Under his leadership, the Free State seized the land west of the Caledon River from the Sotho, and would have taken more had not Britain annexed Basutoland in 1868. Brand was then able to say that the Free State had 'solved' its 'native [African] problem'. Unable to obtain the diamond fields for the Free State, he got £90,000 in compensation from the British in 1876. An able administrator – the Free State became known as the 'model republic' – Brand acted as conciliator between the Transvaal and Britain in the Anglo-Transvaal War in 1881. He continued to prefer closer co-operation with the Cape than with the Transvaal, but became more favourably disposed towards the Transvaal in his later years. [T. Barlow, *President Brand and His Times* (Cape Town, 1972)]

BRITAIN IN SOUTH AFRICA. From the end of the 16th century, British ships engaged in trade with India and the East began calling at the Cape of Good Hope to allow their crews to rest. It was not until September 1795, however, that Britain occupied the Cape, out of anxiety about the growth of French military power in Europe, which occurred partly at the expense of the Dutch, and fearing for the safety of its trading routes. Britain was concerned to prevent the French from capturing the Cape, and sought to maintain the status quo at the Cape as far as possible, guaranteeing Dutch language rights, the legal system and religious freedom. In terms of the Treaty of Amiens between Britain and France, the Cape was handed back to the Dutch, now the Batavian authorities in the Netherlands, in 1803. The British reconquered the Cape in January 1806 after relations with France deteriorated. Again, Britain regarded its presence as temporary, emphasizing only the importance of protecting the sea route, and doing little to disturb social structures in the colony. British troops were, however, used in the frontier war of 1811–1812 to help expel the Xhosa from the disputed Zuurveld. British rule became permanent in terms of the London Convention of August 1814, when the Dutch formally ceded the Cape to Britain. Thereafter, the British swiftly established a stronger and more efficient colonial state, and remained the dominant power in southern Africa for the remainder of the 19th century.

British troops continued to play an important role on the Cape's eastern frontier in a series of wars from 1819 to 1878. Britain was anxious that commercial expansion should occur at the Cape, so that it could be an effective part of its imperial system of free trade and private enterprise. To this end, economic reforms were sporadically implemented in the first decades of British control. Monopolies and trading restrictions were loosened, roads and communications were improved, the land-tenure system was reformed, and banks and insurance companies were founded. Wheat and wine production increased until the 1820s, after which eastern Cape wool began to take over as the colony's chief export. Economic imperatives also led to the ending of slavery in 1834. The British made far-reaching administrative, legal and bureaucratic reforms, which culminated in a new constitution; this conferred representative government on the Cape in 1854, and in essence transferred political power from London to the Cape's white inhabitants, though the franchise* was non-racial.

From the beginning of the century, but particularly from the 1830s, British traders, hunters, speculators and missionaries moved beyond the borders of the Cape into the interior of the subcontinent. In Natal, conflict between Voortrekkers, English traders and Africans led to British annexation in 1843. Thereafter, Natal became a second major territorial and political focus for the British in southern Africa. The constitution granted to Natal in 1856 allowed Britain to continue controlling executive appointments, but permitted the white minority to elect a legislature.

Conflict between and within Boer, Griqua, Tswana and Sotho polities on the Cape northern frontier during the 1830s and 1840s increasingly occupied Britain's attention. The Orange River Sovereignty was annexed in 1848 in the hope of settling territorial disputes, but Britain's military reversal at the hands of Moshoeshoe in 1851 prompted it to withdraw, concluding that military and administrative obligations were too expensive. Britain recognized the independence of the Trans-

31

vaal in 1852 and the Orange Free State in 1854. Out of concern that ongoing disputes between the Orange Free State and Moshoeshoe would threaten its strategic interests and the stability of the Cape's frontiers, Britain again intervened in 1868 by annexing Basutoland as a British colony.

Britain's major motive for involvement in the interior was to ensure the security of its economic interests further south: the control of the Cape sea route and the monopoly of southern Africa's external trade. The discovery of diamonds at the end of the 1860s, however, gave Britain a new economic interest in the interior. In 1871 Britain annexed Griqualand West, which was incorporated into the Cape in 1880; major industrialists and local diggers effectively controlled the area with the support of British officials. During the 1870s, the economic necessity of securing a stable labour supply to the diamond fields became a priority for the British, and political solutions were sought in the form of confederation. Confederation schemes failed, but this did not put paid to the powerful interests who argued that the political fragmentation of southern Africa into British colonies, independent Boer republics and autonomous African societies was disadvantageous to Britain. Britain adopted a more forceful stance, annexing the Transvaal in 1877, defeating the Pedi in 1879, and provoking the Anglo-Zulu War in 1879. Britain thus achieved a decisive shift in the balance of power in southern Africa in favour of white colonists and imperial economic interests. During the 1880s, Britain extended its political and economic interests by annexing Bechuanaland in 1885 to prevent the Germans in South West Africa from forming a common boundary with the Transvaal, while Rhodesia was brought under the British flag by Cecil Rhodes in 1890.

The discovery of gold in the Transvaal deepened Britain's commitments and economic interests significantly. The majority of the 44,000 Uitlanders on the Witwatersrand were British, and their grievances with the government of Paul Kruger gave impetus to a process of more aggressive British involvement. Under Joseph Chamberlain, the Colonial Secretary, and Sir Alfred Milner, the High Commissioner, British policy led to increasing tension with the Transvaal, culminating in the outbreak of the South African War in 1899. The war proved unexpectedly difficult to win and enormously costly to Britain, which had anticipated the rapid demise of republican power. Although Britain emerged victorious in 1902, and Milner valiantly attempted to cement British supremacy through autocratic government and anglicization policies in the immediate aftermath of the war, Britain began to reassess its approach to southern Africa. After the election of a Liberal government in Britain at the beginning of 1906, self-government was granted to the Transvaal and Orange River Colony, and negotiations for a unified South Africa began formally at the National Convention in 1908. The Union of South Africa was inaugurated in 1910. This suited Britain's interests: its military, financial and political obligations were lessened, while as long as South Africa remained within the empire there was little threat to its economic and strategic concerns.

Though the British government was much less directly involved in South African affairs after 1910, strong links between the two countries were retained. South Africa actively fought in both world wars on Britain's side, despite the opposition of Afrikaner nationalists and a measure of discord between the two main white groups in the country. Britain remained South Africa's chief trading partner and largest source of foreign investment even after South Africa declared itself a republic* and withdrew from the Commonwealth* in 1961. [J. Benyon, *Proconsul and Paramountcy* (Pietermaritzburg, 1980); G. le May, *British Supremacy in South Africa* (Oxford, 1967); J. Barber and J. Barratt, *South Africa's Foreign Policy* (Cambridge, 1990)]

BRITISH KAFFRARIA. Territory between the Keiskamma and Kei rivers which was annexed in 1847, at the end of a frontier war, by Sir Harry Smith (1787–1860), Governor of the Cape and High Commissioner, who sought by so doing to control a major section of the Xhosa.* But the annexation helped provoke a larger Cape–Xhosa frontier war in 1850. British Kaffraria was ruled directly by the High Commissioner until 1860, when it was constituted a separate crown colony. In 1866 it became part of the Cape Colony, and was sometimes known as the Ciskei. White settlement was encouraged in the area after the cattle-killing* of 1857, which severely weakened Xhosa power, and again after the last frontier war in 1878. [N. Mostert, *Frontiers* (London, 1992)]

BRITISH SOUTH AFRICA (BSA) COMPANY. Founded by Cecil Rhodes* and granted a royal charter by Queen Victoria in October 1889 to operate in a large territory north of the Limpopo River, the BSA Company played a role in the Jameson Raid.* This was launched from a strip of territory which Joseph Chamberlain, the British Colonial Secretary, gave it for a railway. Otherwise, the history of the Company belongs to that of Rhodesia/Zimbabwe.* [J. Galbraith, *Crown and Charter* (Berkeley, 1974); A. Keppel-Jones, *Rhodes and Rhodesia* (Pietermaritzburg, 1983)]

BROOM, Robert (1866–1951). Prominent palaeontologist, who worked at the Transvaal Museum, and contributed important insights into the origins of mammals, based on his work on reptilian fossils found in the Karoo. In 1947 he discovered an adult skull, named Mrs Ples, at Sterkfontein near Johannesburg, which he identified as belonging to the species *Australopithecus*, and by means of which the earlier studies of Raymond Dart on the Taung skull were verified.

BULHOEK MASSACRE (1921). When the Israelites, a religious sect led by Enoch Mgijima, refused to move from land near Queenstown in the eastern Cape, the government of General Jan Smuts resorted to force, and 163 Israelites, armed only with ceremonial weapons, were killed. Bulhoek became a symbol of white savagery against Africans. [R. Edgar, *Because They Chose the Plan of God* (Johannesburg, 1988)]

BURCHELL, William John (1781–1863). Traveller, botanist, artist and author. Burchell travelled extensively, building up valuable and extensively annotated botanical collections. His *Travels in the Interior of Southern Africa*, written in the early 1820s, is one of the most important accounts of the environment and peoples of early 19th-century southern Africa.

BUREAU OF STATE SECURITY (BOSS). Created by Prime Minister Vorster in 1969, BOSS co-ordinated and evaluated intelligence, and engaged in clandestine operations both within South Africa and abroad in support of apartheid. It infiltrated agents into a number of anti-apartheid organizations and engaged in 'dirty tricks' campaigns. Under Vorster, it became the elite security apparatus of the state; its head, General Hendrik van den Bergh, was Vorster's close friend. After Vorster's fall, the discredited BOSS was restructured and renamed the Department of National Security, which became the National Intelligence Service and, after 1994, the National Intelligence Agency. [G. Cawthra, *Policing South Africa* (London, 1993); J. Brewer, *Black and Blue* (Oxford, 1994)]

BURGERS, Thomas François (1834–1881). Liberal, reformist Dutch Reformed Church theologian who served as President of the South African Republic from 1871 to 1877. During his presidency, he initiated reforms in administration, the judiciary and education, and strongly supported the construction of a railway between the Transvaal and Delagoa Bay as a way to limit British influence in the interior of southern Africa. But he was disliked by many Transvaal Boers, who refused to pay taxes and serve on commando, and his government was easily ousted by Theophilus Shepstone* in April 1877. [M. Appelgryn, *Thomas François Burgers* (Pretoria, 1979)]

BUSHMEN. See SAN

BUTHELEZI, Mangosuthu Gatsha (1928–). Zulu politician, descended from both Cetshwayo* and Cetshwayo's chief minister at the time of the Anglo-Zulu War*; also a nephew of Pixley Seme.*
Expelled from Fort Hare in 1952 for African National Congress (ANC) activities, he became an adviser to the Zulu king. Having attempted unsuccessfully to resist the imposition of the bantustan system on his people, Buthelezi decided to work through it, becoming chief minister of KwaZulu* in 1972. He emerged as the most outspoken bantustan leader, rejecting independence for his fragmented and impoverished territory. Accused of lending credibility to the bantustan policy, he argued that use should be made of any platform to fight apartheid, even a platform created by apartheid. He supported federalism as a device which would allow for redistribution of wealth to Africans, while allaying white fears, and he encouraged foreign investment in South Africa on the ground that it provided jobs for Africans.
In the mid-1970s he revived Inkatha* as a mass organization with the tacit support of the ANC. In the Soweto uprising,* he backed the Zulu hostel-dwellers against the youth. Black Consciousness* supporters condemned him as a sell-out, and threatened his life at the funeral of Robert Sobukwe* in March 1978. He broke decisively with the ANC at a meeting with the exile leadership in London in 1979, refusing to adopt a different strategy and rejecting the armed struggle. Though he continued to work for the release of Nelson Mandela* from jail, from the mid-1980s his party was involved in a virtual civil war with the United Democratic Front* in KwaZulu-Natal. This became a conflict between Inkatha and the ANC itself in the early 1990s, and in all perhaps ten thousand people lost their lives.

Having rejected the interim constitution negotiated at the World Trade Centre in 1993 because of its failure to accept federalism, he held out against participation in the April 1994 election, but was persuaded to join in at the very last minute on 19 April. His party won over 10% of the vote and control of KwaZulu-Natal.

After the 1994 election, he became Minister of Home Affairs in the Government of National Unity.* In 1997 there was speculation that he might be offered the post of Deputy President. [G. Maré and G. Hamilton, *An Appetite for Power* (Johannesburg, 1987); Mzala, *Gatsha Buthelezi* (London, 1988)]

BYWONER (from the Dutch *bijwoner*, meaning 'one who lives with another'). White tenant farmer. There had been *bywoners* at the Cape from the late 17th century, but they came to prominence as a group only towards the end of the 19th century, when land had become scarce and their numbers had increased in consequence. The Roman-Dutch system of partible inheritance led to the subdivision of land into small and uneconomic units, forcing increasing numbers of landless men to work for others. *Bywoners* were given the use of land in exchange for a share of their crop or herd, and sometimes for seasonal labour service. Some were virtually independent farmers, while others could be little distinguished from wage labourers. Pressures on *bywoners* became intense at the end of the 19th century: as land values rose and agriculture became more commercialized, *bywoners* were ejected from many farms. Some became transport riders, but the completion of the railways to the Witwatersrand in the 1890s put most transport riders out of business. Many *bywoners* were hit hard by the rinderpest epidemic among their cattle in 1896 and 1897, and the South African War escalated the process by which many were transformed into an impoverished urban proletariat. In the early 20th century, *bywoner* became virtually synonymous with the term 'poor white'. [R. Morrell, ed., *White But Poor* (Pretoria, 1992)]

C

CALEDON CODE (1809). A systematic collection of laws relating to the Khoikhoi issued by Lord Caledon, Governor of the Cape. It provided that there had to be a written contract between employer and employee, and contained clauses designed to protect the Khoi, but also to encourage them to work: they were required to have a fixed place of abode and to carry a pass if they moved about. It was these restrictive clauses, along with others in the apprenticeship law of 1812 tying the Khoikhoi further to their white masters, which John Philip* of the London Missionary Society* campaigned against, and which were repealed in Ordinance 50* of 1828.

CAPE, BRITISH OCCUPATIONS OF. The strategic value of the Cape of Good Hope on the sea route to India, and a desire to prevent the capture of the Cape Peninsula by France during the Napoleonic Wars, persuaded the British to take over the Cape in September 1795. A large British garrison was stationed in Cape Town, and the trading monopolies of the Dutch East India Company were loosened, but the British authorities otherwise did little to alter patterns of government and life in the Cape. They also failed to bring stability to the troubled eastern frontier.

In 1803, one of the terms of the Treaty of Amiens between Britain and France provided for the handing back of the Cape to the Dutch, and the new Batavian regime in the Netherlands assumed control. The resumption of the Napoleonic Wars, however, resulted in the reoccupation of the Cape by the British in January 1806. Again, Britain regarded its presence there as temporary, and did little to disturb the status quo. In August 1814, at the end of the Napoleonic Wars in Europe, the Cape was formally ceded by the Dutch to Britain, which as a result became the dominant power in southern Africa for the remainder of the century. [R. Elphick and H. Giliomee, *The Shaping of South African Society* (Cape Town, 1989)]

CAPE COLONY (1652–1910). The name 'the Cape' was first given to the south-western tip of the African continent by the Portuguese, the first Europeans to see it. The colony was founded by Jan van Riebeeck,* an employee of the Dutch East India Company (VOC). When he landed on the shore of Table Bay in 1652, at the site of present-day Cape Town,* Van Riebeeck did not intend to establish a colony of settlement, but merely a refreshment station for Dutch ships trading between the Netherlands and the VOC's eastern possessions. The aim was to grow sufficient crops and to establish favourable trading relations with the indigenous Khoikhoi.* But in 1657 farms beyond the VOC's area of jurisdiction, behind Table Mountain, were allocated to nine free burghers.* The following year the first slaves were imported; from then on, the slave community remained an important component of the colonial population, and indeed for most of the 18th century exceeded in number the colonists. In 1659 the first conflict took place between the colonists and the Khoikhoi pastoralists, who found themselves excluded from the land on which the colonists had settled. Some Khoi retreated into the interior, others became labourers for the whites.

By the beginning of the 18th century the colonists had settled almost all of the south-western Cape, whose Mediterranean climate made possible the growing of wheat and the cultivation of vines. From early that century increasing numbers of colonists trekked north and east into the more barren interior, where they engaged in pastoralism on large tracts of land. This trekboer* movement greatly enlarged the area of the colony, for the colonial boundary was moved progressively further into the interior in their wake. The trekboers demanded extensive tracts of land for their livestock and hunting activities, and the VOC granted them 'loan' farms, the boundaries of which the farmers were able to set themselves.

San hunter-gatherers and Khoikhoi offered sporadic but limited resistance to the white advance, and many of these indigenous people had no choice but to become serfs on white farms. By the end of the 1770s the colonial boundary in the east was fixed some six hundred miles from Cape Town, on the Fish River. To the west of this frontier the advancing trekboers had encountered their first serious obstacle, Bantu-speaking pastoral farmers, who effectively blocked significant further east-ward expansion for a period of one hundred years, from the time of the first frontier war in 1779 until the ninth and last in 1878.

The British occupied the Cape in 1795, and although the Cape reverted briefly to Batavian control between 1803 and 1806, the British consolidated their rule after 1806. During the 19th century, the Cape doubled in size. The northern boundary was extended to the Orange River in 1847, and separate crown colonies on the frontiers were incorporated during the latter part of the century: British Kaffraria in 1866, Griqualand West in 1880, and Bechuanaland in 1895. Basutoland was annexed in 1871, but reverted to British government control in 1884; the Trans-keian territories were incorporated in stages between 1879 and 1894.

Until the 1880s the Cape was by far the most powerful state in southern Africa, but then the political and economic balance swung towards the gold-rich Transvaal. Although the South African Republic was defeated during the South African War,* the Transvaal was quickly able to reassert its power thereafter, and its representa-tives dominated the crucial debates during the National Convention,* particularly on the franchise* question. The Convention refused to allow the extension of the Cape's non-racial franchise to the rest of what would become the Union of South Africa. So although the Cape entered the Union of 1910 as the largest province by area, its political influence was secondary to that of the Transvaal, and it was the Witwatersrand which remained the economic powerhouse of the country. [W. James and M. Simons, eds., *The Angry Divide* (Cape Town, 1989)]

CAPE TOWN. The place of the first permanent European settlement in South Africa, and hence known to many white South Africans as the 'mother city'. The Table Bay area had been inhabited for centuries by San hunter-gatherers and Khoikhoi pas-toralists before the Dutch East India Company established a small settlement in 1652. As the number of houses in the white town grew, from 155 in 1710 to about 550 in 1770 and 1200 by the early 19th century, so De Kaap became Kaapstad and then Cape Town. In 1806 the population (excluding government employees and the British garrison) was 16,500, of whom almost 10,000 were slaves and 800 free blacks. The number of slaves declined after the end of the slave trade in 1808, and

37

with growing British immigration whites became a majority of the town's population in about 1840.

Cape Town was the military headquarters of the expanding Cape Colony, the administrative centre of the hinterland, and the marketing centre for the wine and wheat farmers of the south-western Cape, but until the mid-19th century it was chiefly dependent on its trade with passing ships and its position as port of entry to the interior. After the wool boom in the eastern Cape during the 1840s and 1850s, Cape Town lost its pre-eminent commercial position, although its merchants remained powerful, providing the capital for commercial expansion in the east. Only in 1860 was work begun on the harbour breakwater, to give protection from the gales in Table Bay. After the discovery of diamonds and gold, Cape Town became one of the main ports of entry into the interior; with the increase in shipping the docks became the largest employer of labour in the city by the end of the 19th century.

At the turn of the century, the population of the city reached 77,000. Africans only began to move to Cape Town in significant numbers during the last decade of the 19th century. No enforced residential segregation existed until 1901, when Africans were placed in a location at Ndabeni, outside the city, during a plague epidemic. Ex-slaves and their descendants lived on the fringes of the city, in the Malay Quarter, and in the area which became known as District Six.* Cape Town enjoyed a reputation for racial tolerance and political liberalism, partly because of its non-racial municipal franchise based on property.

During the 20th century, Cape Town became an industrial city, and the textile industry in particular developed as a key economic enterprise. From 1910 the city was the seat of the Union parliament. After 1945 the pace of urbanization increased. Afrikaner migrants tended to settle in the northern suburbs, while Africans were placed in the new locations of Nyanga and Guguletu. Residential apartheid was strictly enforced after 1966, when District Six was proclaimed a white area, and thousands of people were forced to move to the Cape Flats. This coercion attracted international attention, as did conflict during the 1980s within the squatter settlement of Crossroads, close to Cape Town's airport. Crossroads was one of several areas housing a large number of Africans attracted to Cape Town in the hope of finding employment, despite legislation to keep them away.

By the 1990s, Greater Cape Town had a population of almost three million people, and a high rate of unemployment, particularly in some of the newer townships such as Mitchell's Plain and Khayelitsha, to which Coloureds and Africans respectively had been forced to move. In the Coloured areas in particular, a gang culture flourished, which in turn led to the formation of the anti-gang group People Against Guns and Drugs (PAGAD) in 1995. It was from the balcony of Cape Town's City Hall that Nelson Mandela delivered his first speech after walking out of jail on 11 February 1990; he was made a freeman of the city in 1997. After the successful completion of the democratic transition, parliament continued to meet in Cape Town, although there was much agitation for it to be moved to Gauteng. Cape Town became the seat of the new provincial government of the Western Cape. In 1997, Cape Town won a place on the short-list of five cities bidding for the summer Olympic Games in 2004, but in September that year heard that its bid had not been successful. [V. Bickford-Smith, *Ethnic Pride and Racial Prejudice in Victorian Cape Town* (Johannesburg, 1975); J. Western, *Outcast Cape Town* (Berkeley, 1996)]

CARNARVON, Henry Howard Molyneux Herbert, Fourth Earl of (1831–1890). Secretary of State for the Colonies from 1874 to 1878. Having confederated Canada, Carnarvon was keen to do the same in South Africa. He began by attempting to bring together the leaders of the various white-ruled states at a conference. When that failed, he appointed Sir Bartle Frere* as High Commissioner to pursue the goal of confederation* and steered enabling legislation through the British parliament. But he left office before Frere led Britain into the Anglo-Zulu War,* after which confederation was abandoned as British policy. Though confederation was not achieved, in trying to confederate South Africa Carnarvon set in motion forces which were to transform the subcontinent.

CATTLE-KILLING (1856–1857). In 1856 a Xhosa girl by the name of Nongqawuse prophesied that if cattle were killed and no crops cultivated a new age would dawn for her people. The Xhosa paramount chief Sarili believed her, and a large number of his followers, devastated by recent intense frontier conflicts and an epidemic of lungsickness among their cattle, did what she advised. On 16 February 1857, she claimed, the ancestors would arise and provide abundant cattle and food. When this did not happen, the unbelievers (who had refused to believe the prophecy) were blamed for the catastrophe by the desperate majority who had slaughtered their cattle. Well over 20,000 people starved to death, and many more were forced as refugees into the Cape Colony to seek work. The Cape's Governor, Sir George Grey, took advantage of the situation by driving Sarili from his land east of the Kei River, and he resettled whites and Mfengu in the cleared area. The ability of the Xhosa to resist colonial advance was destroyed for almost a generation.

Xhosa tradition ascribes the cattle-killing to the manipulation of Grey, the missionaries and white traders, all of whom did indeed benefit from the subsequent events. At the time, Grey himself blamed Sarili and Moshoeshoe for plotting to instigate these events in order to force their people into the colony. The cattle-killing is best understood as a millenarian response to the processes of colonization, which had been eating into the fabric of Xhosa society for decades. [J. Peires, *The Dead Will Arise* (Johannesburg, 1989)]

CENSORSHIP. Censorship of the press began at the Cape as early as the 1820s. Political censorship took on new meanings in the apartheid era. The Suppression of Communism Act (1950 and later amendments) prevented banned and listed persons from being quoted, or anything they wrote from being published. Radical newspapers were suppressed. While such censorship fell under the Ministry of Justice, the Publications and Entertainments Act of 1963 created a government-nominated Publications Control Board under the Ministry of the Interior, which could ban publications for a number of reasons, one of which was 'harming relations between sections of the community'. Few bans were appealed against, because of the costs involved. New legislation in 1974 provided for decisions on banning to be taken by local committees of censors, with appeals going to a Directorate of

Publications. A new category of 'possession prohibited' was added to earlier bans on distributing material, so that mere possession became a crime, whether or not the publication had been acquired legally and in good faith, and whether or not the owner knew of the findings of the censor board. In the early 1960s many of South Africa's black writers had their works proscribed, and by the late 1980s well over 30,000 works had been banned, the majority for 'endangering the state'. Censorship helped prevent whites from realizing the nature of apartheid's crimes and understanding the opposition to apartheid. With the end of apartheid in the 1990s censorship disappeared. [C. Merrett, *A Culture of Censorship* (Cape Town, 1994)]

CETSHWAYO (c.1826–1884). The son of the Zulu king Mpande, Cetshwayo showed considerable political and military skill in surviving intense power struggles with both his father and brother in the 1850s and 1860s. On the death of his father in 1872, he inherited a united and loyal kingdom. He agreed to be 'crowned' by Theophilus Shepstone,* but was determined to maintain the independence of his kingdom. Within a few years, however, the Natal settlers, Shepstone himself and the High Commissioner had all come to view him as a danger to imperial and settler interests. He was portrayed as a military dictator who posed a threat to white-ruled Natal and who prevented his people from leaving the kingdom to work for whites. In December 1878 Sir Bartle Frere presented him with an ultimatum which he could not accept, and in January 1879 British forces invaded his kingdom. Within months his armies had been defeated and he was arrested and sent to Cape Town. After a visit to England to meet Queen Victoria, he was allowed to return to Zululand, now divided by internecine feuding, in 1883. He died shortly afterwards in mysterious circumstances. [C. Webb and J. Wright, eds., *A Zulu King Speaks* (Pietermaritzburg, 1978); J. Laband, *Rope of Sand* (Johannesburg, 1995)]

CHAMBERLAIN, Joseph (1836–1914). British Secretary of State for the Colonies from before the Jameson Raid until after the South African War. Coming into office in 1895, he helped Cecil Rhodes prepare for the coup he was planning against the Transvaal. When the Raid failed, Chamberlain denied knowledge of it, and survived. A staunch British supremacist, he was responsible for the appointment of Sir Alfred Milner as High Commissioner, and worked closely with him in formulating British policy towards the Transvaal. He was therefore responsible in part for pushing South Africa towards war in 1899, believing, like Milner, that the war would be a short one and was necessary for the maintenance of British supremacy. [A. Porter, *The Origins of the South African War* (Manchester, 1980); P. Marsh, *Joseph Chamberlain* (New Haven, 1994)]

CHAMBER OF MINES. Formed in 1887, the Chamber of Mines was a co-ordinating body that represented the interests of the mining houses, particularly in seeking to formulate policy regarding labour recruitment and conditions of service for workers. Centralized organizations were established to handle labour recruitment from Mozambique in 1896 and within South Africa's borders and the High Commission territories in 1912. The Chamber of Mines largely succeeded in eliminating competition between its members and different mines for labour, and remained a powerful voice within the country's most important wealth-generating industry for much of the 20th century.

CHINESE. Though Chinese labourers were brought to the Cape in the 18th century, the present-day Chinese community in South Africa is descended from 19th-century traders and merchants. Like Indians, early immigrants suffered from trading and immigration restrictions. Many were imprisoned at the beginning of the 20th century for resisting registration laws.

After the South African War, the gold mines on the Witwatersrand faced a critical labour shortage: the need to bring them back to full production as rapidly as possible, and the shortage of African labour, prompted Sir Alfred Milner,* the High Commissioner, to recruit labour from North China. The first 10,000 workers arrived in South Africa in May 1904. Over the next four years, 63,296 Chinese indentured workers were sent to the Witwatersrand on three-year contracts. They were housed in compounds, prevented from holding skilled positions, and were not allowed to trade or to own land. Whites, who feared competition, strongly opposed their presence, and by 1910 all the Chinese labourers introduced under this scheme had been repatriated. They played an important role in the rehabilitation of the mines, and their acceptance of low wages undercut the bargaining power of African miners, who after 1906 began to seek work on the mines again in significant numbers.

During the apartheid era, the small Chinese community – estimated to be under 9000 in 1980 – experienced some statutory discrimination, but not as far-reaching as other ethnic groups. They were classified as 'Coloured' under the Population Registration Act of 1950, and the Group Areas Act of the same year made provision for separate residential areas for Chinese people, but few such areas were in fact proclaimed. Most Chinese benefited from their 'honorary white' status: they were allowed to live and trade in white areas, send their children to white schools, and attend recreational venues in white areas. Few participated actively in politics, either in support of or against the apartheid political order. [P. Richardson, *Chinese Mine Labor in the Transvaal* (Atlantic Heights, 1982); M. Yap and D. Man, *Colour, Confusion and Concessions* (Hong Kong, 1996)]

CHRISTIAN INSTITUTE of Southern Africa (CI). An independent ecumenical organization for promoting dialogue and witnessing to reconciliation, founded in 1963 by Beyers Naudé, former Moderator of the Dutch Reformed Church. As the CI became more involved in work with Africans, it grew more radical. It promoted the study of the Christian role in apartheid society and reacted sympathetically to the development of 'black theology', which was ideologically tied to the Black Consciousness* movement. In 1975 the CI was declared an 'affected organization', which meant it could no longer receive financial aid from outside the country, and in October 1977 it was banned,* along with its journal *Pro Veritate*, Beyers Naudé and other officials. [P. Walshe, *Church Versus State in South Africa* (Maryknoll, 1983)]

CHRISTIANITY. Bartolomeu Dias erected a limestone pillar capped by a Christian cross at Kwaaihoek, near Bushman's River mouth on the southern Cape coast, on 12 March 1488. A permanent Christian presence in southern Africa began with the founding of the refreshment station at Table Bay by the Dutch East India Company in 1652. The Company established the Dutch Reformed Church as the only lawful religious organization at the Cape. No other religious body could function in public until 1778, when Lutherans were permitted public worship. Despite formal commitment to the spread of Christianity, little missionary activity occurred during the 18th century. Because whites appear to have regarded their identity as 'Christians' as a key characteristic distinguishing them from other groups, they did not consider religious conversions to be a priority.

By contrast, the 19th century, the period of British colonial and commercial conquest, saw determined work by Christian missionaries. Evangelical concerns were conspicuous ingredients of the message of the missionaries, but these were closely linked to the advance of European notions of civilization and education, the promotion of trade and commerce, and the expansion of British political and military hegemony. The influence of missionaries varied from region to region, as did the responses of Africans to Christianity. Many African societies rejected the Christian gospel, while using missionaries for their own purposes, particularly the exploitation of material and technological benefits such as firearms and ammunition, irrigation and the plough. Missionaries and Africans frequently found themselves in deep confrontation on the material as well as the spiritual and cultural levels. Only after the weakening of African societies during the latter half of the 19th century did missionaries achieve significant numbers of conversions.

Also during the 19th century, various denominations founded institutional structures and congregations. The majority of these were Protestant and, despite different historical and cultural origins, often shared similar values. The Dutch Reformed Church, divided into three separate churches, established itself among the Dutch-speaking white population, and set up racially separate congregations for Coloureds and Africans. Among the English-speaking population, Anglicans, Methodists, Presbyterians, Congregationalists and Baptists were the prominent denominations. Roman Catholicism grew steadily after the arrival of the first bishop in 1838.

The 20th century saw the most rapid growth of Christianity, which developed from a mainly white, minority and imported faith to one embraced by a majority of South Africans, and expressed in a wide variety of ways. Christianity was used during the 20th century to justify apartheid and Afrikaner nationalism, but many of the mainline churches, whose membership crossed social and racial divides, opposed apartheid, often in pronouncements issued by church leaders.

By the 1990s, some 80% of the population claimed some form of Christian allegiance. Whites had become a numerical minority within most denominations; there were also 5000 African independent churches* who had a following of over eight million people, and encompassed a wide range of religious, ritual, faith-healing and prophetic expressions. [J. de Gruchy, *The Church Struggle in South Africa* (Cape Town, 1979); R. Elphick and R. Davenport, eds., *Christianity in South Africa* (Cape Town, 1997)]

CHURCH OF THE PROVINCE. See ANGLICAN CHURCH

CISKEI (land 'this side', i.e. west, of the Kei River). The Ciskei, home of the Xhosa, was annexed as Queen Adelaide Province by Governor Benjamin D'Urban in 1835, but the authorities in London insisted it be given up the following year. It was not until 1847, at the end of the War of the Axe, that it once again became British territory, this time permanently. The Xhosa who lived there tried to maintain their independence, but were defeated in the War of Mlanjeni (1850–1853) and then suffered the disaster of the cattle-killing. They nevertheless went into a final rebellion in 1878. By then numerous whites had been given land in parts of the Ciskei, which became a chequerboard of black and white areas of settlement.

The African areas were brought together under a 'homeland' administration and the bantustan of Ciskei was then granted 'independence' in December 1981. At that time it had a *de facto* population of 650,000, almost all Xhosa-speakers, but its 'independence' meant the loss of South African citizenship for some 1.5 million others who were classified as Ciskeian but who did not live in the territory. In the 1970s, the Ciskei served as the dumping ground for at least 150,000 people forcibly removed there, and an additional 250,000 Africans were moved from the port city of East London and settled within the Ciskei at Mdantsane, which was by 1980 the second largest dormitory town for Africans in the country after Soweto. By independence half the Ciskeian population lived below the poverty datum line, and well over half of all earnings came from migrant labour outside the bantustan. Malnutrition was rife and it was estimated that half of all children died before the age of five.

Once 'independent', the Ciskei, with its capital at Bisho, was run by an authoritarian oligarchy headed by Lennox Sebe, whose Ciskei National Independence Party had won every seat in the rigged 1978 election, and who accepted 'independence' against the advice of a commission he himself had appointed. In a referendum on the issue in 1980, though almost everyone supported independence, only 60% of the population voted and widespread intimidation was alleged. Sebe, who made himself president-for-life, was eventually ousted by Brigadier Oupa Gqozo, whose troops fired on ANC demonstrators in the Bisho massacre of September 1992, and who left office in March 1994 after Lucas Mangope had been forced from power in Bophuthatswana. From April that year the Ciskei was reincorporated into South Africa as part of the new Eastern Cape province. [L. Switzer, *Power and Resistance* (Madison, 1993)]

CIVIC ORGANIZATIONS. Community-based organizations became important in black townships from the late 1970s. The Soweto uprising led to the creation of a Committee of Ten in Soweto, from which emerged the Soweto Civic Association, headed by Dr Nthato Motlana. Other prominent civics included the Port Elizabeth Community Organization (PEBCO), in which Thozamile Botha was the leading figure, and the Alexandra civic, led by Moses Mayekiso, a union organizer. Many civics affiliated themselves to the United Democratic Front (UDF) in 1983, and played an important mobilizing role in the township revolt of 1984–1986. They participated in rent and consumer boycotts, and in some areas became *de facto* local administrations. In the new era after 1990, in which they could openly support the African National Congress, their importance declined. The South African National Civic Organization (SANCO), launched in March 1992 under Moses Mayekiso, did not strengthen the civics on the ground, and a number of their leading figures moved into government. SANCO declined further when it engaged unsuccessfully in business-type operations after the 1994 election and by early 1998 it was reputedly bankrupt.

CIVIL CO-OPERATION BUREAU (CCB). In 1986 approval was given – at what level remains unclear – for the establishment of a covert organization operating under the Special Forces of the South African Defence Force and linked to Military Intelligence. Its main objective was maximum disruption of South Africa's enemies, perceived to be the African National Congress and its allies. It was not until 1990 that news of some of its projects began to be leaked to the media. They included attempts at intimidation, arson, bombing and the assassination of left-wing activists, such as the University of the Witwatersrand activist-anthropologist, Dr David Webster, in May 1989 and the Namibian lawyer Anton Lubowski, shot in Windhoek in September 1989.

In August 1990 the government announced that the CCB would be disbanded, but over two years later some of its projects had not yet been wound up. Some commentators saw the CCB as a product of the P.W. Botha securocrat era, and believed that F.W. de Klerk* had acted to the best of his abilities to end covert operations against his main negotiating partner; others believed that such operations had been allowed to continue because weakening the ANC served the interests of the National Party government. [P. Laurence, *Death Squads* (Johannesburg, 1990); J. Pauw, *In the Heart of the Whore* (Halfway House, 1991)]

COLENSO, John William (1814–1883). Controversial Bishop of Natal, who took up his post in 1853. His theological ideas split the Anglican Church during the 1860s, and his support for the Zulu,* particularly at the time of the Langalibalele affair in the 1870s, earned him the censure of the majority of white settlers in Natal. The Zulu knew him as 'Sobantu', 'father of the people'. [J. Guy, *The Heretic* (Pietermaritzburg, 1983)]

COLOURED LABOUR PREFERENCE POLICY (CLPP). Its origins lie in the 1920s, with attempts by the Cape Town City Council to ensure that jobs went to Coloureds rather than Africans. It became official policy of the apartheid government in 1954, the aim being to reduce the number of African workers in the western Cape. It fell away in the late 1980s, by which time the number of Africans in the western Cape had increased greatly despite the CLPP. [I. Goldin, *Making Race* (Cape Town, 1987)]

COLOURED PERSONS REPRESENTATIVE COUNCIL (CRC). The apartheid government established the CRC in 1968 as an attempt to delegate certain powers to Coloured people, but the majority of Coloureds boycotted elections for the council. When the Labour Party gained control of the CRC in 1975, it set out to make it unworkable, and the CRC was disbanded.

COLOUREDS. In the early 19th century, white colonists at the Cape distinguished themselves from 'people of colour', a category which included Khoikhoi,* free blacks and people of mixed descent. Slaves formed a separate legal category. During the 19th century, and particularly in the decades after the emancipation of slaves in 1838, a nascent shared identity developed among these diverse components of the labouring class in the western Cape. As the social changes brought about by industrialization and the mineral revolution began to take hold at the end of the 19th and beginning of the 20th centuries, a more distinct 'Coloured' identity emerged. The arrival of significant numbers of Africans in the western Cape led Coloureds to assert their difference, on the basis of partial descent from European settlers and generations of incorporation into colonial society, but the category was an extremely fluid and ill-defined one.

Though Coloureds had long had close contact with whites, and spoke the same language (Afrikaans rather than English), they were not accepted into white society and came to occupy an intermediate position in South Africa's racial hierarchy. Light-skinned Coloureds were able to 'pass' into white society, and the Cape Supreme Court found in 1911 that there was no clear way in which such people could be distinguished from whites. Coloureds were not subject to the same discrimination as Africans: for example, they did not have to carry passes and could enter cities as they wished. Segregationist measures and treatment were nonetheless applied, although white supremacists remained divided on whether Coloureds belonged on the white or African side of the racial divide. The Cape School Board Act of 1905, for example, excluded most Coloureds from the new system of general public education. Franchise privileges were not extended to Coloureds in the northern provinces at the time of Union. The economic position of Coloureds, particularly the educated elite, was undermined during the 1920s and 1930s by government policies designed to favour whites over blacks in the competition for jobs. When the franchise was extended to white women, as well as to all white males over the age of 18, at the beginning of the 1930s, only Coloured males over the age of 21 who met the predetermined economic and literacy criteria retained the right to vote.

During the apartheid era, Coloureds endured far more severe restrictions. The Population Registration Act of 1950 emphasized association and ancestry rather than colour to establish who was 'Coloured', with Griquas and Malays as specified sub-groups. Mixed marriages were outlawed, public facilities segregated, and remaining franchise rights lost, for Coloureds in the Cape were removed from the common voters' roll in 1956. During the 1960s, tens of thousands of Coloureds were forcibly relocated to live in their own 'group areas' in terms of the Group Areas Act; white extremists even toyed with the idea of establishing a Coloured 'homeland'.

Considerable division existed among Coloureds about the wisdom of forming separate political parties. This reflected the ambivalent position of Coloureds within the wider society. The need to oppose spreading segregation, however, led to the founding of the first major political body for Coloureds, the African Political Organization, in Cape Town in 1902. Under its president for 35 years, Abdullah Abdurahman, the APO was moderate in its approach to white racism and exclusivity, and advocated assimilation and co-operation with whites as far as possible. More radical groups, which rejected the APO's restrained strategies, established themselves during the 1930s and 1940s. The most prominent of these were the National Liberation League (founded 1935) and the Anti-CAD (Anti-Coloured Affairs Department), affiliated to the Non-European Unity Movement (founded 1943). After the Coloureds were removed from the voters' roll in 1956, they were given the right to elect four white members to parliament on a separate roll. The Anti-CAD movement organized a successful boycott of these elections. In 1959, a Coloured Affairs Department was established, with its own Minister of Coloured Affairs. In 1968, the system of representation of Coloureds in parliament by whites was abolished, and replaced by a Coloured Persons Representative Council (CRC), which was empowered to administer 'Coloured affairs' in areas such as local government, finance, education, welfare and pensions. A boycott of elections to this council was again advocated, but the Labour Party decided to contest the elections, although it rejected the body as an apartheid creation. After the CRC was closed in 1975, the authorities sought new ways of incorporating Coloureds into the political process.

With the inauguration of the tricameral parliamentary system in 1983, a separate House of Representatives was created with powers to administer Coloured 'own affairs'. Coloured people again split over the desirability of participation in these structures, and many Coloureds became involved in various extra-parliamentary movements, led by the broadly based United Democratic Front. In these movements the label 'Coloured' was rejected as an artificial category imposed by an authoritarian and racist state. The idea that Coloureds had specific group interests was rejected, and people identified themselves as 'blacks' or as belonging to 'the oppressed'. But a 'Coloured identity', distinct from that of the white minority or the black majority, proved enduring. In the democratic election of 1994 both the National Party and the African National Congress appealed to some extent to Coloured identity; one key factor in the National Party's victory in the provincial election in the Western Cape was its successful play on Coloured fears about the security of their homes and employment under a black majority government.

In the 1990s the approximately three million Coloureds in South Africa constituted some 8% of the country's population. Over two-thirds of them lived in the Western Cape, while there are sizeable Coloured communities in the Eastern Cape, Northern Cape and Gauteng. [R. van der Ross, *The Rise and Decline of Apartheid* (Cape Town, 1986); G. Lewis, *Between the Wire and the Wall* (Cape Town, 1987); W. James and M. Simons, eds., *The Angry Divide* (Cape Town, 1989); W. James et al., *Now That We are Free* (Cape Town, 1996); I. Mandaza, *Race, Colour and Class in Southern Africa* (Harare, 1997)]

COMMANDOS. As white settlement began to expand from the south-western Cape in the 17th century, free burghers began to organize their own militia units, which were officially sanctioned by the Dutch East India Company* in 1715. The commandos, usually mounted, were largely independent of Company control; the Company supplied them with ammunition, but allowed them to operate independently under the command of their elected leaders. During the 18th century, commandos undertook frequent punitive expeditions against the Khoisan and the Xhosa.* The San* were hunted like vermin, thousands were killed, and many children captured and forced into labour on white farms. Commandos were unable to dislodge the Khoisan from the Sneeuberge or the Nuweveldberge in the last quarter of the18th century, and were similarly blocked in the Zuurveld* by the Xhosa; in both cases, British aid in the early 19th century was required to establish white supremacy. In the late 1830s, the Voortrekkers* took the commando system into the interior, where it was used extensively against African enemies. Commando service was compulsory for males in the two Boer republics, and commandos fought the British in the Anglo-Transvaal War* and the South African War* with considerable success.

During the Rand Revolt* of 1922, striking white miners organized themselves into paramilitary units known as commandos to enforce the strike. In the early 1950s, the Torch Commando,* which was an ex-servicemen's organization of World War II veterans, staged large marches to protest against the Bill proposing the removal of Coloured voters from the common voters' roll. Local citizen units consisting of part-time soldiers in the South African Defence Force* were also known as commandos.

COMMONWEALTH. South Africa played an important role in the evolution of the British Empire into the Commonwealth. Largely in response to pressure from J.B.M. Hertzog,* the Imperial Conference of 1926 declared that Britain and the dominions, including South Africa, were 'autonomous communities within the British Empire, equal in status, in no way subordinate the one to the other in any aspect of their internal or external affairs'. South Africa then adopted its own flag. Although Hertzog favoured South Africa becoming a republic,* he did not consider that practical politics. Once South Africa took full power to alter or amend any legislation by the Status of the Union Act (1934), he accepted the new relationship with Britain, and on that basis entered fusion* with Smuts.* In 1939 he split with Smuts over South Africa's entry into World War II.

The republican movement gathered pace in the 1950s, and after a referendum among whites had endorsed the idea, Verwoerd* attended a Commonwealth Prime Ministers' conference in London in March 1961 to ask that South Africa remain a member of the Commonwealth after the change in status. But when it became clear that South Africa's continued membership was contentious and would result in others leaving the Commonwealth, he formally withdrew South Africa's application. From 31 May 1961, when it became a republic, South Africa ceased to be a member of the Commonwealth. This helped increase the country's international isolation, and South Africa lost its privileged access to markets in Britain. The South African issue both helped hold the Commonwealth together in the 1970s and 1980s, and proved divisive at meetings of heads of government when Mrs Thatcher refused to support sanctions against the country. The ANC, meanwhile, made it clear that when it came to power it would ask that South Africa be readmitted to the Commonwealth; this happened in July 1994. [J. Barber and J. Barratt, *South Africa's Foreign Policy* (Cambridge, 1990)]

COMMUNIST PARTY OF SOUTH AFRICA (CP). Founded in July 1921 as a result of the amalgamation of the International Socialist League, which had been formed by those who broke with the Labour Party in 1915 over its support for the war effort, and other left groups. A section of the Communist International, the CP from the beginning maintained relatively close links with Moscow. During the Rand Revolt* some of its members attempted to combine radicalism and racialism, their slogan in support of the strikers being 'Workers of the world unite and fight for a white South Africa'. Three communists on the executive of the Industrial and Commercial Workers' Union were expelled in 1926, but the communists won recruits in the African National Congress in the late 1920s before the ANC too swung to the right. The party had only 200 African members in 1927, and 1600 in 1928, out of a total membership of 1750. Orders then came from Moscow that it should work for a 'Native Republic' in South Africa. S.P. Bunting, the general secretary, and other leading white members opposed the new policy, because they still hoped to radicalize the white working class and make it the vanguard of a class-conscious proletariat. The expulsion of Bunting's group from the party as deviationists (1931) decimated the party, which by the mid-1930s had very few members but was nevertheless the only non-racial party in the country.

In the 1930s the CP did pioneering work in organizing African workers. Some of its African members served on the executive of the ANC, and the Africans of the western Cape elected three white communists to parliament as 'Native Representatives', two of whom were prevented from taking their seats. In 1950, under the threat of the apartheid government's Suppression of Communism Act, the party dissolved itself, but in 1953 formed itself into the underground South African Communist Party.* [B. Bunting, comp., *South African Communists Speak* (London, 1981); R. and H. Simons, *Class and Colour* (London, 1989); E. Roux, *S.P. Bunting* (Bellville, 1994)]

COMPOUNDS. The compound system introduced on the Kimberley diamond fields* in 1885 was an extended variant on the use of prison labour from the Kimberley convict station, and was designed to accommodate black migrant workers during their period of employment on the mines. Between 1885 and 1889 the bulk of the African labour force of 10,000 men were placed in twelve large closed compounds. Mineowners justified the system as a measure to prevent the theft of diamonds, and also argued that it would cost the workers less, allowing them to return to their homes with a greater proportion of their earnings. The compound system, however, was devised to keep labour as cheap as possible. It served primarily as a means of control, designed to prevent workers from breaking their contracts, to reduce their freedom of movement, and even to enable management to force workers underground, which many tried to resist.

The term 'compound' was also used more loosely from the late 19th century to include any living quarters for a number of African workers, whether or not they were subject to controls. In Cape Town, for example, there was a large harbour compound, as well as smaller compounds housing African workers for private concerns. The compound system extended to the Witwatersrand gold mines was similar to that of Kimberley, although these compounds were not as totally closed as in

Kimberley. Both Chinese* and African workers were required to live in barrack-like, single-sex hostels for the duration of their contracts. Conditions were harsh, with workers sleeping on bunk-like concrete slabs in very overcrowded circumstances. The compounds limited the independence of workers and isolated them from society at large and from other workers in particular. During strikes,* such as those of 1920 and 1946, compounds were surrounded and became virtual prisons, enabling the strikes to be broken. Compounds, and the hostels which took their place, remained crowded and unsanitary places until the 1990s. They were political flashpoints on the Witwatersrand during township conflict in the early 1990s, sometimes serving as bases for armed groups to attack surrounding township residents. Demands for their dismantling became a complex political issue during negotiations between the National Party government, the African National Congress and the Inkatha Freedom Party during this period. [N. Levy, *The Foundations of the South African Cheap Labor System* (Boston, 1982); D. Moodie and V. Ndatshe, *Going for Gold* (Johannesburg, 1994)]

CONCENTRATION CAMPS. During the last quarter of 1900, in an attempt to prevent Boer guerrillas from receiving assistance from civilians in the South African War, the British military authorities established concentration camps for Boer women and children, families of Boers who had surrendered, as well as for Africans who had the potential to supply provisions to Boer commandos. In all, 44 camps, largely ill-equipped and disease-ridden, were established in the Transvaal and Orange River Colony for the Boers; almost 28,000 people died in these camps, the majority of them children under the age of 16. The loss of life helped to force the Boers to negotiate peace with the British in 1902, but also left deep and indelible scars on the Afrikaner consciousness. The concentration camps for Africans were similarly unsanitary and overcrowded; over 100,000 were interned in some 66 camps, and more than 14,000 deaths were recorded. It is likely that almost as many Africans died in such camps as Boers. [S. Spies, *Methods of Barbarism* (Cape Town, 1977)]

CONFEDERATION. In the late 1850s Sir George Grey, the Cape Governor, proposed a federal union of southern Africa's white-ruled states, but the idea was not developed. In 1867 the British Colonial Secretary, Lord Carnarvon, steered the British North America Act through the British parliament and hoped to accomplish a similar arrangement in South Africa during his second term as Colonial Secretary between 1874 and 1878. Carnarvon and his advisers were keen to secure British strategic and economic interests in South Africa, particularly after the discovery of diamonds and with the need to secure a regular flow of migrant labour.

Carnarvon initially attempted to arrange a conference at which representatives of the various states would meet to discuss political unity. This proved a failure; he subsequently authorized Theophilus Shepstone to annex the Transvaal, sent out Sir Bartle Frere (1815–1884) as High Commissioner with instructions to bring about confederation, and carried legislation permitting such a confederation through the British parliament in 1877. Although Carnarvon resigned as Colonial Secretary in 1878, the search for confederation continued. The British army's defeat at Isandlwana* in January 1879 proved a major setback, as did the Cape parliament's rejection of the idea in June 1880; subsequently Frere was recalled. After the Transvaal revolt against British rule later in 1880, plans for confederation were finally shelved. Although the scheme failed, attempts to achieve it did much to transform southern Africa. [C. Goodfellow, *Great Britain and South African Confederation* (Cape Town, 1966); D. Schreuder, *The Scramble for Southern Africa* (Cambridge, 1980)]

CONGRESS ALLIANCE. Joint anti-apartheid front established in the mid-1950s, in which the African National Congress was the leading member. Other members included the South African Indian Congress and the Congress of Democrats. The high point of the Alliance was the Congress of the People, held at Kliptown in Soweto, outside Johannesburg, in June 1955, at which the Freedom Charter was approved. Many of the leading individuals involved in the Alliance were arrested and charged with high treason in 1956. [T. Lodge, *Black Politics in South Africa since 1945* (Johannesburg, 1983)]

CONGRESS OF SOUTH AFRICAN TRADE UNIONS (COSATU). Formed in 1985, when it claimed 450,000 members, COSATU had by 1994 more than 1.3 million members and was by far the largest trade union federation in the country. Its three largest affiliates were the National Union of Mineworkers, the National Union of Metalworkers of South Africa, and the Transport and General Workers' Union. In the debate in the 1980s over the political role the trade unions should play, the populists, who favoured playing a direct role, won out over the workerists, and COSATU aligned itself first with the United Democratic Front and then the African National Congress. Among its leading figures were Jay Naidoo, its general secretary, and Alec Erwin, both of whom became cabinet ministers in the Government of National Unity. COSATU played a leading role in formulating the Reconstruction and Development Programme, but once the ANC was in power, it found itself sidelined, though it remained part of what was loosely termed the Triple Alliance, the third member of which was the South African Communist Party.* [J. Baskin, *Striking Back* (Johannesburg, 1991)]

CONSERVATIVE PARTY. Right-wing white party founded by Andries Treurnicht and 22 other MPs in 1982 after they had broken from the National Party. It became the official opposition in 1987, and in the September 1989 election won 31% of the white vote. Most of its support was from the rural areas, and from lower-middle-class whites. After the decision by De Klerk to negotiate with the African National Congress, it became sidelined. It refused to participate in most of the negotiations, and it boycotted the 1994 democratic election and associated itself with other Afrikaner parties calling for self-determination. [J. van Rooyen, *Hard Right* (London, 1994)]

CONSTITUTIONAL ASSEMBLY (CA) (1994–1996). When negotiations began at the Convention for a Democratic South Africa in 1991, the African National Congress followed the Pan Africanist Congress and demanded an elected CA, but the National Party opposed the idea. The compromise reached in 1993, and embodied in the interim constitution, was that the first election of April 1994 would establish a CA, but that it would be bound by Constitutional Principles agreed to at the Multi-Party Negotiating Forum. The CA comprised the members of the House of Assembly and the Senate sitting together, and it began its work soon after the new parliament assembled in May 1994. It had two years in which to draw up a final constitution. It completed its task in May 1996 just within the two-year deadline. When the Constitutional Court rejected the initial draft, the CA met again later in 1996 and prepared a new draft, which the court then approved. The final task of the CA was to popularize the new constitution, millions of copies of which were distributed in early 1997.

CONSTITUTIONAL COURT. This new eleven-member body was created in 1994 to adjudicate on issues relating to the constitution and to certify that the new constitution adhered to the 34 Constitutional Principles laid down during the negotiations. It was headed by Arthur Chaskalson, who had been the ANC's chief legal adviser during the negotiations, and initially comprised nine men and two women, seven whites and four blacks. Its first contentious ruling was that the death penalty was unconstitutional. Critics who did not understand the concept of the rule of law maintained that the court was undemocratic in its ruling, given that there was widespread popular support for the death penalty. In 1997 the Constitutional Court approved the constitution drawn up by the Western Cape legislature.

CONSTITUTIONAL PRINCIPLES. Some 34 principles were included in the interim constitution adopted at the Multi-party Negotiating Forum in 1993, approved by parliament in December of that year, and amended early in 1994. They were meant to provide a framework for the final constitution, to be drawn up by the Constitutional Assembly (CA), and were binding on that body. They provided that South Africa must be a multi-party democracy, with a justiciable Bill of Rights. The last principle to be added provided for the possible right to self-determination of a community sharing a common cultural and language tradition (to allow for a *volkstaat* and a Zulu kingdom). When the Constitutional Court reviewed the first draft of the new constitution for the country, it sent it back to the CA, largely because it did not meet the principle that the powers and functions of the provinces would not be less than those in the interim constitution. The amended draft was later approved [S. Friedman and D. Atkinson, eds., *The Small Miracle* (Johannesburg, 1994)]

CONVENTION FOR A DEMOCRATIC SOUTH AFRICA (CODESA). This negotiating body convened on 20 December 1991 at the World Trade Centre near Johannesburg's airport, to draw up a new constitution. The 19 delegations included eight main parties and various bantustan governments. When F.W. de Klerk berated the African National Congress for not having disbanded Umkhonto weSizwe, a furious Nelson Mandela insisted on the right to reply and accused De Klerk of pursuing a double agenda, negotiating in public while encouraging units in the security forces to destabilize the ANC. A Declaration of Intent was adopted and five working groups were appointed to prepare the way for a non-racial democratic government. These reached agreement, except that Working Group 2 deadlocked on the number of votes needed for the adoption of the constitution (the National Party wanted three-quarters, and the ANC would not go higher than 70%). A second CODESA was held in May 1992 to try to resolve the issue, but when the ANC suggested the deadlock should be broken by a referendum after six months in which a simple majority would decide the issue, the meeting broke up in disarray. When a similar negotiating body was constituted in 1993, it was called the Multi-Party Negotiating Forum and not CODESA 3, because CODESA seemed a failure. [S. Friedman, *The Long Journey* (Johannesburg, 1993)]

CROSSROADS. See CAPE TOWN

CUITO CUANAVALE, Battle of (1987/1988). Large, conventional battle around the town of Cuito Cuanavale in southern Angola,* in which South African Defence Force troops and their UNITA allies faced the forces of the Angolan army, crack Cuban troops and members of the armed wing of SWAPO, the People's Liberation Army of Namibia.* The result was a stalemate, rather than defeat for the South African forces, which the Cubans claimed it to be, but the stalemate was an important factor promoting negotiations in 1988: these led to the decision to implement UN Resolution 435, providing for the independence of Namibia. The huge cost of the battle for South Africa – the shells fired from the G5 and G6 guns alone cost over R200 million – put strong pressure on the South African government to negotiate independence for Namibia, as did the need to extricate the South African troops from Cuito Cuanavale once the Cubans had moved close to the Namibian border. [F. Bridgland, *The War for Africa* (Gibraltar, 1990)]

CURRENCY. As part of the apartheid government's policy of severing links with Britain, pounds, shillings and pence were replaced by rands and cents. The rand, issued by the South African Reserve Bank, was briefly linked to the British pound but from October 1972 the rand–US dollar rate became the only fixed one. In September 1975, the rand was devalued from R1 = $1.4 to R1 = $1.15. From January 1979, the rand's value against the dollar was permitted to float. The currency depreciated sharply against the dollar after the political situation deteriorated from mid-1984: it fell from R1 = $0.8 in January 1984 to R1 = $0.42 in January 1985 and R1 = $0.35 by August 1985. A two-tier system of a commercial and a financial rand was then introduced to protect the currency; this lasted until March 1995, when the financial rand was phased out. Owing to currency speculation in early 1996, the rand lost 18% of its value against the US dollar and several other currencies, and stood at R1 = $0.23 in June 1996. South Africa's inflation continued to be considerably higher than that of the countries with which it conducted the bulk of its trade, and in April 1998 the rand was worth 5 to the dollar.

d

DADOO, Yusuf (1909–1983). Leading member of the Communist Party* and the South African Indian Congress (SAIC). As head of the SAIC, in 1946 Dadoo led a passive resistance campaign against anti-Indian legislation. He then took the SAIC into an alliance with the African National Congress. A key figure in the Congress Alliance* in the 1950s, he went into exile in 1961, and remained active in anti-apartheid work until his death. [E. Reddy, *Yusuf Mohammed Dadoo* (Durban, 1991); S. Bhana, *Gandhi's Legacy* (Pietermaritzburg, 1997)]

DA GAMA, Vasco (c.1460–1524). Commander-in-chief of the first Portuguese expedition to sail around the entire South African coast en route to India. He and his men encountered Khoikhoi pastoralists in November 1497 at St Helena Bay and then at Mossel Bay, the furthest point reached by Dias.* In December 1497 Da Gama gave the name Natal to the Pondoland coast, which his ships were passing at Christmas time.

DEBT. Until the 1980s South Africa's national debt was relatively small, but it began to increase very rapidly from the early 1980s, because of the need to pay for the huge cost of the war in Angola* and numerous very expensive apartheid projects, such as the Mossgas off-shore gas development and the production of long-range missiles capable of carrying the nuclear warheads then being built. The transition after 1990 from apartheid to democracy was also very expensive, with vast amounts paid for the negotiations themselves, for integrating the armed forces and running the April 1994 election. By the end of 1994, South Africa's total public-sector debt stood at R215.1 billion, of which only R1.64 billion (or 0.7%) was said to consist of foreign debt. The 1996/7 budget made provision for the borrowing of R2.5 billion from foreign funders. By the end of 1997 the national debt had soared to over R325 billion, and more than 20% of the budget was going to service the debt itself. There were calls for the debt incurred in the apartheid era to be written off; South Africa's agreement after 1994 to take over Namibia's debt, incurred during the years of South African occupation, was cited as a precedent.

DEFENCE FORCE. A Union Defence Force was established in 1913 to bring together Boer and Brit in the armed forces of the four ex-colonies. The army comprised a relatively small permanent force, which grew to 60,000 in the 1980s, and a much larger citizen force of national servicemen, a part-time citizen army. In World War I,* 231,000 South Africans volunteered; in World War II* almost 400,000. African volunteers served in both world wars in non-combatant roles, and as soldiers in the regular army from the late 1970s. In the Korean War, the South African Air Force lost 74 aircraft and 34 pilots. In the Namibian border war, conscripts were sent into Angola*: in 1975 South African Defence Force troops came within sight of the Angolan capital, Luanda, before they withdrew. Between 1966 and 1989 some 788 servicemen (police and military) lost their lives in Namibia* and Angola, excluding those who died as members of the South West African Territory Force or in 32 Battalion, most members of which were non-South Africans. Soon after a new national service scheme was introduced in 1993, compulsory service was abandoned. The transition from apartheid in the 1990s allowed a vast cutback in defence expenditure. Some in Umkhonto weSizwe (MK) and the Azanian People's Liberation Army (APLA) had called for the South African Defence Force (SADF) to be dissolved and a new force created, but in negotiations from 1992 a process was agreed which provided for continuity, and in effect the SADF absorbed the forces of MK and APLA, though under the new name of the South African National Defence Force. The SANDF was born with the new order in April 1994. Before the election of that month, the Transitional Executive Council's* sub-council on defence had established a National Peacekeeping Force, which proved a disastrous and short-lived experiment. [G. Cawthra, *Brutal Force* (London, 1986); J. Cilliers, *About Turn* (Halfway House, 1995); A. Seegers, *The Military in the Making of Modern South Africa* (London, 1996)]

DEFIANCE CAMPAIGN (1952). A civil disobedience campaign launched by the African National Congress (ANC) and the South African Indian Congress in June 1952 to bring about changes in government policy relating to pass laws, livestock limitation, Bantu authorities, Group Areas,* separate representation of voters, and the suppression of communism. Large numbers of volunteers, most of them in the Transvaal and Cape, deliberately courted arrest by disobeying minor regulations, hoping this would disorganize authority by filling the prisons and courts to capacity. By the time the campaign ground to a halt in November 1952, 8326 people had been arrested and, in nearly all cases, convicted of an offence. Police countermeasures, aided by the new Public Safety and Criminal Law Amendment Acts, brought an end to the campaign, whose main achievement lay in gaining widespread popular support for the ANC. The ANC's membership rose to 100,000 as a direct consequence of the Defiance Campaign. [L. Kuper, *Passive Resistance in South Africa* (New Haven, 1967); T. Lodge, *Black Politics in South Africa since 1945* (Johannesburg, 1983)

DE KLERK (Frederik Willem) (1936–). State President from 1989 to 1994, and one of the architects of the negotiated settlement of 1990–1994. Born into a political family in the Transvaal, De Klerk received an early training in politics through his membership of the Jeugbond, the youth section of the National Party (NP). He graduated from Potchefstroom University, practised as an attorney, and then entered parliament in 1972, becoming a cabinet minister in 1978 and leader of the Transvaal NP in 1982. When elected leader of the NP in early 1989, he had the reputation of being on the conservative wing of the party. He became Acting State President in August that year, after the resignation of P.W. Botha, and State President the following month. On becoming President he quickly revealed himself to be a pragmatist. Realizing that he had to make drastic changes, and that the collapse of communism in Eastern Europe presented new opportunities for decisive action, he chose the opening of parliament on 2 February 1990 to announce the unbanning of the liberation movements and the unconditional release of Nelson Mandela.*

He played a leading role in the negotiation process which followed, holding face-to-face meetings with Mandela when the negotiations themselves were dead-locked. Mandela had called him a man of integrity in early 1990, but relations between the two men became very strained as Mandela accused him of not doing enough to bring the political violence in the country to an end. Throughout the shift in policy, he carried his cabinet and party with him, and the NP evolved from a racially based party to a non-racial one. In early 1992 he decided to hold a refer-endum among whites to test his support, and won a clear victory. In 1993, with Mandela, he won the Nobel Peace Prize. In early May 1994 he accepted defeat gracefully and became a Deputy President in the new Government of National Unity*(GNU). Once the final constitution had been agreed to, he took his party out of the GNU, and from June 1996 was leader of the opposition. In early 1997 he came under fire from commentators who claimed that he had proved himself a poor negotiator, inasmuch as he had failed to secure the guarantees for his Afrikaner constituency that he had promised he would. He was also criticised for failing to provide an adequate apology before the Truth and Reconciliation Commission.* In August 1997 he suddenly announced his resignation as leader of the NP and from parliament, after which he spent some time on the North American lecture circuit and devoted himself to the writing of his memoirs. An extramarital affair he had been carrying on for some years became public knowl-edge in early 1998. [D. Ottaway, *Chained Together* (New York, 1993); A. Sparks, *Tomorrow is Another Country* (Sandton, 1994); P. Waldmeir, *Anatomy of a Miracle* (London, 1997)]

DELAGOA BAY. The finest natural harbour in south-east Africa, on which Maputo, cap-ital of present-day Mozambique, is situated. The Portuguese began trading from Delagoa Bay in the 1510s, and trade routes ran from the port to the mining areas of the eastern Transvaal and to the elephant hunting lands of Natal. During the 18th century, the port became an important base for both slave and ivory traders. Some historians argue that this trade was a central factor in explaining the process of political centralization which led to the emergence of the Zulu kingdom* early in the 19th century.

Ownership of Delagoa Bay was contested by the British, Dutch and Portuguese, as well as by the Transvaal, in the 19th century. A French arbitrator awarded the port to Portugal in 1875. After the discovery of gold on the Witwatersrand, the Transvaal built a railway line to Delagoa Bay in order to avoid Cape and Natal ports. Completed in 1895, the line continued to serve as an important link during the 20th century. Much of the Witwatersrand's exports left southern Africa through Delagoa Bay, while thousands of migrant labourers from Mozambique were trans-ported along the line to the mines. After 1975, when Mozambique achieved its independence from Portugal, links between South Africa and Mozambique were largely severed, but in the 1990s the railway again transported goods between the two countries, and an ambitious plan was unveiled for a Maputo corridor linking the Rand with the port.

DE LA REY, Jacobus Hercules (1847–1914). Boer general and politician, whose opposition to South African involvement in World War I led him to plan a rebellion in an attempt to restore the independence of the Boer republics. Shot dead by a police patrol while en route to Potchefstroom to begin the military rising, he became a martyr for Afrikaner nationalists. (See also AFRIKANER REBELLION.)

DEMOCRATIC PARTY (DP). To form a unified parliamentary party to the left of the government, the Progressive Federal Party (PFP),* the National Democratic Movement (NDM) and the Independent Party (IP) decided to merge, and the DP was launched in April 1989. Initially, its joint leaders were Denis Worrall, who had resigned as ambassador in London to oppose his erstwhile National Party (NP) colleagues as leader of the IP; Wynand Malan, who had left the NP caucus on the issue of reform and established the NDM; and Zach de Beer, leader of the PFP and subsequently sole DP leader. In the 1989 general election the DP increased the number of its seats from 20 to 33. DP representatives played important roles in the negotiations which followed, and though the DP fared badly in the 1994 election, its handful of MPs performed capably as a critical opposition in the new parliament, advocating the principles of liberal democracy. The party remained a mostly white body, strongly committed to free market principles. It rejected an offer by Mandela to join the Government of National Unity* in early 1997, but at the end of that year agreed to join the National Party-led government in the Western Cape.

DESTABILIZATION. As part of the 'total strategy' of P.W. Botha,* South African security forces acted in a variety of ways to try to prevent neighbouring states from assisting the African National Congress. Massive military incursions into Angola* became routine, while 'dirty tricks' of various kinds were used, along with support for opposition movements and covert interference with cross-border trade. In the late 1980s, with the move towards independence for Namibia* and the beginnings of the transition to democracy in South Africa, the policy was abandoned in relation to South Africa's neighbours, but new forms of internal destabilization, aimed at destroying the negotiations and preventing the ANC from coming to power, were undertaken by elements in the security forces.[J. Barber and J. Barratt, *South Africa's Foreign Policy* (Cambridge, 1990); P. Johnson and D. Martin, *Destructive Engagement* (Harare, 1986) and *Apartheid Terrorism* (London, 1989); J. Hanlon, *Beggar Your Neighbours* (London, 1986)]

DIAMONDS. Alluvial diamonds were found along the Orange River in 1867, but only after further discoveries in 1870 did digging begin in earnest in the pipes of blue ground at the so-called dry diggings, where Kimberley* developed. Work at the Kimberley mine itself, which was to become the richest diamond mine in the world, began in 1871. By 1872, over 50,000 people had converged on the area; some 3000 individual diggers acquired small claims, and worked them with the assistance of labourers, using picks, shovels and buckets. By the mid-1870s, amalgamation of these claims began to take place on a large scale, because of the collapse of the reef, the accumulation of water in the diggings and the need for expensive steam machinery to facilitate more extensive underground digging. Overproduction of diamonds by the beginning of the 1880s intensified competition between the larger organizations, leading to further amalgamation and the emergence in 1888 of De Beers Consolidated Mines, owned by Cecil Rhodes,* with a monopoly of mining operations in Kimberley. De Beers eventually won control of other diamond deposits discovered later, in the Transvaal and in South West Africa.

Ownership of the diamond fields was much disputed, and conflicting land claims by the Orange Free State,* the Transvaal and the Griqua* state under Nicholaas Waterboer were resolved in 1871, when Waterboer's claims to the fields were recognized by the British High Commissioner, who extended British protection to the Griqua and annexed the area as the Crown Colony of Griqualand West. A cash payment of £90,000 was given to the Orange Free State in 1876 in compensation, and in 1880 the Cape was finally persuaded to incorporate Griqualand West.

By 1872 Kimberley was a town second only to Cape Town in size in the subcontinent. As southern Africa's first industrial community, it created a new market for farmers. It also brought new prosperity to the ports of Cape Town and Port Elizabeth, and railways linking Kimberley to the coast were constructed. Capital accumulation on the diamond fields made possible the rapid exploitation of gold on the Witwatersrand from the end of the 1880s. Patterns of labour that became conventional elsewhere in the country were also first established in Kimberley Migrant labourers from as far as the Delagoa Bay hinterland and the north-eastern Transvaal journeyed to the diamond fields, and were often paid in kind rather than in wages. The small number of black diggers were put out of business by the mid-1870s; pass laws were introduced to control the labour force in 1872; and a much tighter system of control was instituted through the closed compound system begun in 1885. [S. Kanfer, *The Last Empire* (New York, 1993); C. Newbury, *The Diamond Ring* (Oxford, 1989); R. Turrell, *Capital and Labour on the Kimberley Diamond Fields* (Cambridge, 1987)]

DIAS, Bartolomeu de Novaes (c.1450–1500). Commander of the first European ship to round the southern tip of Africa, in January 1488. He dropped anchor in Mossel Bay at the beginning of February 1488. Two caravels under his command sailed further east to Algoa Bay before the crews demanded that they return to Portugal. His voyage opened the way for Vasco da Gama* to sail on to India.

DINGANE (c.1795–1840). Zulu king, who assumed power after participating in the assassination of his half-brother Shaka* in 1828. Determined to maintain Zulu domination, he sent a large force onto the highveld to attack the Ndebele under Mzilikazi,* who had fled from Shaka in the early 1820s. Though the Ndebele defeated Dingane's army in 1832, he retained his control in Natal, where he was obliged to deal with Voortrekker* incursions under the leadership of Piet Retief* in 1838. After initially concluding an agreement with the Voortrekkers, Dingane had Retief murdered in February that year, and then attempted to drive the Voortrekkers out of Natal. The Zulu army was overcome at Blood River* by a trekker commando under Andries Pretorius in December 1838, and Dingane's authority was much weakened. Ousted by his half-brother Mpande in 1840, he escaped to Swaziland, where he was murdered. [J. Laband, *Rope of Sand* (Johannesburg, 1995)]

DINGISWAYO (c.1770–1818). Chief of the Mthethwa chiefdom. Though he seized power in a violent manner in 1809, he displayed considerable skill in winning loyal followers and extending the influence of his chiefdom. He played a leading role in developing the fighting methods of the Mthethwa army, and won control of the lucrative trade routes to Delagoa Bay, which made him the most influential figure in south-east Africa until his murder by the chief Zwide* of the Ndwandwe c.1818. Dingiswayo's death paved the way for the rise to power of Shaka* of the Zulu,* to whom he had given refuge.

DINUZULU (c.1870–1913). The son of the Zulu king Cetshwayo,* he was caught in a bitter struggle for succession with Zibhebhu, a relative and a powerful chief, after the death of his father in 1884. He defeated Zibhebhu with the support of Transvaal Boers, to whom he ceded land in return for military assistance. After the British annexed Zululand in 1887, Dinuzulu was exiled to St Helena for ten years on charges of rebellion. On his return in 1898 he enjoyed the status of only a minor chief. He was again put on trial for treason, public violence and sedition after being implicated in the Bambatha Rebellion* of 1906, and was sentenced to four years' imprisonment. He was released in 1910, and spent the remainder of his life in exile on a farm in the Transvaal. [C. Binns, Dinuzulu (London, 1968); J. Guy, The Destruction of the Zulu Kingdom (London, 1982)]

DITHAKONG, Battle of (June 1823). Dithakong, the Tlhaping capital, north-east of Kuruman, was defended successfully by the Tlhaping, with the assistance of Griqua troops who had horses and firearms, from attack by thousands of invaders in June 1823 at the time of the Mfecane.* This prevented disruption from spreading further west in the southern African interior.

DOMINION PARTY. Founded in 1934 by Colonel C.F. Stallard (1871–1971). Most members were English-speakers from Natal who would not follow Jan Smuts* into fusion* with J.B.M. Hertzog's Nationalists. They distrusted Hertzog* and feared that fusion would endanger the Imperial connection. They voted against Hertzog's legislation on land and franchise passed in 1936, and supported Smuts in 1939 over entering World War II. When Smuts broke with Hertzog, the rationale for a separate party faded away, and most members soon cast in their lot with Smuts's United Party.

DRAKENSBERG (Afrikaans for 'dragon mountain'). Mountain range which runs for 650 miles, with major peaks over 11,000 feet, separating the coastal corridor from the interior plateau (the highveld) of South Africa. To Nguni-speakers, the central portion of the range, a formidable barrier, was known as Qathlamba, meaning 'mountain of spears'. The southern and northern sections were relatively easy to cross, e.g. by those uprooted from Natal by the Mfecane* in the early 1820s, and by Voortrekkers* moving in the opposite direction in 1837. The Drakensberg offered a relatively secure refuge to the San* in the 19th century. Langalibalele* fled into the Drakensberg in 1873, and the mountains saw fighting during the Anglo-Transvaal War* and the South African War.* In the 20th century, the mountains became a major tourist attraction.

DUBE, John Langalibalele (1871–1946). Educationist, journalist and politician. Educated in Natal and the United States, he founded the Ohlange Institute outside Durban in 1901 as an educational centre. He established Natal's first black newspaper, *Ilanga lase Natal*, in 1903, and edited it until 1915. He was the first president-general of the South African Native National Congress, later the African National Congress, serving from 1912 until 1917. Thereafter, he ceased to play a role in national politics, but continued to be active in political and educational work in Natal. [S. Marks, *The Ambiguities of Dependence* (Baltimore, 1988)]

DUNCAN, Sir Patrick (1870–1943). One of the Milner Kindergarten,* Duncan was Colonial Secretary for the Transvaal from 1903 to 1907, a member of parliament, cabinet minister under Smuts,* legal adviser on Bechuanaland to the British High Commissioner, and then Governor-General of South Africa from 1936. He supported the Unionist Party,* was then a leading member of the South African Party,* and a founder member of the United Party.* Keen to reconcile English and Afrikaners, Duncan worked with Smuts, Hertzog* and Havenga to form a coalition in 1933 and fusion* in 1934. As Governor-General in 1939, he played an important role in the decision that South Africa should participate in World War II.* He died in office in 1943.

DURBAN. White settlement began in 1824, when a small party of traders from the eastern Cape was granted a cession of land from the Zulu ruler Shaka* at a natural harbour, which they named Port Natal. In 1835, its name was changed to honour Sir Benjamin D'Urban, then Cape Governor. After Britain annexed Natal in 1843, greater numbers of British immigrants arrived; by 1854, when Durban received a municipal charter, it had a population of 1200 whites and a smaller number of Africans. The development of the harbour mouth, which chiefly required the elimination of a sandbar to enable large ships to enter the harbour, was completed in 1904; by then it was connected by rail to the Transvaal, and in the 20th century the port handled more cargo than any other in the country.

By 1950 Durban was the country's third-largest city, and its population comprised Africans, Indians and whites in almost equal numbers. A manufacturing centre, and the headquarters of the country's sugar industry, it was a popular tourist destination. By the end of the 1980s, when it was reputed to be Africa's fastest-growing city, and its port the busiest in Africa, Durban's population exceeded three million people, the large majority of whom were Africans. By the mid-1990s large numbers of foreign tourists were visiting the city, attracted in part by its cosmopolitanism. [P. Maylam and I. Edwards, eds., *The People's City* (Pietermaritzburg, 1996)]

DUTCH. The official language of the Cape under the rule of the Dutch East India Company* and the British until 1822, when English was proclaimed the language of government and justice; English also increasingly became the language used in Cape schools. In the Boer republics established after the Great Trek,* Dutch was the language of government, law, the church and the schools. In the Cape, meanwhile, campaigns on behalf of the Dutch language undertaken by J.H. Hofmeyr ('Onze' Jan), editor of *De Suid-Afrikaan*, during the 1870s began to bear fruit: in 1882, Dutch was recognized as an official language of the Cape parliament, and it gradually gained equal recognition with English as an official language in the colony. The South Africa Act of 1909, which created the Union* of South Africa, provided that Dutch and English should both be official languages and be treated equally. In 1925, the Union parliament passed legislation declaring that 'Dutch' was to be understood as including Afrikaans*; Afrikaans in effect became an official language of the country from that date.

DUTCH EAST INDIA COMPANY. Private commercial trading company, commonly known as the VOC, derived from the initials of its Dutch name, *Verenigde Oost-Indische Compagnie*. The VOC was founded in 1602 to co-ordinate Dutch trading expeditions to the East Indies. Under its charter from the States General (the government of the Netherlands), it enjoyed a monopoly of all Dutch trade east of the Cape of Good Hope, a position which enabled it to build enormous commercial and political power and become the largest company in the world by the end of the 17th century. In 1652, the VOC established a base at the Cape of Good Hope to service and supply its ships on the sea route between the Netherlands and the East. This refreshment station was intended to be a contained supply post, and it was never envisaged that a colony of settlement would develop at the Cape. The growth of the station into a large colony occurred under the supervision of the VOC, whose officials ruled the Cape until 1795.

VOC rule at the Cape was directed towards narrow Company goals: the maximization of profit and minimal expenditure. For most of the period to 1795, VOC rule at the Cape was characterized by corruption and inefficiency. The Governor and the seven-member Council of Policy at the Cape were all VOC officials; although technically responsible to the VOC's board of 17 directors in the Netherlands, they had extensive local power. They presided over a colony characterized by extreme inequality, though it never experienced any serious rebellion: a combination of repressive government, brutal punishment, bribery and close networks of officials kept VOC power intact. By the 1780s, however, the VOC was in terminal decline as a result of competition from English and French traders and domestic events in the Netherlands. Its survival became dependent on loans from the States General after 1783, and in 1794 the Company was declared bankrupt. At that stage, a commission of inquiry was compiling a large volume of evidence of VOC corruption and misgovernance at the Cape and elsewhere. In 1795 the British conquest of the Cape brought to an end VOC control of the Cape; the Company was taken over in 1796 by the new Dutch government, the Batavian Republic, which terminated the Company's operations shortly thereafter. [R. Elphick and H. Giliomee, eds., *The Shaping of South African Society* (Cape Town, 1989)]

DUTCH–KHOIKHOI WARS (1659–1660; 1673–1677). Wars fought between newly arrived Dutch settlers and Khoikhoi hunter-pastoralists in the south-western Cape. The first was confined to the Peninsula, near the fledgling white settlement, where the first white farms encroached on Khoikhoi grazing land; it ended in stalemate after a year of inconclusive fighting, with the Khoikhoi having failed to expel whites from the Peninsula. The Dutch, having expanded gradually beyond the Peninsula, attempted in the second war to defeat Gonnema, leader of the Cochoqua. He was subjugated in 1677, after the Dutch obtained the assistance of other Khoikhoi, and he agreed to pay an annual tribute to the Dutch Governor. His defeat marked the end of serious Khoikhoi resistance to Dutch expansion in the south-western Cape. [R. Elphick, *Kraal and Castle* (New Haven, 1977)]

DUTCH REFORMED CHURCHES. The Reformed Church was the official church in the Cape Colony during the Dutch East India Company* period. Its activities and ministers were controlled by the Company and by the mother church in Holland, but these links were severed after the British occupation of the Cape. Its life was invigorated by a number of Scottish Presbyterian ministers who joined it from the 1820s. One result of this was the beginnings of missionary work on a large scale, something which had not been deemed necessary during the 18th century. In 1843, the church was given virtual self-government by the state, and adopted the name Nederduits Gereformeerde Kerk (NGK). NGK work began among the Voor-trekkers* during the 1840s, though the Cape-based church was initially reluctant to support the trekkers. In the early 1850s the trekkers at Potchefstroom* decided to sever links with the church, associated as it was with the British-ruled Cape, and formed the Nederduitsch Hervormde Kerk, which was given official recognition in the republican constitution of 1856. Further religious dissension occurred, when those who objected to the singing of hymns in public worship formed a separate Gereformeerde Kerk in Rustenburg in the Transvaal in 1859. A strict Calvinist church, its members developed close bonds with neo-Calvinists in Holland, and became known as 'Doppers'. Although only a minority of Afrikaners supported it, the Gereformeerde Kerk nevertheless experienced strong growth, and developed the Potchefstroom University for Christian Higher Education in the 20th century.

The Cape synod of the NGK decided in 1857 that separate services could be held for whites and blacks because of the 'weakness' of the former; this was under-stood to be a practical solution to cultural differences rather than desirable on scrip-tural or doctrinal grounds. Separate congregations became the norm, and led to the establishment of 'daughter' mission churches defined on racial grounds: the 'Sendingkerk' for Coloureds (founded in 1881), the NGK in Afrika for Africans, and the Indian Reformed Church. During the early 1930s, this arrangement of 'con-venience' underwent profound reorientation, as white church leaders developed theological and biblical justifications for the racial separation of the churches. In 1948, a report entitled 'Racial and National Apartheid in the Bible' was accepted as official policy, and became a foundation of the theological defence of apartheid.

By the end of the 1940s, the NGK was largely isolated from mainstream ecu-menical life and theological trends in the wider Reformed Church, and devoted its attention to the creation of a federal structure for the four provincial churches. This was achieved in 1962. Widely perceived to be the National Party at prayer, the NGK was by far the largest of the three DRC churches: in 1980, it had 1.7 million white members, as opposed to the 258,000 of the Nederduitsch Hervormde Kerk and the

127,000 of the Gereformeerde Kerk. The NGK's 'daughter' churches were similarly strong, with a combined total of 1.8 million adherents. During the 1980s, the NGK was riven by failed attempts to unite the mission churches with the main church, as well as by its official stance over apartheid. Its pronouncements on church and society were largely uncertain and ambiguous, and the church experienced a decline in membership of close to 20%. In 1997 it formally apologised for its role in apartheid before the Truth and Reconciliation Commission.* [W. de Klerk, *Puritans in Africa* (Harmondsworth, 1976); D. Chidester, *Religions of South Africa* (London, 1992)]

DU TOIT, Stephanus Jacobus (1847–1911). Writer, educationist and cultural leader, remembered most for his early campaigns on behalf of the Afrikaans language. He founded a cultural organization, Die Genootskap van Regte Afrikaners (1875), the first Afrikaans newspaper, *Die Afrikaanse Patriot* (1876), and produced the first Afrikaans grammar book (1876) and history (1877). He also founded the Afrikaner Bond,* the first organized party in the Cape parliament.

e

EASTERN CAPE. New province created on 27 April 1994 from the Transkei and Ciskei bantustans and the former eastern part of the Cape Province, including the Port Elizabeth–Uitenhage industrial complex and much of the scenic Garden Route. (For its history, see CAPE COLONY, CISKEI, TRANSKEI.) Bisho, the former capital of Ciskei, adjacent to King William's Town, became the capital of the new province. The ANC won a large majority in the Provincial Assembly in the 1994 election, and Raymond Mhlaba, who had been imprisoned on Robben Island with Nelson Mandela,* became the first provincial premier, but proved unable to deal with the administrative problems caused by integrating two former bantustans with a portion of the former Cape Province. In early 1997 Mhlaba was succeeded by Arnold Stofile.

EASTERN CAPE SEPARATISM. Movement to promote the economic and political concerns of colonists in the eastern Cape in the 19th century. From 1823 colonists there called for 'separation' from the government in Cape Town, which they perceived to be antagonistic to their interests. For some, separatism meant the development of a loose federalism in the Cape. Others wanted the transfer of the seat of government from Cape Town to the eastern districts, a move they believed would dispose parliamentarians more favourably towards eastern problems. Yet others desired complete independence from the Cape Colony. Separatist issues were articulated most vociferously in the *Graham's Town Journal*, under the editorship of Robert Godlonton (1794–1884), a leading spokesman for the settlers. Farming, commercial and urban groups in the eastern districts never achieved more than transient unity, however. In 1860 a Separatist League was established, led by wool producers fighting the imposition of a tax on wool, and in the early 1860s separatism appeared to be a serious force. The Cape parliament met in Grahamstown in 1864, in part to assuage separatist feeling. Tensions between competing interests within the eastern Cape were never far from the surface, however, and after the discovery of diamonds rivalry between towns and interest groups intensified, weakening irrevocably any chance of a unified separatist movement. Separatist ideas surfaced from time to time in Grahamstown in the late 19th century, particularly in the late 1870s at the time of the confederation schemes, but never again carried significant weight. [B. le Cordeur, *The Politics of Eastern Cape Separatism* (Cape Town, 1981)]

ECONOMIC CHANGE. Some 2000 years ago, Khoikhoi pastoralists practising a nomadic lifestyle settled alongside hunter-gatherers, who had long inhabited the region. Some two centuries later, Bantu-speaking agriculturists and pastoralists settled south of the Limpopo River, bringing further economic diversification. They introduced mining, particularly for iron and copper. Both the Khoikhoi and Bantu-speakers engaged in considerable trade (mainly in livestock and manufactured goods such as iron objects, leather and wood crafts, and beads) over long distances, and ties were forged with traders beyond what is now South Africa.

With the establishment of the white settlement by the Dutch East India Company* in 1652, trade increased as Khoikhoi bartered increasing numbers of livestock and hunting products with whites for beads and manufactured European goods. Fruit and vegetables were supplied to passing ships, and the production of wheat and wine in the south-western Cape slowly expanded during the 17th and 18th centuries, until viticulture became the main industry of the area by the beginning of the 19th century.

After the second British occupation in 1806, the Cape was drawn into the British imperial economy. The tight trading and monopolistic restrictions of the Dutch East India Company were lifted, exports were encouraged by a lowering of tariffs, immigration was promoted, and agriculture, commerce, banking and transport all developed markedly during the first half of the 19th century. Merino sheep farming was introduced into the eastern Cape in 1827, and from the 1830s wool* began to overtake wine* as the Cape's major export. Production rose dramatically: 144,000 pounds weight in 1834, 1 million pounds in 1841, 5 million pounds in 1851, and 25 million pounds in 1862. Although the drought of the 1860s and the slump in world prices after the American Civil War greatly reduced production, wool remained the country's most important agricultural export. In Natal after 1860, but particularly from the 1870s, sugar-cane became a valuable cash crop for white farmers, while black peasants supplied a large proportion of the grain market. The two Boer republics practised semi-subsistence agriculture.

The discovery of diamonds* in 1867, then gold,* set in motion changes that transformed much of the country's economy. The economic centre of the country shifted from the eastern Cape to the Kimberley–Cape Town axis, and then firmly to the highveld. Foreign capital poured into the country; profits from the diamond mines financed the country's first important railways,* as well as the initial development of the gold-mining industry; and coal mining also grew dramatically from the end of the 19th century. The new urban centres in the interior opened up an enormous new market for agricultural produce. White farmers began to commercialize, aided by the transfer of revenues obtained from mining, and competition from African peasant farmers was eliminated.

The political unification of the country in 1910 underpinned further economic growth during the 20th century, although expansion was unevenly spread. Agriculture experienced severe difficulties during the 1920s and 1930s, as problems arising from soil erosion, drought, population pressure and economic depression battered farmers. After the 1950s, agriculture was transformed by increasing specialization, technological improvements and capital-intensive farming. Agriculture's position in the economy declined, however, during the second half of the century. New mines were opened during the inter- war years, and gold in particular boomed during the 1930s.

In the 20th century, the most important structural change in South Africa's economy was the expansion of manufacturing, at the expense of mining and agriculture, in the contribution to national income. In 1911/12, mining contributed 27.1% of net domestic product, agriculture 17.4% and manufacturing 6.7%. During World War II, manufacturing overtook mining as the leading sector. In

1995, manufacturing contributed 23.5% of gross domestic product (GDP), mining and quarrying 8.7%, and agriculture 4.7%. While mining remained important, and coal exports increased dramatically, the value of mining exports as a proportion of overall exports declined as the manufacturing sector grew. During the first half of the century, significant developments occurred in the textile, food-processing, engineering, and iron and steel industries. After World War II, the industrial base of the country broadened and diversified further. By the late 1980s, however, the economy was suffering severely from sanctions, and only arms production boomed.

The average growth of the economy in the five decades between 1911/12 and 1961/62 was 1.8% per annum; allowing for price increases and population growth, real income per head more than doubled during this period. During the 1960s, growth was exceptionally high, and GDP grew at an average rate of 5.9% per annum. This fell sharply during the decade of the 1970s, when GDP grew at an average of 3.3%. Further declines were recorded in the 1980s, when an average growth of only 1.4% in GDP was recorded (negative real growth rates occurred in 1982, 1983, 1985 and 1990); with the population increase of 2.6% per annum in this decade, income per head was in decline. A similar situation occurred in the period to 1995, when GDP grew at an average of just under 2.5%.

South Africa remained heavily dependent on international trade during the 20th century. At the same time the composition of imports changed markedly during the century. Imports as a proportion of national income did not change much from their average level of 24% in the 1930s, but in 1910 food, drink, clothing and textiles constituted 46% of total imports, whereas these consumer goods comprised only 11.7% in 1994, when intermediate and capital goods made up the bulk of imports. In 1968, 92% of imports were manufactured, whereas only 38% of exports were classified in this category (a large proportion of these were only lightly manufactured agricultural and mineral products). South Africa remains heavily dependent on mining and agriculture to pay for imported products.

The total value of South Africa's exports in 1994 was R87.5 billion, equivalent to 20.9% of GNP. The United Kingdom, traditionally South Africa's main trading partner, had slipped to third position by 1994. In that year, Germany (at 16.4%), the United States (15.7%), the United Kingdom (11.3%) and Japan (9.9%) were the main suppliers of imports. South Africa's exports in 1994 went mainly to Switzerland (6.7%), the United Kingdom (6.6%), the United States (4.8%) and Japan (4.6%). Exports to all African countries totalled 9.6%, while imports from Africa were only 3%. The chief African markets for exports were Zimbabwe, Zambia and Mozambique, while the only substantial supplier of imports was Zimbabwe. South Africa joined the Southern African Development Community in August 1994.

After the 1960s, when the country achieved remarkable economic development (although the results of this were very unevenly distributed), the South African economy performed much less well. While the instability of the world economy was sometimes to blame, domestic political upheaval, a weakening in the gold price, foreign sanctions and periodic drought were more important in restricting economic growth. The country experienced its longest recession of the 20th century between 1989 and 1993, when real GDP fell by 4% and employment fell by

8%. In 1993, gross domestic investment was R59.9 billion, equivalent to 15.6% of GDP. This was financed by gross domestic savings of R65.9 million (17.2% of GDP), allowing for net capital outflows to the rest of the world of R8.8 billion, and a decrease in gold and other reserves of R2.9 billion.

Low levels of investment limited the ability of the economy to generate growth and create employment. More than 100,000 jobs in mining and 60,000 in manufacturing were lost during the first half of the 1990s. Employment levels had been poor, however, since the end of the 1960s. During the 1970s the number of those employed rose only by 2.7% per annum, barely in excess of the population growth, while during the 1980s employment among Africans grew at only 1.4% per annum, well under the population increase. Accurate statistics of unemployment are difficult to obtain, as official statistics cover only the limited number of registered unemployed people. A large migration to towns has occurred in the country since the abolition of influx control in 1986, and disguised unemployment in the rural areas was increasingly registered as overt unemployment in the urban areas. An official survey in October 1994 placed the number of unemployed at 32% of the labour force (about 4.6 million people). The informal sector of the economy has absorbed some of these people, but unemployment remained one of the most serious challenges for the new democratic government.

While South Africa could thus boast a modern economy, its economic performance was hampered by the constraints of population increase exceeding economic growth, and large areas of the country remained underdeveloped. The economy was heavily dependent on the export of primary products, the prices of which had been falling since the early 1960s. After 1994 especially, as sanctions fell away and South Africa entered the global economy more fully, it was forced increasingly to compete on the world market. Basic needs of the entire population had to be addressed, while at the same time the country had to try to be competitive internationally. [S. Jones and A. Muller, *The South African Economy 1910–1990* (Basingstoke, 1992); J. Nattrass, *The South African Economy* (Cape Town, 1988); N. Nattrass and E. Ardington, eds., *The Political Economy of South Africa* (Cape Town, 1990)]

EDUCATION. Before white settlement began, children were educated by their families and communities in different ways, from the transmission of oral traditions and rituals between generations, through the instruction of children at puberty during initiation ceremonies, to the communication of economic skills essential to the continuing survival of communities. Formal schooling began with a school established in 1658 by officials of the Dutch East India Company (VOC)* at the Cape for slave children. This was meant to increase the usefulness of slaves to the colonists. The children of white colonists began to receive formal education from 1663, in a small school run by an official of the Dutch Reformed Church.* This inaugurated a segregated educational system that dominated education for the entire VOC period.

The history and development of formal schooling in South Africa is closely intertwined with the history of the Christian church and missionary activities. The educational responsibilities of the Dutch Reformed Church were widely accepted in the colony, and proposals of the Commissioner-General of the Batavian Republic,*

J.A.U. de Mist, to secularize education under state control were met with considerable suspicion. After the British occupation of the Cape, an anglicization process was begun, and teachers were recruited from England and Scotland. In 1839, a Department of Education was established under a superintendent-general. The first holder of the office, James Rose Innes, initiated a two-tier system of state-maintained schools: 'first class' schools in large towns, and 'second class' schools, providing only primary education, in small centres. Mission schools, as well as smaller farm and community schools, were entitled to state subsidies under certain conditions. Many state-aided schools were formed by local initiative in subsequent years, until the arrangement was formalized in the Cape by the Education Act of 1865. This pattern of state non-denominational schools and state-aided mission and church schools was extended to Natal and the Orange Free State, although private schools, often founded on religious principles, were also permitted to function. In the Transvaal, this British pattern was rejected in favour of a Dutch model with teachers recruited from Holland. From the 1880s, a pattern of Christian National Education (CNE) began to develop, based on Calvinism and nascent Afrikaner nationalism; after the South African War,* CNE schools were strongly promoted in the Transvaal and Orange Free State with the backing of the Dutch Reformed Church in opposition to anglicization and other state initiatives.

After the establishment of Union* in 1910, provincial control was maintained over white schools, while the great majority of blacks who received an education did so in schools which had been founded by missionary societies in the 19th century and which were continued, often with grants from the state, either by those societies or by different churches. Much mission education was limited to vocational and manual training, although this slowly began to change during the early decades of the 20th century. After the election of the National Party to government in 1948, educational policy was reformulated along apartheid lines. A commission under W.M.M. Eiselen recommended in 1951 that control of education be removed from the churches and missions, and, while white education would continue to be run by the provinces, a separate central government department should henceforth supervise what was called Bantu Education. These proposals were taken up in the Bantu Education* Act of 1953, which initiated separate and inferior state-controlled education for blacks, provoking considerable upheaval during the 1950s as churches were largely obliged to sever their links with education.

The Soweto uprising* of 1976 marked the beginnings of overt black rejection of apartheid education, and forced the state to begin planning for educational reform. Changes were very slow in implementation. Although the De Lange Commission of 1981 recommended the abolition of racially based education, the tricameral constitution of 1983 continued to categorize education along racial lines. After 1983, together with various bantustan authorities, no fewer than 14 different official departments were responsible for education in various areas of the country and for separate sections of society. Private schools began to implement non-racial education during the 1980s, but it was only in the 1990s that state schools began to admit pupils of all backgrounds.

The challenges of education posed formidable challenges to the post-1994 government as it grappled with the legacy of apartheid and the enormous disparities in the quality and funding of education. While considerable progress was made in rationalizing various educational authorities and examining bodies, the allocation of resources and funding remained contentious issues, as did syllabus changes. In 1997 a major new 'outcomes-based' approach to learning, called Curriculum 2005 after the expected date of final implementation, was launched by the Ministry of National Education, to be phased in from 1998. [A. Behr and R. Macmillan, *Education in South Africa* (Pretoria, 1971); J. Marcum, *Education, Race and Social Change in South Africa* (Berkeley, 1982); P. Kallaway, ed., *Apartheid and Education* (Johannesburg, 1984); E. Unterhalter et al., eds., *Apartheid Education and Popular Struggles* (Johannesburg, 1991)]

ENGLISH. English-speaking settlers and their descendants have lived in close proximity to speakers of other languages for two centuries, and a form of English easily recognized as 'South African' has emerged. Many words from Afrikaans, Khoesan and Bantu languages have been adopted, and South African English has many distinctive pronunciations, adaptations and constructions. A rich literature developed; some South Africans writing in English won international acclaim, such as Alan Paton for *Cry, the Beloved Country*, and Nadine Gordimer, who was awarded the Nobel Prize for Literature in 1991.

In the 1990s English was the first language of over three million South Africans, or 8% of the population: about 39% of whites, 15% of Coloureds, and 95% of Indians spoke English as their first language. Its influence as a medium of communication between people of different backgrounds, and as the major language of public life, was vastly more important than was suggested by its status – merely one of eleven official languages.

ENGLISH-SPEAKING WHITES. When the British first occupied the Cape in 1795, there were few English-speakers anywhere in southern Africa. After the second British occupation in 1806, their numbers grew steadily, and reached 4000 by 1820. In that year, a further 5000 settlers were recruited in England, and were located by the Cape authorities in the Albany district on the eastern frontier of the colony. While English-speakers remained a distinct minority of the white population despite this influx of immigrants (there were some 43,000 Dutch-speakers), they soon exercised a predominant influence in the colony.

The settlers of 1820 were socially and politically diverse. Though the majority of males were artisans and tradesmen, they included farmers, soldiers, teachers and a handful of professionals; few had any substantial financial resources. They were ill equipped for conditions in the eastern Cape, where the colonial authorities wished to use them as small-scale agriculturists to secure the defence of the frontier against the Xhosa.* By 1824, almost two-thirds had abandoned their farms and moved to Grahamstown* and other emerging small towns in the eastern Cape. Most of them quickly established themselves in a range of commercial pursuits, and legal and illicit trade across the frontier enriched many. Merchants and shopkeepers also moved into the interior, and small towns founded in the Orange Free State and the Transvaal often had a strong English-speaking presence. Those who stayed on farms began to prosper on larger holdings of land, particularly after the introduction of merino sheep farming. By the end of the 1830s, wool* had become the principal export of the Cape.

The colonial authorities in Cape Town actively consolidated English influence in the Cape. During the 1820s, the autocratic Governor, Lord Charles Somerset, sought to replace the use of Dutch in public life by English through his anglicization policies. English became the sole language of government from 1825 and of the courts from 1827. Anglicization was pursued less aggressively after 1827, but English enjoyed preferential treatment in schools, churches and public life. English speakers dominated Cape politics for most of the century, though the Afrikaner Bond* challenged their position from the 1880s.

In contrast to the Cape, the majority of white colonists in British-ruled Natal* were English-speaking. The earliest permanent white settlers there in 1824 were English-speaking, and after annexation in 1843 English-speaking immigrants arrived in considerable numbers, particularly between 1849 and 1852, when just under 5000 English and Scottish people arrived in Durban with government assistance. Many settled in Durban, Pietermaritzburg and other towns, while others prospered from growing sugar and fruit crops, from indigenous timber and wattle cultivation, and from cattle and sheep farming. Large numbers of English-speakers, particularly artisans and skilled workers, were attracted to South Africa after the discovery of diamonds* and gold* in the interior. Their presence in the Transvaal provoked considerable tension between them and the government, especially after the Jameson Raid.* The South African War* and Milner's* post-war attempts at anglicization deepened divisions between English-speakers and Afrikaners. A measure of reconciliation was achieved between these two groups after Union* in 1910, and the status of English was enshrined alongside Dutch* (later Afrikaans) in the constitution. English-speakers were outnumbered by Afrikaners in the Union, despite ongoing immigration from Britain until 1948; this restricted their political influence. Between 1910 and 1948, most English-speakers offered their political allegiance to the South African Party,* which was committed to reconciling Afrikaners and English-speaking whites, and then to the United Party.* The more chauvinistic Unionist* and Dominion* parties, which relied exclusively on English-speaking support, never became significant political forces.

Despite their political weakness, English-speaking whites dominated commerce, industry, business and banking. English was the principal language of South African urban life, even in places such as Pretoria and Bloemfontein, until the urbanization of Afrikaners during the inter-war years. Considerable economic inequality between English and Afrikaans-speaking whites persisted in towns until the 1960s. English-speaking immigration to South Africa, which stopped when the National Party (NP) came to power, began to increase again during the 1960s, and as many as 20,000 English-speaking immigrants entered the country each year by the late 1970s. Most immigrants from Europe, and from former European colonies in Africa, were absorbed into the English-speaking community, although few took out citizenship: in the 1980s at least one-fifth of English-speaking whites were not citizens.

The political influence of English-speaking whites declined markedly after 1948. Most gave their allegiance to the white-supremacist United Party,* which slowly declined until its demise in 1977. After the NP achieved its goal of a republic* in 1961 and toned down its aggressive Afrikaner nationalist rhetoric, it began to win English-speaking support, and gained a significant number of votes from English-speakers by the end of the 1970s. More liberal English-speaking whites found a political home in the Progressive Party* (the Progressive Federal Party after 1977), whose support base lay largely in more affluent constituencies in the major cities. Among whites, most of the strongest critics of apartheid were English-speakers: people such as Helen Suzman, the Progressive Party MP; Alan Paton, who was active in the Liberal Party*; and Helen Joseph, who worked closely with the African National Congress. Several English-language newspapers won international prominence for their anti-apartheid campaigns. [R. de Villiers, *Better Than They Knew* (Cape Town, 1972, 1974); J. Lazerson, *Against the Tide* (Boulder, 1994)]

ESAU, Abraham (c.1856–1901). Martyr from Calvinia in the north-western Cape, whose support for the British during the South African War* earned him the hostility of invading Boer commandos and Cape rebels. Because he had raised a force of Coloureds to fight on the British side, the Boers murdered him when they occupied Calvinia in 1901. [B. Nasson, *Abraham Esau's War* (Cape Town, 1991)] *f*

FAIRBAIRN, John (1794–1864). Journalist and politician. He edited the *South African Commercial Advertiser* in Cape Town from 1824 until 1859, and was widely known for his unyielding commitment to the freedom of the press, his campaigns against slavery, his leadership of the anti-convict movement of 1849, and his support for representative government at the Cape. He served as member of the Legislative Assembly from 1854 until 1864, and was prominent in promoting commercial activity at the Cape. [H. Botha, *John Fairbairn in South Africa* (Cape Town, 1984)]

FAKU (1780–1867). Paramount chief of the Mpondo from 1820 until his death. Through his links with Wesleyan missionaries as well as the Cape and British authorities, he successfully consolidated a large measure of Mpondo autonomy after the Mfecane.* During the 1850s, however, he was increasingly drawn into confrontation with the British over conflicting land claims, and his power base eroded markedly after the Xhosa cattle-killing* of 1857.

FIRST, Ruth (1925–1983). Radical political activist, scholar and journalist. An active communist, she was detained and forced into exile in 1963. Her account of her detention provided a key exposure of security police methods. She was assassinated by a parcel bomb sent her by South African agents when she was working in Mozambique; she was probably a target because of the role her husband Joe Slovo* played in Umkhonto weSizwe.* [D. Pinnock, *Ruth First* (Cape Town, 1995)]

FISCHER, Abram (Bram) (1908–1975). Anti-apartheid activist lawyer. Grandson of a Prime Minister of the Orange River Colony and son of a Judge-President of the Orange Free State, he studied law at Oxford and while a student travelled to the Soviet Union. From 1935 he worked at the Johannesburg Bar, and was active in the Communist Party.* In the 1950s and early 1960s he defended those accused of treason in the Treason trial,* and in 1963–1964 Nelson Mandela and the members of Umkhonto weSizwe* arrested at Rivonia.* He was then himself arrested and charged with being an office-bearer in an unlawful organization, the South African Communist Party* and for unlawful acts to further the aims of that organization. Jumping bail, he went underground to continue this work. Arrested after ten months underground, he was sentenced to life imprisonment in 1966 and was released only when on the point of death. From 1990 he was often held up by the ANC as a model Afrikaner, who courageously worked against an Afrikaner government committed to evil policies and who suffered for the cause of freedom. [S. Clingman, *Bram Fischer* (Cape Town, 1998)]

FITZPATRICK, Sir James Percy (1862–1931). Politician, capitalist, author. A prominent leader of the Uitlanders* in Johannesburg during the 1890s, FitzPatrick enjoyed close ties with many of the leading mining magnates, and was imprisoned for his part in the Jameson Raid. He played an active role in politics after the South African

War,* as a member of the Unionist Party.* He is best remembered as author of the novel *Jock of the Bushveld*, first published in 1907, which portrayed his life on the goldfields of Barberton. [A. Duminy and B. Guest, ed., *FitzPatrick* (Johannesburg, 1976) and *Interfering in Politics* (Johannesburg, 1987)]

FOREIGN INVESTMENT. Foreign investment has played a vital role in the development of South Africa's economy, particularly the mining industry. By 1936, almost half of total foreign investment in Africa was in South Africa. Further foreign investment arrived after World War II, mainly drawn to the gold mines of the Orange Free State. There was an outflow of foreign capital between 1960 and 1964, following the Sharpeville massacre,* the consequent State of Emergency, and the banning of African political organisations, but from 1965 to 1976 capital inflows into the country were again positive, except in 1973.

A sharp decline in investment from abroad occurred in the years 1977–1980, when negative outflows of both long-term and short-term capital took place after the Soweto uprising.* From 1981 to 1983, foreign investment was again positive, but was sharply negative from 1984, following the tricameral* constitution and the State of Emergency from mid-1985. With deepening recession and serious political disturbances, negative short-term capital movements reached record levels. A two-tier system of exchange rates for foreign investments (financial rand and commercial rand) was introduced in September 1985 to prevent further deterioration, and the government was obliged to declare a moratorium on the repayment of foreign debt, as well as reschedule the repayment of loans. Negative outflows of capital occurred until 1993, although international sanctions* on trade and investment were widely abandoned in 1991; only after 1994, as the lengthy negotiations towards resolving the country's political turmoil were completed and a democratic government came to office, did foreign investment in the country begin to turn around from the very negative period of the 1980s. Major investment then came from Malaysia, Britain, Germany and the United States.

FOREIGN RELATIONS. Within the British Empire or Commonwealth, South Africa began to develop its own foreign policy from the time of the Balfour Declaration of 1926. It became a member of the League of Nations, and then the United Nations.* Jan Smuts's* reputation as an international statesman brought considerable international credit to his country. But under the National Party government after 1948, with the implementation of apartheid, South Africa gradually moved into increasing isolation. This grew markedly after the Sharpeville* crisis, and with South Africa's departure from the Commonwealth* in 1961. It was even more marked after the Soweto uprising* of 1976.

In the mid-1980s various kinds of sanctions* were imposed on the apartheid regime, which developed ties with such other pariahs as Israel and Paraguay. Then after 1990 the country's international position was dramatically transformed. Not only were links much strengthened with Britain, Germany and France, links which had never been severed during the sanctions period, but ties were again established with the likes of Russia, the Netherlands and the Scandinavian countries, which had given massive support to the African National Congress (ANC). After the April

1994 election, South Africa rejoined the Commonwealth (in July), became a member of the Organization of African Unity (in June) and the Non-Aligned Movement (in May), and joined the Southern African Development Community (SADC) (in August). Nelson Mandela's moral standing in the world brought his country great credit, and after he became chair of the SADC, he began to play a more active role in trying to bring about peace on the African continent, mediating in May 1997 in the Zairean crisis on board a South African ship off the Central African coast. He continued to regard Cuba, Syria and Libya as friendly nations, because of their support for the ANC in its years of exile, despite strong international pressure to distance himself from them. From the beginning of 1998 South Africa switched recognition from Taiwan to China, a move designed in part to help South Africa win a permanent seat on an enlarged United Nations Security Council. [J. Barber and J. Barratt, *South Africa's Foreign Policy* (Cambridge, 1990); G. Mills, *From Pariah to Participant* (Johannesburg, 1994)]

FORT HARE. J.T.Jabavu* and others campaigned for the establishment of a college for Africans early in the 20th century. It opened as the South African Native College in 1916 on land given by the Church of Scotland adjacent to Lovedale, the leading mission high school for Africans, at Alice in the eastern Cape. Those who attended Fort Hare included Nelson Mandela,* Mangosuthu Buthelezi,* Kaiser Matanzima* and Robert Mugabe of Zimbabwe. Affiliated to Rhodes University in 1949, Fort Hare was, after 1959, taken over by the government and reconstituted as an ethnic college for Xhosa-speaking students. In the late 1960s it emerged as one of the leading centres of Black Consciousness.* [A. Kerr, *Fort Hare* (Pietermaritzburg, 1968)]

FRANCHISE. The constitution granted to the Cape in 1853 gave the colony a non-racial franchise with a low qualification: every male citizen over 21 years who owned property valued at £25, received a salary of £50 per annum, or received a salary of £25 per annum plus free board and lodging, was entitled to vote. By the 1880s, African and Coloured voters were acquiring the vote in significant numbers, particularly in the eastern Cape, as the Transkeian territories were progressively incorporated into the colony. Legislation was passed to limit the number of African voters: in 1887 land held on communal tenure was deemed unacceptable as a qualification for the franchise, and in 1892 the property qualification was raised from £25 to £75, the wage qualification was eliminated, and voters were required to sign their name when registering. By 1909, about 10% of voters at the Cape were Coloured, and 5% were African.

In Natal, the franchise was theoretically colour-blind, but in practice blacks were ineligible in terms of legislation of 1865, which disqualified all Africans who had not been exempted from customary law. Indians were barred from the vote in 1896. In the Transvaal and the Orange Free State the franchise was limited to white males. Article 8 of the Treaty of Vereeniging* of 1902, which concluded the South African War,* provided that there would be no change in the franchise before the restoration of self-government, after which the two former republics could decide the issue themselves. This meant there was no chance of the franchise being extended to blacks in territories so implacably opposed to a non-racial franchise.

The National Convention* of 1908–1909 decided that each of the four provinces of the Union* would retain their own franchise arrangements. Only whites could stand for election to the House of Assembly or the Senate. Cape delegates hoped that in time the non-racial franchise would be extended to the northern provinces, but the Cape franchise instead came to be seen as anomalous. In 1930 the franchise was extended to white women, and in 1931 property and educational requirements for all whites were removed. The effect of these two measures was to reduce drastically the proportion of black voters in the Cape, from 20% in 1929 to 8.5% in 1935. In 1936, African voters (who only numbered 10,000, a mere 1.4% of the total number) were removed from the common voters' roll: the privilege of the franchise meant that they could not be subject to coercive and racially discriminatory measures. Cape Africans were then placed on a separate voters' roll, and were entitled to vote for three 'Native Representatives' to parliament, who had to be white. This system was abolished in 1960.

After the National Party (NP) came to power in 1948, it was determined to remove Coloureds from the common voters' roll in the Cape, where Coloured voters held considerable influence in several constituencies. This provoked a prolonged and bitter constitutional crisis, but the NP achieved its goal in 1956. Coloureds were thereafter entitled to vote for white representatives to parliament, a system that was abolished in 1968, when a Coloured Persons Representative Council* was established with limited powers to administer local government, education, welfare and pensions for Coloured people. Africans, meanwhile, were expected to exercise political rights in their 'homeland' (bantustan*) of origin; in 1963 the first election of a bantustan government took place in the Transkei.*

In 1983, the constitution was altered to provide for a racially based tricameral* parliament. Separate legislative chambers for whites, Coloureds and Indians were established, for which elections on separate voters' rolls took place. The white chamber was larger than the other two combined. Africans were excluded from the system, which never won acceptance among the majority of Coloured or Indian people. Fierce opposition to the tricameral constitution gave birth to the broad-based United Democratic Front,* which channelled most anti-apartheid activity within the country during the 1980s. In terms of the 1993 interim constitution, the franchise was extended to all South African adults over the age of 18 years, and in the April 1994 election Nelson Mandela* and other black leaders and their black followers cast their votes for the first time.

FREE BLACKS. Blacks at the Cape who were neither slaves nor of Khoikhoi, Bastard* or Bantu-speaking descent. They were of Asian and African origin, and most were ex-slaves; a few entered the Cape as free persons. They were always a small minority of the Cape's population: in 1670 they constituted 7.4% of the total free population, and only 4.4% in 1770, when they numbered just over 1000 people. In the 18th century, most lived in Cape Town in conditions of poverty, and, though they were in charge of the town's fire brigade, they suffered statutory discrimination: the curfew, for example, applied to 'slaves and people of colour', and so to free blacks. Ordinance 50 of 1828 removed such legal disabilities, and thereafter the free blacks were gradually absorbed into the Coloured population. [R. Elphick and H.

Giliomee, eds., *The Shaping of South African Society* (Cape Town, 1989)]

FREE BURGHERS. Initially, former officials of the Dutch East India Company (VOC)*
who were given land to farm, but the term came to be used for all whites who were
not Company officials. In 1657, hoping to reduce expenditure, the VOC released
nine employees from their contracts of service and gave them smallholdings of land
in the Liesbeek River valley, east of Table Mountain. These first farmers bound
themselves to supply produce at fixed prices. By the end of the 17th century, there
were 1334 free burghers, their numbers having increased partly due to immigration
(for example, 180 Huguenot refugees from France arrived in 1688). Little immigration occurred during the 18th century, however, and mainly through natural
increase the number of free burghers rose to 15,000 by 1795. Relations between the
free burghers, particularly the wealthier farmers, and the VOC were frequently
tense. Free burgher grievances focused mainly on economic restrictions imposed by
the VOC, though frustrations were also expressed with the denial of political rights
and the corruption and incompetence of officials. [R. Elphick and H. Giliomee,
eds., *The Shaping of South African Society* (Cape Town, 1989)]

FREEDOM CHARTER. See AFRICAN NATIONAL CONGRESS, CONGRESS
ALLIANCE

FREEDOM FRONT. White Afrikaner political party born in early 1994 under the leadership of General Constand Viljoen,* which campaigned for self-determination for
white Afrikaners and for the establishment of an Afrikaner *volkstaat* in a part of
South Africa. In the April 1994 election it won 640,000 votes. Its acceptance of
negotiation rather than confrontation helped avert a civil war in early 1994, and in
return the ANC agreed to set up a Volkstaat Council, a talking shop as there was no
question of allowing self-determination, and to the provision in the 1996 constitution for a commission for the promotion of rights of cultural, linguistic and religious communities.

FRERE, Sir Henry Bartle (1815–1884). After a distinguished career in India, Frere was
offered the post of Governor of the Cape and High Commissioner in 1877 as the
best person to bring about confederation.* Frere came to South Africa determined
to achieve that goal and expected to become first Governor-General of a new British
dominion. But at the Cape he first found himself involved in another war with the
Xhosa,* then dealing with the Zulu kingdom,* for he believed that before a self-
governing white-ruled dominion could be left to defend itself, white supremacy
had to be established throughout South Africa. He therefore took actions which
brought on the Anglo-Zulu War* in January 1879. The war opened with the British
defeat at Isandlwana,* and as a result of this disaster, the High Commission was
divided, and Frere was kept in South Africa only while some possibility of a confederation remained. The annexation of the Transvaal, however, roused its white
inhabitants against the British, and the Cape parliament opposed confederation.
Frere was recalled in 1880, his hopes shattered.

FRONTIERS. The term 'frontier' is most often associated with the eastern Cape region, where conflict between Xhosa* and whites occurred over the period of about one hundred years (from the mid-1770s until the last frontier war of 1878–1879). There were, however, numerous other frontiers, where different societies encountered one other and attempted to resolve their conflicting interests. As white trekboers* began to move inland from the Cape at the beginning of the 18th century, for example, frontiers opened in which many different forms of conflict and co-operation existed. Another frontier situation occurred between the mid-18th and mid-19th centuries in the Orange River area, where numerous communities experienced profound transformation through their dealings with one another; new societies emerged, and co-operation for mutual economic benefit frequently occurred across cleavages of race or status. Further frontier situations manifested themselves in the southern African interior during the 19th century, as white conquest shifted to the areas which became Natal,* the Orange Free State* and the Transvaal.*

Historians have long debated the best ways of conceiving the South African frontiers and their significance. Pro-colonist historians of the early 20th century, as well as Afrikaner nationalist historians, viewed the frontier as a clash between heroic Christian whites who brought order and civilization to hostile, barbaric blacks. A different view emerged in the 1930s, articulated by liberal historians, most notably Eric Walker, who argued that white frontiersmen, through their disregard for black society and land on the frontiers, developed racist attitudes, which took root during the 19th century, particularly in the Boer republics, and were carried into the 20th century, when segregationist and apartheid policies developed. The psychologist I.D. MacCrone extended Walker's arguments in his *Race Attitudes in South Africa* (1937), by providing detailed evidence about the isolation of frontier life; in his view whites lost touch with civilization and thus evolved racist attitudes which were carried forward into the 19th and 20th centuries.

More recently, scholars have challenged the notion of conflict and racism as essential features of southern African frontier communities. Liberal Africanist work, notably *The Oxford History of South Africa* (1969 and 1971), stressed co-operative forms of interaction as well as conflict. The revisionist historian Martin Legassick, in a powerful critique of the liberal 'frontier tradition' (1970), argued that some of the least colour- and race-conscious interaction between different societies occurred on the frontier, and the origins of white racism should be sought elsewhere. Together with other revisionists, he maintained that 18th-century racism was quite different from the systematic and overt racism of the late 19th and 20th centuries, which was the product rather of the industrial and mineral revolutions. South African frontiers can thus no longer be viewed in terms of two or more sharply divergent societies coming into conflict with one another. Internal cleavages, changing alliances, peaceful interchanges and complex forms of interaction all occurred in addition to, and parallel with, conflict and warfare. While in some ways frontiers undoubtedly strengthened white racist attitudes, the precise influence of frontiers in shaping white racism remains elusive. [S. Marks and A. Atmore, eds., *Economy and Society in Preindustrial South Africa* (London, 1980); N. Mostert, *Frontiers* (London, 1992)]

g

GANDHI, Mohandas Karamchand (often known by the title 'Mahatma', or great soul) (1869–1948). The central figure in South African Indian* politics between 1893 and 1914. Gandhi settled in Natal in 1893 after obtaining legal training in England. Almost immediately, he became involved in campaigns for Indians to be accorded equal treatment with whites. He founded the Natal Indian Congress in 1894, and served as its first secretary. He led an unsuccessful campaign in 1895 against legislation which denied Indians the vote in Natal. During the South African War,* he organized an Indian ambulance corps, and in 1903 he founded the influential weekly newspaper *Indian Opinion*.

After the war, Gandhi tackled discrimination against Indians in the Transvaal. He developed his famous philosophy of *satyagraha* ('keep to the truth') and launched a non-violent resistance campaign based on its principles in September 1906, to persuade the post-war British administration to lift restrictions on the number of Indians entering the Transvaal. An agreement was reached which stipulated that the registration of Indians would be voluntary rather than compulsory. Later campaigns focused on the poll tax paid by Indians and the non-recognition of marriages solemnized under Indian rites; after Gandhi was himself imprisoned, concessions on these issues were granted by the authorities. He also organized strikes on the Natal coalfields and sugar plantations, and in 1913 led a march of Indians from Natal to the Transvaal, which temporarily bridged class divisions within the Indian community. Gandhi left South Africa in July 1914 for India, where he led the struggle for Indian independence from Britain. [R. Huttenback, *Gandhi in South Africa* (Ithaca, 1971); M. Swan, *Gandhi* (Johannesburg, 1983); J. Brown and M. Prozesky, eds., *Gandhi in South Africa* (Pietermaritzburg, 1996)]

GAUTENG (Sotho, 'place of gold'). South Africa's richest province, which not only included Johannesburg, the largest city, but also Pretoria, the administrative capital, and Johannesburg International Airport, the main point of entry for visitors to South Africa. Part of the former Transvaal* province, Gauteng came into being in April 1994, with the transition to democracy and the coming into force of the interim constitution. Initially called PWV (Pretoria–Witwatersrand–Vereeniging), its name was changed in 1995. Gabriel 'Tokyo' Sexwale of the ANC, a former prisoner on Robben Island,* became its first premier, and Johannesburg was chosen as its capital. In January 1998 Sexwale left office to pursue a business career, and was succeeded as premier by Mathole Motshekga. One of the major issues he had to deal with was crime, for Johannesburg was the crime centre of the country.

GENADENDAL. The oldest mission station in South Africa, founded in 1737 by George Schmidt of the Moravian Missionary Society, it served Khoikhoi in the district of Swellendam. Originally called Baviaanskloof, the mission was closed after six years because of hostility from the Dutch Reformed Church and white colonists. It was reopened in 1792, and prospered. Many of the early missionaries* to southern

Africa, from a range of missionary societies, visited Genadendal and organized their missions along lines similar to the Genadendal pattern of closed settlement around the mission church. [B. Kruger, *The Pear Tree Blossoms* (Genadendal, 1966)]

GERMAN IMMIGRANTS. More German than Dutch immigrants entered the Cape under Dutch East India Company* patronage during the 18th century, but the Germans, mainly single men, were absorbed into the local Dutch population. During the 19th century, colonial authorities in the Cape and Natal sponsored immigration from Germany on a larger scale, and immigrants entered southern Africa with their families or in large parties. In Natal, a group of immigrants settled at New Germany outside Durban in 1848, while in 1857 soldiers of the disbanded Anglo-German Legion from the Crimean War were settled with their families in British Kaffraria.* They were followed shortly afterwards by some 4000 peasants from north Germany, who founded communities such as those of Stutterheim, Berlin and Hanover.

During the 20th century, immigrants from Germany continued to enter the country, though not as part of large state-sponsored programmes. The National Party government after 1948 encouraged immigration from Germany more actively, and implemented a scheme to settle German children orphaned by World War II with Afrikaner families. By 1991 there were approximately 33,000 German-speaking whites in South Africa.

GLEN GREY ACT (1894). Introduced into the Cape parliament by Cecil Rhodes,* the Glen Grey Act was initially designed for the Glen Grey district of the eastern Cape, but was extended to the whole Transkei* in 1898. Rhodes hoped it would become a blueprint for southern Africa, and spoke of it as a 'Bill for Africa'.

The Act had three main elements. Firstly, it altered the system of land tenure, replacing communal tenure with small individual lots; land held under the new system, however, did not count towards the qualifications for the Cape franchise.* As there were not enough individual lots, some Africans found themselves permanently landless. Secondly, in order to force Africans into migrant labour, a tax was imposed on all men who could not prove they had been in *bona fide* wage employment for any three months in any single year. The tax, to which there was much hostility and which proved unworkable, was withdrawn in 1905. Thirdly, a system of district councils was introduced to provide for African participation in local government on an advisory basis.

GOLD. Africans mined gold at several places in the Transvaal – those later known as Lydenburg, Pilgrim's Rest, the Soutpansberg and the Limpopo River valley – during the precolonial period, but gold was used only for ornamentation or trade, on a fairly small scale. In the early 1870s, considerable deposits of alluvial gold were worked by white prospectors in the eastern Transvaal. Small amounts were also found at Rustenburg and on the Witwatersrand before the discovery of the Witwatersrand main reef in 1886. The potential of the goldfields was not fully appreciated until the early 1890s, when the invention of the cyanide process revealed the extent of the deep-level ores and made their exploitation possible. In

1930, new prospecting methods exposed vast new reefs to the south-west of the Witwatersrand, and after World War II a number of new mines were opened up in the northern Orange Free State.*

Though the Witwatersrand gold deposits were the largest and richest in the world, the average gold content per ton of rock was very low. The gold-bearing reef, hundreds of metres underground, required deep-level mining. which meant large-scale operations and huge amounts of capital. The few mining houses which could function in such an environment drew on capital from the Kimberley diamond fields* or from abroad. Of the £200 million invested between 1887 and 1934, 60% came from foreign sources. With the price of gold fixed, and high development costs inevitable, attempts were made to keep labour costs as low as possible. Skilled jobs went to whites, mostly immigrants from Europe, who were able to command high wages; remuneration for the large numbers of African migrant workers was pushed down to the minimum.

The discovery of gold turned the Transvaal, which had been the poorest state in southern Africa, into the wealthiest within a few years. By 1896, gold accounted for 96% of its exports. Gold played a major part in bringing about both the South African War* and the Union* of South Africa in 1910. It remained the backbone of the South African economy, contributing massively to state revenue and earning large quantities of foreign exchange.

The international price of gold played a significant part in South Africa's prosperity during the 20th century. South Africa's departure from the gold standard in 1933 increased the price of the commodity by 65%, boosting domestic economic activity and making possible the opening of new mines. Until 1970, the price was fixed at $35 a fine ounce, but the introduction of a second-tier free market in gold resulted in a greatly increased gold price, heralding a decade of enormous profit for the gold industry. By 1978, 36 active mines produced almost 700 tons a year, roughly half the world's total production. An average price of $613 per fine ounce in 1980 created a record year of growth for the South African economy.

For most of the 1980s and early 1990s, however, the gold price averaged between $300 and $400 an ounce, placing increasing pressure on the gold-mining industry, and the amount mined per year went down steadily. In 1996 less than 500 tons was produced. Growing competition from mines abroad, ongoing enormous capital expenditure, and more organized and militant labour activity combined to reduce profits and yields. Marginal mines found it increasingly difficult to operate, and some were forced to close. Though gold remained significant in the South African economy, it was by the 1990s very much less significant than it had been. In late 1997 the price collapsed to below $300 dollars an ounce, once again threatening many shafts, though the development of gold futures, productivity agreements with workers, and a restructuring of the industry all helped mitigate the effects of the falling price. [J. Lang, *Bullion Johannesburg* (Johannesburg, 1986); R. Macnab, *Gold Their Touchstone* (Johannesburg, 1987); R. Ally, *Gold and Empire* (Johannesburg, 1994)

GOLDSTONE COMMISSION. The Prevention of Public Violence and Intimidation Act of 1991 established a standing commission to investigate such violence and make recommendations for its prevention. Chaired by Judge Richard Goldstone, the commission acquired further powers in 1992, and in November that year announced that some of its investigators had uncovered a secret Military Intelligence operation designed to carry out 'dirty tricks' against opponents of the government. Further revelations followed prior to the April 1994 election, after which the commission ceased operating.

GOVERNMENT OF NATIONAL UNITY (GNU). This came into being, in terms of the interim constitution of 1993, in May 1994. The idea of a coalition government for a limited period of five years was advocated by Joe Slovo* in the negotiations in 1992 as a compromise, to meet the National Party's concern for 'power- sharing', to allay white fears, and as a device for constitutional continuity in a period when threats from the far- right seemed serious. An African National Congress document entitled 'Negotiations: A Strategic Perspective' supported the idea. Nelson Mandela later said it was essential for national reconciliation. The interim constitution provided that the GNU was to last for five years, but the NP was frustrated in the coalition, and once the new constitution was drawn up in May 1996, the NP announced that it would withdraw from government in the middle of the year. Inkatha* then remained the only other member besides the ANC.

GRAHAMSTOWN. Town in the eastern Cape founded as a military post by Colonel John Graham in 1812 to prevent the Xhosa from re-entering the Zuurveld.* Many British immigrants who settled as farmers in the Zuurveld after 1820 moved to Grahamstown, which grew to become the most important trading and administrative centre in the eastern Cape and, by the middle of the 19th century, second in size only to Cape Town. The Cape parliament met in Grahamstown in 1864, when the town was a political focus of the eastern Cape separatist movement.* Its economic decline began in the 1870s, when railway development between the coastal ports of East London and Port Elizabeth and the interior bypassed the town. During the 20th century, Grahamstown became chiefly known for its educational institutions, which included Rhodes University and a number of leading schools. In the 1980s and 1990s it was home to the National Festival of the Arts, South Africa's most important arts festival.

GREAT TREK. The organized migration of Afrikaner farmers from the Cape into the interior of South Africa in the late 1830s. Small exploratory parties surveyed conditions in Natal and on the highveld in 1834 and 1835 and reported the existence of fertile and apparently unpopulated land. In 1836 the first of several large organized groups of Voortrekkers* left the eastern Cape. Leaders such as Piet Retief,* Andries Pretorius, Louis Trichardt and others guided some 14,000 people out of the Cape by 1840, about one-tenth of the Cape Afrikaner population.

Most of the trekkers were pastoral farmers from the eastern Cape, who were responding to a shortage of land and fears of a scarcity of labour. They were also rebelling against the British government at the Cape, whose interference in their lives they found intolerable. Ordinance 50* of 1828 and the emancipation of Cape slaves* unsettled the eastern Cape Afrikaners. By outflanking the Xhosa* and moving into the interior, the trekkers hoped to rule themselves and their labourers as they wished, re-creating as far as possible the conditions of the trekboers of the 18th century. The land of the interior proved far from empty, and the trekkers clashed with both the Ndebele* and the Zulu* during the late 1830s. Most of the trekkers who went to Natal* returned to the highveld after 1843, when the British annexed Natal; those who had settled on the highveld had by then successfully acquired sufficient land for their needs. In 1852, the independence of the trekkers north of the Vaal River was recognized, and they formed the South African Republic* or Transvaal,* while the independence of those between the Orange and Vaal rivers was recognized in 1854.

For much of the 20th century, the Great Trek occupied a major place in the mythology of Afrikaner nationalism. Afrikaner historians, particularly Gustav Preller (1875–1943), regarded the Trek as a central event in Afrikaner history, portraying it as the formative moment in the assertion of Afrikaner identity. The Trek echoed the movement of Israelites from captivity in Egypt into the promised land; it was presented as a heroic tale of small numbers of self-reliant people escaping oppressive British dominance and conquering hostile African forces with the assistance of God. Such ideas were popularized in the decades after the South African War, most particularly at the centenary celebrations of the Trek held across the country in 1938, which the National Party successfully used to mobilize political support and consolidate its following. The foundation stone of the Voortrekker Monument outside Pretoria was laid in that year, and the building completed in 1949, a year after the party came to power and began to implement its apartheid policies. The day on which the trekkers in Natal defeated the Zulu army in 1838, 16 December, was celebrated by Afrikaners as a sacred day throughout the apartheid era. During the 1980s, however, the resonance of the Great Trek waned, and only Afrikaners of the far-right continued to view it in the terms in which it was formerly regarded. [E. Walker, *The Great Trek* (London, 1934); T. Moodie, *The Rise of Afrikanerdom* (Berkeley, 1975); T. Keegan, *Colonial South Africa* (Cape Town, 1996)]

GREY, Sir George (1812–1898). Governor of the Cape and High Commissioner from 1854 until 1861. He disapproved of the treaties which had recognized the independence of the Transvaal and the Orange Free State, and was the first British administrator to regard South Africa as a potential federation. One of Grey's main motives for suggesting a federation was the formulation of a common 'native policy' in the region. He believed blacks should be 'civilized' by being gradually 'assimilated' into white society. He pursued this goal with vigour among the Xhosa* on the Cape's eastern frontier, encouraging their participation in the money economy, reducing the power of chiefs in British Kaffraria,* and building schools for their education. Grey exploited the cattle-killing* of 1856–1857, in particular, to further these ends. [J. Rutherford, *Sir George Grey* (London, 1961); J. Peires, *The Dead Will Arise* (Johannesburg, 1989)]

GRIQUA. Pastoralists of Khoikhoi and mixed descent, initially known as Bastards* or

Basters, who left the Cape in the late 18th century under their first leader, Adam Kok I (c.1710–c.1795). As they moved north through Namaqualand, their possession of horses and guns enabled them to gain dominance in the middle Orange River region at the beginning of the 19th century. With the encouragement of the London Missionary Society,* they settled at Klaarwater, later called Griquatown, in 1804. Here missionaries sought to create an ordered settlement, based on agriculture, and provided the Griqua with a constitution; many, however, were reluctant to abandon their nomadic pastoralist, hunting and trading economic activities. Griqua raiding bands were active in the interior in the 1820s and played an important role at the Battle of Dithakong in 1823. One semi-nomadic group, mostly Bergenaars (mountain people), settled at Philippolis, an LMS mission in southern Transorangia,* in 1825 under the leadership of Adam Kok II (c.1790–1835). Many Griqua at Philippolis became successful commercial farmers, particularly in response to the economic opportunities offered by merino sheep farming.

Towards the end of the 1830s, the Griqua at Philippolis began to suffer white encroachment on their lands. In 1843, Adam Kok III (1811–1875) entered an agreement with the Cape government, promising to keep order along the frontier. A further treaty in 1846 divided Griqua lands into a leasable portion, in which Griqua could lease their farms, and an unleasable reserve, in which no whites were to have access to land. After the proclamation of the Orange River Sovereignty* in 1848, however, Kok was stripped of jurisdiction outside the reserve and lost the leasable land, while whites steadily encroached on the reserve itself. In 1861, the Griqua decided to sell their remaining farms to the Orange Free State, and some 2000 people moved across the Drakensberg, suffering considerable privations en route to 'Nomansland' on the eastern side of the mountain range, which became known as Griqualand East.* Kokstad was founded as the main settlement, but in the early 1870s the east Griqua began to lose their farms to whites, a process which accelerated after Cape officials arrived in Kokstad in 1874 and after Kok's death in 1875. A rebellion in 1878 against the Cape administration was quickly suppressed, and the territory was formally incorporated into the Cape the following year. The demoralized and impoverished east Griqua never recovered their cohesion as a community or their independence.

Meanwhile, the inhabitants of Griquatown and the surrounding country experienced considerable economic hardship as a result of cattle disease, declining resources of game, and drought during the 1840s and 1850s. Their land rights, however, were not seriously challenged until the rich diamond reserves of the region were discovered towards the end of the 1860s. The Griqua claim to the land was asserted by David Arnot, who was of Scottish–Griqua descent, and their leader Nicholaas Waterboer. When Britain sought to take over the diamond fields, it accepted the Griqua claim, granted them British protection, and annexed Griqualand West in 1871. Thereafter, the Griqua were given individual tenure, but many sold their farms to whites, while others lost their land when they went into rebellion in 1878. By the end of the century, only a few Griqua retained any claim to land; the great majority were landless and impoverished. In the 1990s some of their descendants talked of claiming compensation from the British government for being robbed of their land. [R. Ross, *Adam Kok's Griquas* (Cambridge, 1976)]

GRIQUALAND EAST. Territory on the eastern slopes of the Drakensberg, south of Natal, settled by Griqua* refugees from Philippolis in 1861–1862 and formally annexed to the Cape in 1879. A century later, Griqualand East was transferred from the provincial administration of the Cape to that of Natal.

GRIQUALAND WEST. Territory north of the Gariep or Orange River,* settled by Griqua* pastoralists from the Cape at the beginning of the 19th century. It was named Griqualand West when it was annexed by the British in 1871, four years after the discovery of diamonds in the area. Though the legitimacy of the Griqua title was recognized, British annexation led to the rapid alienation of the Griqua people from the land. Griqualand West was incorporated into the Cape in 1880.

GROOTE SCHUUR MINUTE (May 1990). Document agreed to at a meeting between the newly unbanned African National Congress and the government at Groote Schuur, then the presidential residence in Cape Town. The minute sought to clear obstacles in the way of negotiations, in particular those relating to the release of political prisoners. It was followed by the Pretoria Minute* of August 1990, which continued the process and provided for the suspension of the ANC's armed struggle.

GROUP AREAS ACT (1950). A central pillar of apartheid, it provided for residential segregation on the basis of race in urban areas. In terms of the Act, mainly Coloured and Indian people were removed and relocated, usually far from their places of work. (Africans were removed to separate areas under different legislation.) One of the most notorious proclamations under the Group Areas Act provided that Cape Town's District Six, mainly inhabited by Coloured people, would be reserved for whites only. The buildings of District Six were demolished, and the people who had lived there were forcibly removed, mostly to new accommodation on the Cape Flats, away from the city centre. Immense bitterness was caused by the Group Areas Act before it was repealed in 1991. By then it had shaped the social geography of most South African cities and towns in ways which were likely to last a very long time. [D. Smith, *Apartheid in South Africa* (Cambridge, 1990); A. Lemon, *Homes Apart* (Cape Town, 1991); J. Western, *Outcast Cape Town* (Berkeley, 1996)]

h

HANI, Martin Thembisile (Chris) (1942–1993). A devout Christian in his youth, Hani joined the African National Congress (ANC) in 1957 while at school in the eastern Cape. At the University of Fort Hare* he was influenced by Marxist ideas and became a lover of Latin and of literature. He left South Africa in 1963 to undergo military training and fought in Rhodesia. From 1974, based in Lesotho, he worked to create a political structure for the ANC in the eastern Cape. He rose through the ranks of Umkhonto weSizwe* to become chief of staff in 1987. After the ANC and the South African Communist Party (CP)* were unbanned, he returned to South Africa and soon became a very popular speaker in the townships. Long an active member of the CP, he was elected its general secretary in 1991. In the last year of his life he repeatedly urged militant youth to work for peace. His assassination in April 1993 sent shock waves through South Africa. A massive funeral was held and, in the aftermath of the assassination, violence increased markedly and racial tensions grew. On the other hand, his assassination helped persuade the negotiators in the Multi-Party Negotiating Forum* to agree to a date for South Africa's first democratic election. [T. Mali, *Chris Hani* (Johannesburg, 1993); M. Berger, *Chris Hani* (Cape Town, 1994)]

HIGH COMMISSION. The first High Commission was added to the Cape Governor's charge in 1846. It was devised to assist the Governor to settle the colony's eastern frontier, giving him vague powers to act beyond it. Successive holders of the office used it as an informal means of extending British sovereignty. British Kaffraria was established under the High Commission in 1847, and the Orange River Sovereignty* in 1848. Though it doubted the High Commission's legal power to act in this way, the Colonial Office in London accepted both cases as *faits accomplis*. In 1868 Basutoland* was likewise annexed in terms of the High Commission, as was Griqualand West* in 1871. In 1877 the High Commission was enlarged, for the new holder of the office, Sir Bartle Frere,* arrived as Cape Governor and High Commissioner for all southern Africa, to work for confederation.* After the defeat of the British forces at the beginning of the Anglo-Zulu War* in 1879, a separate High Commissioner for South-East Africa was appointed. The unity of the office was restored in 1881, and in 1884 the first official High Commission territory* came into being, when Basutoland was taken back from Cape rule.

Milner* actively used the High Commission in the build-up to the South African War,* and after the war he was the first High Commissioner to attempt to reshape all of South Africa. His successor, Lord Selborne (1859-1942), gave public backing to closer union.* From 1910, the High Commissioner retained responsibility for the High Commission territories, and until 1930 was also Governor-General of the Union, representing the Crown in South Africa. After the declaration of the Republic in 1961, and with the impending independence of the High Commission territories, the High Commission was abolished in 1964. (After 1994, when South Africa rejoined the Commonwealth,* the British ambassador to South Africa became known as the High Commissioner, but that title did not confer the responsibilities of previous High Commissioners.) [J. Benyon, *Proconsul and Paramountcy* (Pietermaritzburg, 1980)]

HIGH COMMISSION TERRITORIES These were the three British territories of Basutoland,* Bechuanaland* and Swaziland,* ruled in terms of the High Commission.* They were sometimes, less accurately, referred to as the Protectorates. Although the South Africa Act of 1909 envisaged their transfer to the Union* of South Africa, they were excluded from the Union in 1910 because of Britain's special relationship with them and the concern that South Africa would not safeguard the interests of their African inhabitants. Every Union prime minister sought their transfer, J.B.M. Hertzog* most vociferously, for he disliked the constant reminder of Britain's continued direct involvement in southern African affairs; the inhabitants of the territories, however, opposed any transfer.

After the election of the National Party (NP) to power in 1948, transfer of the territories to South Africa became highly unlikely; after the declaration of the Republic* in 1961, it was out of the question. In 1963 H.F. Verwoerd* made a final appeal to Britain to allow South Africa to lead them to independence. When it became clear that Britain would guide this process, he became the first prime minister to accept that they would not be incorporated, and spoke of a friendly neighbour policy towards them.

When referring to land in African hands, the NP sometimes added the three territories to the South African reserves to obtain a more impressive, but misleading, figure. The territories were, however, locked into the migrant labour system* and so were heavily dependent on the South African economy, to the extent that some used the term 'South Africa's hostages' to describe them. [J. Halpern, *South Africa's Hostages* (Baltimore, 1965); R. Hyam, *The Failure of South African Expansion* (London, 1972); J. Benyon, *Proconsul and Paramountcy* (Pietermaritzburg, 1980)]

HINTSA (*c.*1790–1835). Chief of the Gcaleka people and paramount chief of the Xhosa* from 1804. The British believed him to have been the prime mover behind the Xhosa invasion of the Cape in 1834. In 1835, while being held hostage by Sir Harry Smith,* he was shot when allegedly trying to escape. His body was then mutilated and it was later rumoured that his skull was taken back to Britain. His brutal death under mysterious circumstances made him a national martyr among the Xhosa. [J. Peires, *The House of Phalo* (Johannesburg, 1981); N. Mostert, *Frontiers* (London, 1992)]

HOBHOUSE, Emily (1860–1925). British philanthropist who exposed conditions in Boer concentration camps* during the South African War,* so bringing the conduct of British policy into question in Britain. She also assisted impoverished Boer women to establish self-help schemes after the war.

HOFMEYR, Jan Hendrik ('Onze Jan') (1845–1909). Cape political leader and champion of the Dutch language. He led the Afrikaner Bond,* representing Afrikaner agrarian interests, in the Cape parliament during the 1880s and 1890s, and used this base to make and break several prime ministers. His alliance with Cecil Rhodes* between 1890 and 1895 was to their mutual advantage, but he broke with Rhodes after the Jameson Raid,* of which he disapproved strongly. He actively promoted reconciliation between white South Africans before and after the South African War.* [T.R.H. Davenport, *The Afrikaner Bond* (Cape Town, 1966)]

HOTTENTOTS. Name given to Khoikhoi* by the Dutch in the 17th and 18th centuries, derived from what seemed to the Dutch to be their unintelligible speech. By the 19th century it had become a general term for all Khoisan people and their descendants at the Cape. The terms 'Hottentot' and 'Hotnot' gradually acquired a strongly pejorative connotation. [R. Elphick, *Kraal and Castle* (New Haven, 1977)]

HUDDLESTON, Trevor (1913–1998). Anglican priest and member of the Community of the Resurrection, who lived in Johannesburg from 1943 until 1956. His work in Sophiatown and the forced removal of people from the suburb in 1955 by the government in terms of the Group Areas* Act prompted him to write a damning account of apartheid entitled *Naught for Your Comfort* (1956). Banned from South Africa, he served as president of the British Anti-Apartheid Movement, and in October 1987 convened the Harare Conference, which brought together a range of resistance groups from within and outside the country.

HUGUENOTS. French Protestant refugees, about 200 of whom were settled at the Cape by the Dutch East India Company* between 1688 and 1700. They established themselves mainly in the Stellenbosch district, at present-day Franschhoek, where many became involved in the fledgling Cape wine industry. By the mid-18th century, they had become absorbed into the Dutch population.

HUNTER-GATHERERS. See SAN

i

IMVO ZABANTSUNDU ('Opinions of the People'). Influential weekly Xhosa newspaper founded in 1884 by J.T. Jabavu* in King William's Town in the eastern Cape. Published in English and Xhosa, *Imvo* became the leading voice of Xhosa opinion for over a decade. From 1898, however, it was challenged by *Izwi Labantu* ('Voice of the People'), edited from East London. *Imvo* was closed in August 1901 by government order for being critical of the South African War,* and did not resume publication until October 1902. Although it has continued to appear until the present, it has never again been as influential as when Jabavu was its editor.

INDEPENDENT CHURCHES. African independent churches began to be formed in the late 19th century, when a number of individuals and congregations broke away from mission churches, frustrated with paternalistic missionaries, the rejection of African tradition and culture, and the denial of African leadership,. In 1884 Nehemiah Tile (c 1850–1891), a Methodist preacher, established the Thembu Church in the Transkei; in 1892, Mangena Mokone, a Methodist minister, founded the Ethiopian Church in Pretoria, taking the name from Psalm 68:31 ('Ethiopia shall stretch out her hands unto God'). Mokone was joined in 1896 by James Dwane (1848–1916), another disillusioned with Methodism, who went to the United States that year and established a link between the Ethiopian Church and the American Methodist Episcopal Church (AMEC),* a black church which had been founded in Philadelphia in 1816, and which made him its general superintendent in South Africa. Dwane was consecrated Vicar-Bishop of the AMEC two years later, by which time the church in South Africa had over 10,000 adherents. In 1900 Dwane led a large body of followers into the Anglican Church, in which he established a separate Order of Ethiopia, with a measure of autonomy. By the turn of the century, other churches had also been established: the Bantu Presbyterian Church, the Zulu Congregational Church and the Lutheran Bapedi Church were among the most prominent to secede from their white 'parent' churches.

The word 'Ethiopianism' was frequently used when whites in the early 20th century accused independent churches of being a sinister cover for political opposition to white authority. In his classic work *Bantu Prophets in South Africa* (1948), Bengt Sundkler, a Lutheran missionary in Zululand, employed the term 'Ethiopianism' for those independent churches which retained the outward form, structure and much of the theology of their parent churches, while he labelled as 'Zionist' those which were also an expression of African independence but which blended African tradition with Christian beliefs, laying more emphasis on prophecy, healing and purification rituals. Independent churches varied enormously from one another, making such classification difficult. Some were millenarian in character, such as the Israelite sect founded by Enoch Mgijima at Bulhoek* in 1918. They also represented a wide range of political opinion. While a few ministers from independent churches were active in the African National Congress, many of them shunned political involvement altogether.

The potential power of the independent churches was weakened by constant fission; by the 1970s, there were over 3000 of them, and by the 1990s over 5000. Many of these comprised a single congregation with fewer than 200 followers. The combined membership of the independent churches was almost six million by 1991, representing over 30% of all practising Christians in the country. The largest church was the politically conservative Zion Christian Church, based at Moria in the Northern Province, which claimed a membership of between two and three million people. [J. Chirenje, *Ethiopianism and Afro-Americans in South Africa* (Baton Rouge, 1987); J. Campbell, *Songs of Zion* (New York, 1995)]

INDIANS. Some Cape slaves were of Indian origin, but South Africa's Indian community traces its origins to two groups of migrants who settled in the country in the latter part of the 19th century. Between 1860 and 1911, just over 152,000 people from south and north-eastern India arrived in Natal as indentured labourers. The majority of them worked on sugar plantations, but others were employed on the railways, coal mines and wattle plantations. At the end of their five-year contracts, workers could enter a further five-year term, after which they were entitled to a free trip back to India, or could remain in Natal as free Indians. Most elected to stay in Natal, and became itinerant hawkers, shopkeepers, market gardeners and artisans. Some made their way to the diamond fields at Kimberley* or to the Transvaal.*

The other group of migrants were known as 'passenger Indians', as they paid their own passage to Natal. They were traders and merchants, mainly Gujarati-speaking Muslims from the west coast of India, though some were Hindu and some came from Mauritius; a few passenger Indians were Christian teachers and priests. Most remained in Natal, though some proceeded to the Transvaal and the Cape. Passenger Indians were to provide leadership to the Indian communities all over Natal.

In 1911 the Indian community numbered 150,000, 89% of whom lived in Natal. By this time, Indians had encountered official restrictions from various authorities. Natal imposed a £3 tax to encourage them to return to India; they were barred from the vote (1896); trading restrictions were enacted (1897); and new immigrants were required to know a European language (1897), a measure which succeeded in reducing the flow of immigration. In the Transvaal, Indians were denied citizenship rights and could own property only in certain designated areas (1885); they were obliged to carry registration certificates (1907); and immigrants were required to pass a test in a European language (1908). In the Orange Free State, they were unable to own or rent property (1885), nor could they pursue business without permission (1890). Resistance to such measures, led by the Natal Indian Congress (NIC), founded in 1894, and particularly by Mohandas Gandhi,* was largely unsuccessful, though his *satyagraha* campaign which culminated in 1913 did succeed in having the £3 tax abolished in Natal and in securing recognition for Indian marriages.

The new Union* of South Africa government prohibited all further immigration of Indians in 1913, with the exception of the wives and children of Indians already settled in South Africa. For several decades after Union, successive governments regarded the Indian community as temporarily resident in South Africa. The Cape

Town agreement (1927) between the governments of South Africa and India provided for voluntary state-aided repatriation of Indians, but only a minority availed themselves of the opportunity; many passenger Indians in particular had prospered economically.

The war-time government of Jan Smuts* appointed commissions in 1941 and 1943 to investigate Indian 'penetration' of white areas; this resulted in the 'Pegging' Act of 1943, preventing the purchase of property by Indians from whites in Durban. In 1946, a more far-reaching Asiatic Land Tenure and Indian Representation Act divided Natal into exempted and unexempted areas: in the latter Indians were not permitted to own or occupy property without permission. Under the influence of a younger, more radical leadership, the NIC launched another passive resistance campaign, while the government of India withdrew its High Commissioner, broke off trade relations, and raised the issue in the United Nations.* Tougher legislation ensued, however: the Group Areas* Act of 1950 heralded the effective segregation of Indians, large numbers of whom were forced from their homes and businesses in the cities and resettled in small, overcrowded suburbs, where they often had to pay inflated prices for accommodation. The NIC meanwhile forged closer links with the African National Congress, and Indian leaders played an important role in the Defiance Campaign*; many, however, suffered banning,* which significantly weakened the NIC and prevented co-ordinated opposition to removals under the Group Areas Act.

In 1961 the Indian community was finally accepted as a permanent part of the South African population by the National Party government. A nominated National Indian Council was established in 1964, which became the South African Indian Council in 1968. Provision was made at the end of the 1970s for 40 of its 45 members to be elected, but elections were only held in November 1981 after opposition within the Indian community to the council; a mere 6% of voters turned out. The tricameral* constitution of 1983 created the House of Delegates for Indian representation in parliament, giving Indians control of 'own affairs' such as health, housing and education. Less than 20% of the electorate voted for members of parliament in the election of 1984.

In 1991, the Indian population numbered 864,000, just under 3% of the total population. Over 80% of Indians lived in Natal. Significant religious, linguistic, class and political cleavages existed within the community: for example, some 57% were Hindu, 24% Muslim and 18% Christian, and while some Indians participated willingly in the 1980s in government-created structures, others joined a range of opposition movements. Tensions between Indians and Africans also occasionally manifested themselves violently, as in Natal in 1985, when Gandhi's Phoenix settlement was burned down. [B. Pachai, *International Aspects of the South African Indian Question* (Cape Town, 1971); S. Bhana and J. Brain, *Setting Down Roots* (Johannesburg, 1990); S. Bhana, *Gandhi's Legacy* (Pietermaritzburg, 1997)

INDUSTRIAL AND COMMERCIAL WORKERS' UNION OF SOUTH AFRICA (ICU). A trade union formed by Clements Kadalie, a mission-educated Malawian, in 1919 in the Cape Town docks. In the 1920s, as national secretary, he built up the ICU into a massive movement, which expanded especially in the rural areas of Natal, the

Transvaal and the Orange Free State. In 1927 it claimed a membership of 100,000, the majority being rural Africans. It voiced a broad range of popular grievances. In the towns its main success was in organizing workers in the docks, railways and municipal services. In the countryside, it concentrated on issues relating to land, wages and the pass laws. Kadalie consistently sought to win recognition for the ICU as a legitimate union and voice for black workers. Failing to secure acceptance by white-led unions in South Africa, he went abroad in 1926 in a bid to secure international recognition for the ICU. William Ballinger, an adviser sent out by the British Labour movement in 1928, found the affairs of the ICU in chaos, and Kadalie fell out with both Ballinger and A.W.G. Champion, leader of the Natal ICU, who broke away in 1928 and established a rival ICU yaseNatal. The ICU was destroyed in part by mismanagement and internal conflict, but also by action taken against it by the government and employers. By 1929 it was in decline, and by 1933 had virtually disappeared, though Kadalie established an Independent ICU, which for a time had an organized following in East London. The ICU was remembered for having given many a brief 'taste of freedom'. [C. Kadalie, *My Life and the I.C.U.* (London, 1970); P. Wickins, *The Industrial and Commercial Workers' Union of Africa* (Cape Town, 1978); H. Bradford, *A Taste of Freedom* (New Haven, 1987)]

INFLUX CONTROL. Control over the movement of Africans into the urban areas. Smuts's* Natives (Urban Areas) Act of 1923 imposed a system of segregation and influx control on Africans, who were to be allowed into the towns only to serve white labour needs, and in strict proportion to the availability of work. All Africans except domestic workers would be housed in locations outside the towns, thus keeping the towns themselves 'white'. In 1937 male Africans were given fourteen days in which to find work in the towns, or return to the reserves, and from 1938 influx control regulations were applied systematically. In 1952 the notorious 'Section 10' legislation was enacted, which denied the right to live in an urban area to any African, male or female, who was not born there, unless he or she had lived there continuously for fifteen years or served under the same employer for ten years. It also reduced to 72 hours the time allowed blacks for finding employment in an urban area. Despite all such measures, the number of Africans in the towns grew. Influx control caused immense social distress – husbands and wives were separated, homes were broken up – and the administration of the system led to the growth of a vast and corrupt bureaucracy. In 1986 the pass system* which underpinned influx control was abolished by the P.W. Botha* government. [D. Hindson, *Pass Controls and the Urban African Proletariat in South Africa* (Johannesburg, 1987); Y. Muthien, *State and Resistance in South Africa* (Aldershot, 1994); I. Evans, *Bureaucracy and Race* (Berkeley, 1997)]

INFORMATION SCANDAL. Dubbed 'Muldergate' by the press, this scandal in the Department of Information in the 1970s in some ways resembled the Watergate scandal in the United States. The Prime Minister, John Vorster,* was persuaded by the Secretary for Information, Eschel Rhoodie, and the Minister, Connie Mulder, to bankroll various schemes for putting South Africa's case in influential newspapers and journals. The single largest sum went to establish an English-language, pro-government newspaper in Johannesburg, the *Citizen*. When news of this began to emerge, those involved sought to cover up their deeds, and Mulder denied to parliament that any government money had gone to finance the *Citizen*. This may have cost him the premiership, which went to P.W. Botha* instead. Vorster was forced to resign, first as Prime Minister and then as State President. Of those directly involved, only Rhoodie was prosecuted and he was acquitted on appeal. [M. Rees and C. Daly, *Muldergate* (Johannesburg, 1981); E. Rhoodie, *The Real Information Scandal* (Pretoria, 1983); D. O'Meara, *Forty Lost Years* (Johannesburg, 1996)]

INKATHA. First established as a cultural organization in 1922–1923, it was revived by Mangosuthu Buthelezi* in March 1975, and took over the symbols and anthem used by the African National Congress (ANC). By 1985 it claimed to have over one million members, and at the end of the 1980s 1.5 million members, with a youth brigade of 60,000 and a women's brigade of 500,000. Buthelezi's gradualist approach, working within the bantustan policy while rejecting 'independence', was condemned as collaboration by radical black urban youth. After Buthelezi broke with the ANC in 1979, refusing to accept the authority of the exile leadership, Inkatha appeared as a rival to the ANC and the United Democratic Front,* and conflict increased. Inkatha *impis* (armed groups) fought University of Zululand students in 1983. From August 1985 bitter fighting with the UDF also took place in the Pietermaritzburg area as the two organizations struggled for turf. By 1989 they were locked in a low-grade civil war, with Inkatha warlords sending out their men to burn down the homes of 'comrades' in cycles of revenge. Soon after it was announced in July–August 1990 that Inkatha would become a political party – the Inkatha Freedom Party, open to all – the Witwatersrand exploded in a new burst of conflict between Inkatha and the 'comrades' (*amaqabane*).

The IFP stood for multi-party, non-racial democracy supported by a free market system. Its funding came at this time in part from conservative sources in Germany and from the South African government, as was revealed in the Inkathagate* scandal of July 1991, which severely weakened Buthelezi's credibility. Buthelezi signed the National Peace Accord in September 1991, but relations with F.W. de Klerk* were ruptured a year later when the government signed the Record of Understanding* with the ANC, one of the clauses of which was designed to prevent IFP members from carrying their 'traditional' weapons in public. Another clause provided for the fencing of the hostels of migrant workers, most of which were Inkatha strongholds. In direct response to the Record of Understanding, an angry Buthelezi in October 1992 took the IFP into a right-wing Concerned South Africans Group (COSAG), alongside such reactionary parties as the ultra-right, white Conservative Party. In mid-1993, the IFP refused to continue sitting in the constitutional talks at Kempton Park (see MULTI-PARTY NEGOTIATING FORUM) because the talks did not provide for the federal system which the IFP wanted, and because Buthelezi rejected the principle of 'sufficient consensus' in the negotiations. On 19 April 1994, at the very last minute, he was persuaded by a friend, Professor Washington Okumu of Kenya, to join the election battle; he feared that if he did not do so, he and the IFP would become politically irrelevant in the new order. Special stickers were hastily printed and stuck onto the ballot papers. In the election, the IFP won over 10% of the vote and, as the result of some bargaining, a majority in the KwaZulu-Natal legislature. Buthelezi then became Minister of Home Affairs, with a seat in the Government of National Unity,* and talk that the IFP might consider a secession option disappeared. The IFP claimed it had been promised international mediation on certain disputed constitutional issues; because this did not materialize, it again refused to join in the discussions on the final constitution, walking out of the Constitutional Assembly* in both 1995 and 1996. The KwaZulu legislative assembly, dominated by the IFP, went ahead and drew up its own constitution, but this was rejected by the Constitutional Court.* Buthelezi nevertheless remained in the GNU, even after the National Party left it. The first local government election in KwaZulu-Natal in 1996 revealed that the IFP had retained its rural support in KwaZulu, but was losing support in the urban areas. By this time, its support was almost entirely limited to that province. In late 1997 there was talk of a merger between the IFP and the ANC before the 1999 election, but Buthelezi himself rejected the idea. [G. Maré and G. Hamilton, *An Appetite for Power* (Johannesburg, 1987); G. Maré, *Ethnicity and Politics in South Africa* (London, 1993); A. Jeffrey, *The Natal Story* (Johannesburg, 1996)]

INKATHAGATE. A scandal which broke in July 1991, when it was revealed that the National Party (NP) government had secretly funded Inkatha* and its associated trade union, allegedly for anti-sanctions activities. The government had long aided Inkatha, and helped arrange secret military training for IFP recruits in northern Zululand and in the Caprivi strip area of Namibia. As a result of the revelations, the personal reputation of De Klerk* as a man of integrity suffered a major blow, and Inkatha's claim to be an independent player in the negotiations was compromised. Ties between Buthelezi and the NP were loosened, though they were to be severed only as a result of the Record of Understanding in 1992.

IRON AGE. For much of the 20th century, it was commonly believed that southern Africa was populated from the north during the 15th and 16th centuries, at roughly the same time that white colonization began from the south. Incontrovertible archaeological evidence collected since the 1960s shatters this myth. From about AD 200, new groups of farming communities moved south across the Limpopo River and settled in parts of present-day South Africa. Because they smelted and processed ore to make iron tools, they have been defined as belonging to the 'Iron Age'.

These Iron Age people were also the first to practise agriculture, growing crops such as sorghum and millet; they kept livestock, and lived in houses constructed from wood and reeds in small permanent villages. Their settlements were located in low-lying regions near the coast or in river valleys where fertile soil and good summer rainfalls ensured reliable harvests. The remains of pottery and other material such as burnt wood reveal that by AD 800 they were well established in the present-day Northern Province, Mpumalanga, KwaZulu-Natal and the Eastern Cape. Patterns of settlement began to change around AD 800–1000, probably as a result of the increasing importance of cattle. Farming continued in the river valleys, but people also moved onto the grasslands of the interior, and by AD 1200 almost the entire highveld was inhabited by Iron Age people. Settlement patterns differed: villages were much larger, accommodating hundreds of people, and stone building was extensive, both for houses and for livestock enclosures and walls around settlements. Limited timber resources also meant that opportunities for iron smelting were restricted; trade networks consequently developed with the communities in the eastern part of the region. In the main, cattle was exchanged for iron, but long-distance trade also occurred, conducted by Arab traders who established trading posts on the Mozambique coast; their commodities, such as glass beads, were prized in southern Africa.

Perhaps the most important result of trade and control of trading networks was the concentration of wealth in the hands of some Iron Age communities. Between AD 1200 and 1500, powerful centres emerged, the most significant of which were Mapungubwe and Great Zimbabwe. Mapungubwe, situated south of the Limpopo, developed into the dominant power of the region during the 13th century and was home to over 10,000 people at the peak of its power. Wealthy inhabitants lived on the defensible hilltop, which overlooked the valley where poorer people were located. The ruling classes presided over a diversified economy: pastoralism, agriculture, a significant manufacturing sector (in iron, gold, pottery and weaving) and extensive trade. By the end of the 13th century, Mapungubwe's power was waning, as Great Zimbabwe further north rose to prominence.

By the 15th and 16th centuries, the entire interior of South Africa, with the exception of the Karoo semi-desert (which prevented further southern expansion), was settled by Iron Age people who practised mixed agriculture and pastoralism, and who engaged in extensive trade. The majority lived in small villages, while some in the interior occupied larger, more concentrated settlements. By the time they came into contact with white settlers towards the end of the 18th century, they could trace a history of settlement of over 1500 years. [M. Hall, *The Changing Past* (Cape Town, 1990)]

ISANDLWANA. The first major battle of the Anglo-Zulu War.* On 22 January 1879, the invading British troops stumbled unexpectedly across a Zulu army numbering 20,000 men. The British force of some 1250 men, which had been left to guard the encampment at Isandlwana, was completely overwhelmed, and few escaped with their lives. The battle represented a crushing defeat for the British and their plans for confederation in southern Africa. Though it was a Zulu victory, losses among the Zulu were high, and the war ended with their defeat a few months later. [J. Laband, *Fight Us in the Open* (Pietermaritzburg, 1985)]

ISLAM. The first Muslims at the Cape were political exiles, convicts banished from the possessions of the Dutch East India Company* in the East, or slaves. Most of the slaves came from Bengal, the west coast of India, and the Indonesian islands. Slaves of Indonesian origin formed about half of Cape Town's slave population, and many Indonesian customs, relating to clothing, food and ritual, were brought to the Cape.

Towards the end of the 18th century, a remarkable growth of Islam occurred among Cape slaves. The religion appealed to them because *imams* identified with their needs, performing marriages and funerals denied by Christian churches, and it was colour-blind. Slave-owners welcomed the conversion of their slaves to Islam because of official restrictions on the buying and selling of Christian slaves, and because of the Muslim prohibition on alcohol. Many free blacks* were also attracted to Islam. During the first British occupation of the Cape, Muslims in Cape Town were able to persuade the authorities to allow them to practise their religion freely, and the first mosque opened in 1804.

The majority of Cape Muslims followed the Shafi school, though a minority were persuaded by Abu Bakr Effendi (1835–1880), sent to Cape Town by the Sultan of Constantinople in 1862, to adopt Hanafi beliefs. After 1860, Indian* indentured labourers arrived in South Africa to work on the Natal sugar plantations; of the initial groups, which came mainly from Madras, about 12% were Muslim. From the late 1870s, a new class of 'passenger' Indians, mostly Gujarati-speaking Muslims, settled in Natal. By the 1990s, about half of the country's 350,000 Muslims were descended from those in the 19th-century Cape, while the other half traced their roots to the Indian settlers in Natal.

Apartheid radicalized some Muslims, and Muslim youth movements challenged the conservative Muslim Judicial Council. Imam Haron, who died in police custody in 1969, became a martyr, while many Cape Town Muslims joined the militant People Against Gangsters and Drugs (PAGAD) in the mid-1990s. Pan-Islamic contacts grew, and South Africa's Muslims had by the mid-1990s one of the highest rates of *hajj* outside the Middle East. [A. Davids, *The Mosques of Bo-Kaap* (Athlone, 1980); R. Elphick and H. Giliomee, eds., *The Shaping of South African Society* (Cape Town, 1989)]

j

JABAVU, John Tengu (1859–1921). Journalist, educationist and political leader. Jabavu qualified as a teacher at Healdtown Missionary Institution in the eastern Cape, but became prominent through his editorship of *Imvo Zabantsundu*,* which he founded with white Cape liberal support in 1884. Until the end of the century, he was the most powerful African spokesman in the Cape. He lost political credibility in the early 20th century, being accused of personal ambition and over-intimate ties with the white establishment. He refused to champion the South African Native National Congress (later the African National Congress), he supported the Natives Land Act* of 1913, and he split the Cape African vote in standing for election to the Cape Provincial Council in 1914. Jabavu did much to promote the founding of a university college for Africans; the establishment in 1916 of the South African Native College, later Fort Hare* University, owed much to his efforts. His son D.D.T Jabavu taught there. [D. Jabavu, *The Life of John Tengo Jabavu* (Lovedale, 1920); C. Higgs, *The Ghost of Equality* (Cape Town, 1997)]

JAMESON RAID. Leander Starr Jameson, one of Cecil Rhodes's closest friends, led this abortive attempt to overthrow the government of the South African Republic* in December 1895. An administrator in the British South Africa Company* in Matabeleland, Jameson was commissioned by Rhodes, then Prime Minister of the Cape, to head a force of mounted men to invade the Transvaal from Bechuanaland,* and link up with an expected Uitlander* uprising. The attempt failed, and Jameson and his 500 men surrendered to Transvaal troops on 2 January 1896. The Uitlander leaders in the conspiracy were sentenced to death for their part in it, but had their sentences commuted to heavy fines; Jameson served only four months of a 15-month sentence. The Raid had far-reaching political repercussions: Rhodes was forced to resign as Prime Minister, the alliance between him and Hofmeyr* of the Afrikaner Bond* was destroyed, and the Transvaal, more convinced than ever of British bad faith and duplicity, forged a close alliance with the Orange Free State.

In 1965 the Australian historian Geoffrey Blainey suggested that owners of deep-level gold mines supported the raid, seeking to replace the government of Paul Kruger* with one more amenable to their interests, while the owners of outcrop mines, which required less capital, did not. Later research showed this to be too simple, but suggested that those implicated in the raid had longer-term commitments to the industry and were more development-oriented than those who were not involved. [J. van der Poel, *The Jameson Raid* (London, 1951); E. Pakenham, *Jameson's Raid* (London, 1966); J. Carruthers, ed., *The Jameson Raid* (Johannesburg, 1996)]

JEWISH COMMUNITY. Only after the British occupation of the Cape did Jews arrive in any numbers. Some became merchants in Cape Town, where the first permanent Hebrew congregation was formed in 1841, while others traded in the interior, where they formed an accepted constituent of the white rural population. In 1880, there were about 4000 Jews in southern Africa.

During the 1880s and 1890s, a large number of Jews from eastern Europe, particularly Lithuania, settled in South Africa. A literacy test, introduced by the Cape in 1902 to restrict Indian* immigration, threatened to cut off this flow, but in 1906 Yiddish was recognized as a European language, and by 1914 over 40,000 Lithuanian Jews had entered the country. The Immigration Quota Act of 1930 reduced the flow of immigrants from eastern Europe to a trickle. Some 7000 refugees from Nazi Germany settled in South Africa before the Aliens Act of 1937 closed the door to further immigration.

Anti-semitism displayed itself in various guises during the early 20th century, most explicitly in Afrikaner circles during the 1930s, particularly among extremists who viewed Hitler as a hero. After World War II, however, both Jan Smuts* and D.F. Malan* supported the Zionist cause, with which South African Jews closely identified themselves, and the overt hostility of the pre-war years subsided to some extent. Though there were sometimes tensions between the Jewish community and the political establishment during the apartheid period, Jewish people generally prospered, and made notable contributions in commerce, industry, politics and the professions.

Jews formed about 4% of the white population in 1936, but their numbers declined proportionately thereafter, mainly because of restricted immigration and low birth rates. In 1991, the Jewish community numbered almost 120,000 people, about 0.3% of the country's population. [G. Saron and L. Hotz, *The Jews in South Africa* (Cape Town, 1955); G. Shimoni, *Jews and Zionism* (Cape Town, 1980); M. Shain, *The Roots of Antisemitism in South Africa* (Charlottesville, 1994)]

JOHANNESBURG. The largest city in South Africa, centre of the country's gold-mining industry, manufacturing and commerce. Johannesburg emerged as a direct result of the discovery of gold* on the Witwatersrand in 1886. It mushroomed on the farms above the gold-bearing reef: in 1887, the diggers' camp contained 3000 people; by 1899, the population of Egoli, as it became known to Africans, was 120,000; and by 1914, it had grown to 250,000, a figure which excluded Africans living illegally on the outskirts of the town.

By the first two decades of the 20th century, Johannesburg had become a city of immense inequalities of wealth, ranging from Randlords* who lived in great opulence in the northern suburbs to numerous impoverished migrant workers and unemployed people eking out an existence around the mines and factories of the city. By mid-century, Johannesburg was the heart of the country's business activity, and was its largest commercial and industrial centre by far. From the 1960s, as air travel replaced sea travel, it became the main gateway to South Africa. By the beginning of the 1990s, greater Johannesburg had a population of between four and five million people, and was attracting new inhabitants from all over South Africa as well as beyond the country's borders. It became the capital of the newly formed Gauteng province in 1994. [C. van Onselen, *Studies in the Social and Economic History of the Witwatersrand* (London, 1982); N. Mandy, *A City Divided* (Johannesburg, 1994)]

k

KANGWANE ('land of the Ngwane'). A small bantustan created for the Swazi* within South Africa. When it was given a legislative assembly in 1978, only 100,000 of the estimated 600,000 Swazis in South Africa lived in the territory, which was divided into a portion adjoining the northern Swaziland border and another bordering the Kruger National Park. In the 1970s the South African and Swaziland governments entered into secret negotiations on the transfer of the territory to Swaziland, and in June 1982 the South African government announced that KaNgwane was to be incorporated in Swaziland, along with a portion of KwaZulu.* The KaNgwane legislative assembly, which was known to oppose incorporation, was dissolved. But transfer never happened, and in 1994, as with all other former bantustans, KaNgwane was reincorporated into South Africa.

KAROO. Name derived from a Khoikhoi word meaning 'dry country'; it refers to the semi-desert region covering a third of the area of South Africa. It stretches from the Langeberg range in the south to the southern Orange Free State, and is characterized by flat-topped hills and open treeless plains. Khoisan hunters and herders once occupied the area, but Bantu-speaking mixed farmers did not settle here because of its aridity. White trekboers moved across the Karoo from the 1740s, encountering considerable opposition from the San.* During the 19th century, sheep farming became the dominant economic activity, but wasteful farming practices over the past century have caused environmental degradation, resulting in an enlargement of the Karoo. The Karoo has been evoked powerfully by several South African writers, particularly by Olive Schreiner* in *The Story of an African Farm* (1883), Pauline Smith in *The Little Karoo* (1925) and Guy Butler in *Karoo Morning* (1977).

KAT RIVER SETTLEMENT. The right of the Khoikhoi and 'other free persons of colour' to own land was recognized in Ordinance 50* of 1828, but they had no access to land outside the mission stations. The Kat River Settlement was the sole experiment in the granting of land to such people: in 1829, the Cape government made available to some 250 families land in a relatively fertile valley in the eastern Cape, from which the Xhosa chief Maqoma* had recently been ejected. The government intended the settlement to act as a buffer between the colony and the Xhosa.* The inhabitants fought on the side of the colony in the wars of 1834–1835 and 1846–1847, in the second of which the settlement suffered severely.

White colonists increasingly coveted the land of the Kat River valley, particularly when some members of the settlement became successful peasant farmers. Some whites wished to use the settlement as a labour resource; others desired the land for sheep farming. Driven to rebellion, about half the settlers took up arms in 1851 against the colonial authorities, when the Cape was involved in another war with the Xhosa. Andries Botha, a leading rebel, was convicted of high treason, and the land of the rebels was confiscated and given to whites. Loyalists remained in the settlement, and some retained their title to the land. A number of their descendants were finally driven from the area when the Kat River valley was incorporated into the Ciskei* bantustan in 1981. [N. Mostert, *Frontiers* (London, 1992)]

KHOIKHOI. Pastoralists who called themselves 'men of men' ('Khoikhoi'). Those who lived in the south-western Cape during the late 15th century were the first southern Africans encountered by Portuguese explorers. The Dutch who settled at the Cape in the 17th century called them 'Hottentots',* an insulting imitation of their staccato speech.

Although the origins of the Khoikhoi are not entirely clear, it is generally accepted that they first appeared some 2000 years ago among Khoe-speaking hunting groups in the northern parts of present-day Botswana and Namibia. Precisely how these hunters acquired livestock is uncertain, but it most likely occurred through contact with early Iron Age* peoples moving south. The Khoikhoi themselves then moved further south, probably because of the need for additional grazing as well as under population pressure. Some evidence suggests that they migrated south along the coast from northern Namibia until they reached the Cape Peninsula, whereupon they turned east until they reached the present-day eastern Cape. Another theory is that some (the ancestors of the Nama) moved west along the Orange River, while others (the ancestors of the Cape Khoikhoi) migrated southwards into the eastern Cape, and then west along the coast until they reached the Cape Peninsula. By AD 500, Khoikhoi groups were settled along the western, southern and eastern Cape coasts, as well as along the Orange River and in much of Namibia; there was a less dense population in the Cape interior and on the highveld.

Initially the Khoikhoi possessed only sheep, but they later acquired cattle through contact with farmers in the eastern Cape. They practised a semi-nomadic lifestyle, the needs of their livestock – their major source of wealth – taking precedence. They followed regular transhumant patterns, shifting between different vegetation zones during winter and summer. Societal structures were flexible, clans consisting of related families and their clients; clans in turn were often grouped together under the loose control of chiefs, who lacked the power to prevent regular fission of communities. Raiding occurred frequently between groups for cattle and control of water and pasture. The shelters of Khoikhoi consisted of wooden structures and reed mats, which could be easily dismantled and transported on the backs of oxen; their equipment was similarly designed for mobility. Their relationship with hunter-gatherers was complex: the latter sometimes raided their livestock, but also acted as their clients. They had close ties as well with various Bantu-speaking groups, intermarrying in particular with the Tlhaping* north of the Orange River and with the Xhosa* in the eastern Cape.

After the Dutch* settled in the south-western Cape in the 1650s, pressures on Khoikhoi land and livestock resources began to increase. Some of the Dutch wished to enslave the Khoikhoi, but others recognized the need to acknowledge their independence, so as to sustain a reliable trade with them. Two wars were fought between the Khoikhoi and Dutch, in 1659–1660 and in 1673–1677, the second of which saw the Dutch firmly established in the south-western Cape at the expense of continued Khoikhoi autonomy there. Groups were forced to retreat from the region or to take work on white farms, where they became herdsmen, ox-trainers and wagon-drivers. Their numbers were further weakened by serious outbreaks of smallpox between 1713 and 1720, and then later in 1735 and 1767. It is estimated by some that Khoikhoi numbers south of the Orange declined from approximately 200,000 in the mid-17th century to about 20,000 at the end of the 18th century.

Khoikhoi resistance to white expansion should not be underestimated: during the 18th century, many joined bands of San raiders, and seriously hindered white advance into the interior. Khoihkoi who had been reduced to a landless proletariat in the eastern Cape took up arms in 1799 and joined Xhosa resistance to the colonists; it took the British over two years to suppress this rebellion. Some succeeded in escaping to the middle Orange area, where they became known as the Korana* during the 19th century, while others formed the nucleus of Griqua* groups. Most independent Khoikhoi communities were unable to cope with the commercial pressures of white colonization. Those who survived within the colony remained legally free, but in practice their position was not much different from that of the Cape slaves.* The pass laws to which they were subject were removed by Ordinance 50 of 1828, and gradually Khoikhoi people were absorbed into the emerging community of those called Coloureds.* Some Khoi managed to survive at the mission stations of Namaqualand, which were designated as reserves for Coloureds in 1909 by the Cape government. [R. Elphick, *Khoikhoi and the Founding of White South Africa* (Johannesburg, 1985); E. Boonzaier et al., *The Cape Herders* (Cape Town, 1996)]

KHOISAN. Name used by the anthropologist Isaac Schapera in his book *The Khoisan Peoples of South Africa* (1930), as well as by later scholars, for the Khoikhoi and the San together. Although the Khoikhoi language was distinct from the San languages, historical evidence frequently failed to distinguish adequately between them, or does not tell us whether the people being described were hunters or herders. Khoisan is thus a convenient composite term.

KHOLWA (Zulu word meaning 'believer'). The *amakholwa* were Africans in Natal who were converted to Christianity during the 19th century and received some formal education. By the end of the century, there were an estimated 40,000 African communicants and 100,000 church adherents in Natal. Though often as critical as whites of the 'primitive' practices of unconverted Zulu people, they were not accorded equal status with the colonists, most of whom feared the challenge posed by the growth of the large *kholwa* community. [N. Etherington, *Preachers, Peasants, and Politics in Southeast Africa, 1835–1880* (London, 1978); J. Lambert, *Betrayed Trust* (Pietermaritzburg, 1995)]

KIMBERLEY. Foremost diamond* centre of South Africa, expanding out of the mining camp which developed after the discovery of diamonds in the area in 1869 and 1870. Named after the British Colonial Secretary, the Earl of Kimberley, when the diamond fields were annexed in 1871, the town grew to become the second-largest settlement in southern Africa after Cape Town within two years, with a population of over 50,000. Kimberley was incorporated into the Cape in 1880, by which time it was also the centre of a thriving gun trade. Kimberley was besieged for four months during the South African War*. It remained the headquarters of De Beers Consolidated Mines, the world's largest diamond company, until the early 1990s. In 1994 it became the capital of the new Northern Cape province. [W. Worger, *South Africa's City of Diamonds* (New Haven, 1987); R. Turrell, *Capital and Labour on the Kimberley Diamond Fields, 1871–1890* (Cambridge, 1987)]

KINDERGARTEN. Collective nickname for a group of brilliant young men from Oxford, who were attracted by the reputation of Milner* and came to South Africa to assist him in his administration of the Transvaal and Orange River Colony after the South African War.* Their chief importance was probably as extremely able administrators, but they are remembered more for having, after Milner's departure, promoted the cause of the unification of South Africa. Lionel Curtis drafted the Selborne Memorandum advocating Union,* and he and others founded an influential periodical, *The State*. Most of the Kindergarten went on to distinguished careers elsewhere, but Patrick Duncan* remained and became Governor-General of the Union. [W. Nimocks, *Milner's Young Men* (Durham, 1968)]

KITCHENER, Horatio Herbert (1850–1916). Chief of Staff to Lord Roberts during 1900; Commander-in-Chief of the British forces in South Africa from November 1900 until the end of the South African War* in May 1902. He was responsible for wearing down Boer guerrilla opposition to the British by three deeply unpopular and controversial means: the scorched earth policy, a system of blockhouses, and the establishment of concentration camps.* [S. Spies, *Methods of Barbarism* (Cape Town, 1977)]

KOK, Adam III (1811–1875). Chief of the Griqua* at Philippolis from 1837. White pressure forced him to sell the remaining Griqua land to the Orange Free State* government in 1861, and he led 2000 of his followers on a long, arduous journey across the Drakensberg to the area which was renamed Griqualand East.* He considered himself an independent ally of the British, but his position was undermined by the Cape in the 1870s. [R. Ross, *Adam Kok's Griquas* (Cambridge, 1976)]

KORANA. Khoikhoi pastoralists who settled north and south of the middle Orange River* towards the end of the 18th century. They were distinguished from other Khoikhoi groups by their language, Korana. Through their contact with trading networks from the Cape, they obtained guns and horses, which enabled them to control the entire middle Orange region by the mid-19th century. White pastoral encroachment on Korana lands resulted in a number of clashes in the area during the 1850s and 1860s. Two wars were fought between the Cape government and the Korana (1868–1869 and 1878–1879), which resulted in most Korana being sent into the Cape as labourers, while their chiefs were imprisoned on Robben Island. The middle Orange region was thereafter named Gordonia. [T. Strauss, *War along the Orange* (Cape Town, 1976)]

KROTOA (c.1642–1674). Known to the Dutch settlers as Eva, Krotoa played an important role in facilitating trade between the Khoikhoi and the Dutch in the early days of the Dutch settlement at the Cape. Through her personal ties she had privileged access to the Khoi, and she succeeded her uncle Autshumato as the main interpreter for the Dutch. A servant in Jan van Riebeeck's household, she was probably the first Christian convert in South Africa. She married the Dutch soldier and surgeon Pieter van Meerhoff, but her influence declined in the 1660s, and her husband's death in 1667 marked the end of her links with the Dutch. She was arrested the following year for drunkenness and prostitution and banished to Robben Island, where she died. [C. Malherbe, *Krotoa, Called 'Eva'* (Cape Town, 1990)]

KRUGER, Stephanus Johannes Paulus (1825–1904). President of the South African Republic from 1883 until 1900. The son of Voortrekker parents, he became Commandant-General (military leader) of the Transvaal in 1863. After the British annexation of the Transvaal in 1877, he headed negotiations for the restoration of independence, and led the subsequent armed revolt in 1880, which brought about the return of self-rule. Elected President in 1883, he won three further terms of office. Though respected for his military capabilities, he was not universally popular among the somewhat fractious white electorate, many of whom resented his autocratic style. His last election victory in 1898, however, was a landslide, the Afrikaner electorate unifying in the aftermath of the Jameson Raid* and in the context of increasing British pressure on the Transvaal's continued independence.

After negotiations with Milner* on the position of the Uitlanders* failed in 1898–1899, Kruger took the initiative and, with the support of the Orange Free State, sent the British an ultimatum, which led to the outbreak of the South African War.* He was forced to flee the Transvaal in 1900, and went abroad to seek foreign support. He died in Switzerland in 1904. Portrayed by the British as a dour and inflexible reactionary, he was regarded by Afrikaners in the 20th century as among the greatest of leaders, and his career served as a source of inspiration for resurgent Afrikaner nationalism from the 1930s. [D. Kruger, *Paul Kruger* (Johannesburg, 1961); J. Marais, *The Fall of Kruger's Republic* (Oxford, 1961)]

KWANDEBELE. See NDZUNDZA NDEBELE

KWAZULU. Though the KwaZulu bantustan* became self-governing in 1977, its chief minister, Mangosuthu Buthelezi,* refused to consider accepting 'independence'. In April 1994, Natal and the former KwaZulu bantustan were joined in the new province of KwaZulu-Natal. In the election held that month, the Inkatha* Freedom Party (IFP) won a majority and formed a provincial government, which included some African National Congress (ANC) members. There was much disagreement over whether the provincial capital should be in Ulundi, the former bantustan capital, or Pietermaritzburg.* By the mid-1990s negotiations between the local IFP leadership and Jacob Zuma and Thabo Mbeki* of the ANC began to have some effect on reducing the war that had continued sporadically from the early 1980s between the IFP and its opponents, and had resulted in the deaths of perhaps 12,000 people. A provincial constitution was drawn up, but rejected by the Constitutional Court.* [A. Jeffrey, *The Natal Story* (Johannesburg, 1996)]

LABOUR PARTY (LP) (1965–1994). A Coloured political party, formed in anticipation of the establishment of the Coloured Persons Representative Council (CRC),* with the aim of using this body to help overthrow apartheid. In the CRC elections in 1969, the LP won most seats (23), but the government rigged a majority in its own favour. In 1975 the LP won 34 seats and took over the executive, and worked to destroy the CRC from within. This led to the disbandment of the CRC in 1981. At a conference at Howick in Natal in 1983, the party nevertheless agreed to participate in the tricameral* parliament, giving that body significant legitimacy, even though many Coloureds made clear their rejection of it (see UNITED DEMOCRATIC FRONT). The LP explained that it would work within the new system for the socio-economic advancement of the Coloured community and against apartheid. The party became the governing party in the House of Representatives from 1984, and its leader, the Rev. Allan Hendrickse, was for a time a cabinet minister in P.W. Botha's government. The LP claimed credit for some apartheid reforms, but Hendrickse was humiliated by Botha when he challenged beach apartheid. In the new order inaugurated by De Klerk in February 1990, the LP had difficulty in defining its role. After it was replaced by the National Party as the majority party in the House of Representatives in February 1992, it developed increasingly close ties with the African National Congress, and in 1994 supported the ANC in the first democratic elections.

LAND REFORM AND RESTITUTION. Beginning in the 1650s, indigenous people began to lose their land, as a result of white settlement and conquest. A long history of legislation to restrict African rights to land followed. In that history the Natives Land Act of 1913 occupies a central place. Millions were dispossessed of land, or forcibly removed from it, for segregationist reasons after 1913. The body of discriminatory legislation which had permitted this began to be repealed by the De Klerk government, most notably in the Abolition of Racially-Based Land Measures Act (1991) and the amending legislation of 1993, but such measures did not provide redress, except where the state had itself taken over private or communal land, and was willing to hand it back. The democratic government elected in 1994 had to find a way to give redress without driving those in possession, most of whom were whites, into open defiance. The Restitution of Land Rights Act, steered through parliament by the Minister of Land Affairs, Derek Hanekom, an Afrikaner farmer who had been imprisoned for working for the African National Congress (ANC), established a land rights commission to deal with claims to land held in private as well as public hands, and provided for referral to a land claims court if consensus could not be reached. The year 1913 was the cut-off date for such claims. Expropriated land was to be returned, or alternative land provided, or compensation paid to those whose claims were valid. The process proved slow and cumbersome, and the issue of land reform itself still remained to be tackled. The Pan Africanist Congress and Azanian People's Organization demanded the return of all land seized by white 'settlers'. [T. Davenport and K. Hunt, *The Right to the Land* (Cape Town, 1974); C. Murray and C. O'Regan, *No Place to Rest* (Cape Town, 1990)]

LANGALIBALELE (1818–1889). Ruler of the Hlubi people, who lived in the foothills of the Drakensberg in north-western Natal in the 19th century. Their independence and growing prosperity caused increasing concern to nearby white farmers and to the colonial authorities in Natal. In 1873, Langalibalele refused to comply with a law to register rifles acquired by his men on the diamond fields, and ignored summonses to explain his conduct. An armed force was sent to arrest him; as he fled, a skirmish occurred, in which three whites and two loyal blacks were killed. This 'rebellion' shocked white Natalians; Langalibalele was deposed by Theophilus Shepstone,* captured, given a mockery of a trial and banished for life to Robben Island. Thousands of his Hlubi people and their neighbours were dispossessed of their land and cattle.

The panic reaction of the Natal colonists to this petty episode displayed their insecurity. Lord Carnarvon* took advantage of it to push Natal into support for his plans for confederation.* Natal's Lieutenant-Governor was recalled, and Carnarvon refused to allow Langalibalele to remain on Robben Island. He was imprisoned on the Cape Flats near Cape Town until 1887, when he was allowed to return to Natal. [B. Guest, *Langalibalele* (Durban, 1976); N. Herd, *The Bent Pine* (Johannesburg, 1976)]

LANGA MARCH (March 1960). The single most important act of African protest in the aftermath of the Sharpeville massacre.* On 30 March 1960, some 30,000 Africans marched from Langa township into the centre of Cape Town, to protest against police activity in the aftermath of the events of 21 March at Sharpeville and Langa itself. But the march was not a prelude to insurrection. The large and peaceful crowd was persuaded by Philip Kgosana, the young Pan Africanist Congress (PAC) organiser who became its leader, to return to Langa, being promised by the police a meeting which never took place. Kgosana and others were arrested under the State of Emergency regulations promulgated that day. Kgosana later left the country, and lived in exile until the mid-1990s, when he returned to take up a leadership position in the PAC. [G. Gerhart, *Black Power in South Africa* (Berkeley, 1979); T. Lodge, *Black Politics in South Africa since 1945* (Johannesburg, 1983); P. Kgosana, *Lest We Forget* (Johannesburg, 1988)]

LANGENHOVEN, Cornelis Jacob (1873–1932). Writer, journalist, and politician, he campaigned for Afrikaans to be recognised as an official language and to be used as a medium of instruction in schools. He wrote 'Die Stem van Suid-Afrika' ('The Call of South Africa'), which was sung alongside 'God Save the King' as South Africa's national anthem from 1938 until 1957, when it became the sole national anthem until the first democratic election of 1994, after which it formed part of the new anthem.

LANGUAGES. It was part of the compromise of Union (1910) that there should be two

103

official languages, Dutch and English. Afrikaans replaced Dutch as an official language in 1925 and became the dominant language of government under the National Party after 1948. African languages received no official recognition until the constitutions of 1993 and 1996 provided for the recognition of eleven official languages: Pedi, Sotho, Tswana, Swati, Venda, Tsonga, Afrikaans, English, Ndebele, Xhosa and Zulu. Until 1998 official documents continued to be published in Afrikaans as well as English, but English, which had always been the main language of business, became the *de facto* official language of government.

LEAGUE OF NATIONS MANDATE (1920). In terms of the Charter of the League of Nations, South Africa was provided with a C-class mandate to rule South West Africa.* This enabled it to administer the territory as if it was an integral part of South Africa itself, but South Africa had to concern itself with the well-being of the indigenous inhabitants, which it did not. When the League collapsed, the newly established United Nations* claimed its authority, and in 1966 the UN General Assembly unilaterally terminated the mandate. South Africa never recognized the UN as successor to the League in this respect. [S. Pienaar, *South Africa and International Relations Between the Two World Wars* (Johannesburg, 1987)]

LE FLEUR, Andrew Abraham Stockenström (1867–1941). Griqua leader who fought over several decades for land for Griqua* and Coloured people. Imprisoned for sedition between 1898 and 1903, and barred from returning to Griqualand East, he settled in Cape Town where he tried to establish various self-help schemes. In 1917, he organized a trek of landless Griqua from Griqualand East to Touws River in the western Cape, where he hoped to establish a farming settlement. The venture failed, as did similar settlements on the Olifants River (1922) and at Victoria West (1926) for Coloureds from the mission reserves in Namaqualand. Only one such settlement scheme was successful: a community of landless people trekked from the Cookhouse–Bedford district to the Plettenberg Bay area in the southern Cape, and finally settled at Krantzhoek. The settlement became a symbol of Griqua hopes and endeavours, and remains today the main Griqua establishment in the country.

LEIPOLDT, Christiaan Frederik Louis (1880–1947). Medical doctor, journalist, poet, dramatist and teacher. Versatile in English and Dutch as well as Afrikaans, he published prolifically in various genres, including poetry, short stories, novels, drama, travelogues, and popular and scientific papers. His most important contribution was in the development of Afrikaans as a written language. He is best remembered for several volumes of poetry, the most significant of which was *Oom Gert vertel en ander Gedigte* (1911), and for his greatest drama, *Die Heks* (1923), a pathbreaking dramatic work.

LEMBEDE, Anton Muziwakhe (1914–1947), one of the founders of the African National Congress Youth League and its first president. Son of a Zulu farm labourer, he was educated at Adams College and the University of South Africa. A Catholic and strong anti-communist, he urged Africans to work together to throw off their oppression, and was the first South African to articulate a philosophy of African nationalism. His premature death was widely regarded as a great setback to the cause of African liberation. [R. Edgar and L. Msumza, eds., *Freedom in Our Lifetime* (Johannesburg, 1996)]

LESOTHO. See BASUTOLAND

LIBERAL PARTY (LP) (1953–1968). A non-racial political party, founded by whites who rejected both the feeble opposition which the United Party offered to apartheid, and the pro-communist leanings of the Congress of Democrats. Its members included such people as Margaret Ballinger, Native Representative in parliament, and Alan Paton, author of *Cry, the Beloved Country*, who became its leader. Though the LP began by adopting a policy of a qualified franchise, it accepted universal suffrage in 1960, and the number of its African members began to increase considerably. When its attempts to win white votes in parliamentary elections proved futile, some of its members turned away from non-violence after the Sharpeville massacre, and joined non-liberals in the African Resistance Movement, which organized acts of sabotage to bring home to whites the evils of the apartheid system. This activity gave the government justification for continued and increased harassment of members of the LP. Many were banned. The party was dying even before the government introduced legislation making multi-racial parties illegal. Faced with this legislation, the LP took a principled stand and dissolved itself. Many of the ideas and ideals for which it had fought were realized in the constitutions of 1993 and 1996. [J. Butler et al., eds., *Democratic Liberalism in South Africa* (Middletown, 1987); R. Vigne, *Liberals Against Apartheid* (London, 1997)]

LIMPOPO RIVER. Second in size of the African rivers which enter the Indian Ocean, the Limpopo, unlike the larger Zambezi, often carries little water, and has never been a barrier to human movement. For many centuries before it became the northern and north-western boundary of the Transvaal, it was an important trade route between the interior and Delagoa Bay.* A road to Zimbabwe over Beit Bridge opened in 1929; a rail link across the river at the same place began operating in 1974. The name 'Limpopo' may come from a Sotho word meaning 'river of the waterfall'.

LONDON MISSIONARY SOCIETY (LMS). The most active Protestant missionary society in southern Africa during the first half of the 19th century. Founded in 1795 as an interdenominational organization, the LMS was active in a variety of locations at the Cape, and many LMS missionaries clashed with the Cape authorities over policy towards slaves and indigenous peoples. The most prominent LMS missionaries included Johannes van der Kemp,* founder of the Bethelsdorp mission outside what became Port Elizabeth; John Philip,* superintendent of the LMS in South Africa from 1819 to 1849; Robert Moffat,* who worked at Kuruman; the explorer and missionary David Livingstone; and Van der Kemp's colleague James Read, whose latter years were spent as LMS missionary in the Kat River Settlement.* In the later 19th century the LMS mission stations were gradually incorporated within the Congregational Church. [J. Sales, *Mission Stations and the Coloured*

Communities of the Eastern Cape (Cape Town, 1974); H. Bredekamp and R. Ross, eds., *Missions and Christianity in South African History* (Johannesburg, 1995)]

LUTHULI, Albert John (*c.*1898–1967). Chief, teacher and politician. Luthuli gave up his traditional leadership position at Groutville in Natal to become president-general of the African National Congress,* an office he held from 1952 until his death. A man of great charm and moderation, he was awarded the Nobel Peace Prize in 1960, and spoke of how the African people of South Africa had long knocked at the door and found it locked against them. Restricted to his home, he died while out walking, being hit by a train under circumstances which some found mysterious. [A. Luthuli, *Let My People Go* (New York, 1962)]

LYDENBURG HEADS. Terracotta representations of human heads, found in the eastern Transvaal, now Mpumalanga, in the 1950s. They are thought to date from *c.* AD 500 and to have been the work of Iron Age Bantu-speaking people.

m

MACKENZIE, John (1835–1899). London Missionary Society missionary, author and advocate of British rule in Bechuanaland.* He arrived in South Africa in 1858 and worked first at the missionary centre of Kuruman on the 'missionaries' road', thereafter in what is now Botswana. He believed in the extension of British rule to protect African peoples from settler encroachment. Fearing the Tswana would fall under Transvaal Boer rule, he campaigned in England in 1882 for British rule to be extended, and in 1884 briefly worked as British commissioner in Bechuanaland, the year before Sir Charles Warren proclaimed the establishment of a British protectorate over the country. [A. Sillery, *Mackenzie of Bechuanaland* (Cape Town, 1971)]

MADIKIZELA-MANDELA. See MANDELA, Winnie

MAFEKING. The most northerly town in the Cape Colony and the administrative capital of the Bechuanaland Protectorate from 1885. Mafeking became famous when besieged by the Boers between October 1899 and May 1900 during the South African War; in many ways, the ending of the siege served as a symbol of the resurgence of British pride after the initial setbacks of the war. In 1980 the town was transferred to Bophuthatswana and its name was changed to Mafikeng (Tswana, meaning 'place of stones'). Today it is the capital of North West Province.

MAJUBA. When British and Boer forces clashed on Majuba Hill in February 1881 in the Anglo-Transvaal War,* the British troops were soundly defeated by Boer volunteers determined to restore the independence of the Transvaal.* By then the British government had already decided to restore self-government to the Transvaal, and an armistice was signed between the two sides in March 1881, but the cry 'Avenge Majuba' did not help the cause of British–Transvaal reconciliation.

MAKEBA, Miriam (1935–). Singer whose career began during the 1940s in schools and churches near Pretoria. She worked with various township jazz groups before going into exile and settling in the United States. She was active in civil rights, anti-apartheid and Africanist campaigns during the 1960s and beyond, while achieving an international reputation as a singer and musician.

MALAN, Daniel François (1874–1959). Prime Minister from 1948 to 1954. This dour, unsmiling man, who grew up north of Cape Town, and knew Smuts as a child, left his Dutch Reformed Church ministry to edit the National Party newspaper, *De Burger* (later *Die Burger*). When Hertzog, leader of the NP, came to power in 1924, he joined his government, but broke with Hertzog when the latter moved towards Smuts. He formed a new 'Purified' National Party, which he held together in opposition until in May 1948 it took power, and began to put its policy of apartheid into practice. [D. O'Meara, *Forty Lost Years* (Johannesburg, 1996); R. Schrire, ed., *Malan to De Klerk* (London, 1994)]

MALAYS. See ISLAM

MANDELA, Nelson Rolihlahla (1918–). Born into the Madiba clan of the Thembu in the Transkei, he was the son of the chief councillor to the paramount chief, and the acting paramount chief became his guardian. He attended the Methodist college of Healdtown, then Fort Hare* University, which he left on a matter of principle. He went to Johannesburg, where he worked as a clerk in a law firm while completing his first degree through the University of South Africa. He then studied law at the University of the Witwatersrand while active as a founder member of the African National Congress (ANC) Youth League.* From 1947 he was a member of the executive of the Transvaal ANC. In 1951 he opened a law office, but his political work dominated and he was first banned,* then arrested in December 1956 and charged with treason. After the long-drawn-out Treason trial* ended in 1961, he went underground to establish and organize the armed wing of the ANC, Umkhonto weSizwe (MK).* Known as the Black Pimpernel, he travelled abroad, but in August 1962 was arrested in Natal, and then joined in the dock the other MK leaders arrested at Rivonia. He was sentenced to life imprisonment and sent to Robben Island.* There his moral authority and leadership did much to improve conditions for the prisoners.

In 1976 he rejected an offer by Jimmy Kruger, Minister of Police, that he settle in, and recognize, the Transkei bantustan. Instead, he became the main international symbol of apartheid repression. Probably because of the campaign for his release, he was moved to Pollsmoor prison on the mainland outside Cape Town in 1982. In 1985 he rejected State President P.W. Botha's offer of freedom in return for renouncing violence. When he went to hospital for prostate treatment in November that year, the Minister of Justice, Kobie Coetsee, went to see him, and from May 1988 he was engaged in regular talks with senior government officials. In December 1988, after treatment for tuberculosis, he was transferred to a house at Victor Verster prison near Paarl, and from there he was taken to have tea with P.W. Botha in July 1989. In December that year, he met Botha's successor, F.W. de Klerk.* On 11 February 1990 he walked to freedom, after 10,000 days of imprisonment, at the age of 71, without any bitterness for his lost years. The ANC first elected him its deputy president, and then in July 1991 president.

At a number of points in the negotiations that followed, his leadership was decisive in moving the process forward. In 1993 he and De Klerk were jointly awarded the Nobel Peace Prize. He was the ANC's main drawcard in the 1994 election, the first election in which he was able to cast a vote. On 10 May 1994 he was sworn in as the country's first democratically elected President at the Union Buildings, Pretoria. Later that year, he told his life story in his autobiography, *Long Walk to Freedom*. As President, he worked for national reconciliation, and to promote South Africa abroad. He handed over the leadership of the ANC to Thabo Mbeki* in December 1997, and made clear that he would stand down as President in the elections in 1999.

In April 1992 he separated from his wife Winnie, and in 1996 announced a relationship with Graça Machel, widow of the former President of Mozambique, Samora Machel. [F. Meer, *Higher Than Hope* (Durban, 1989); N. Mandela, *Long Walk to Freedom* (London, 1994); M. Meredith, *Mandela* (London, 1997)]

MANDELA, Winnie Madikizela (1934–). Born in the Transkei, she became involved with the African National Congress (ANC) after moving to Johannesburg, where she became Nelson Mandela's second wife in 1958. In 1962 he was arrested and she was banned for the first time. In 1969 she was detained under the Suppression of Communism Act and spent a long period in solitary confinement; again jailed in 1974 and 1976, she was then banished in 1977 to the small Free State town of Brandfort. After eight years there, she returned to Soweto,* where she organized a Mandela United Football Club of youths to protect her. By early 1989 leading members of the United Democratic Front (UDF) were forced to issue a statement distancing the UDF from her, because of the actions of the football club and its members. After her husband's release, she was charged with kidnapping and with protecting the assailants of youths who had been taken to her home in December 1988 and there beaten. One of them, a young activist by the name of Stompie Seipei, died. She was convicted on the kidnapping charge, but was found not guilty of the more serious ones on appeal. In 1992 her husband announced that they were separating. She became a Deputy Minister in the Government of National Unity in 1994, but increasingly fell out with her ex-husband, who began divorce proceedings against her after she was dropped as Deputy Minister. Despite her record, she retained popular support in the ANC, and headed the Women's League. In 1997 she was re-elected leader of this organization. She then asked for a public hearing before the Truth and Reconciliation Commission,* at which much testimony pointed to her involvement in a series of murders in the late 1980s. Though she denied all, her position was much weakened, and she failed in her candidacy for the deputy presidency of the ANC at the Mafikeng conference in December 1997. [E. Gilbey, *The Lady* (Johannesburg, 1993); M. Meredith, *Mandela* (London, 1997)]

MAPUNGUBWE. Capital of one of the largest precolonial Iron Age states known to have existed in what is now South Africa. It is thought to have been at its peak in the 13th century AD. Today all that remains is some ruins close to the Limpopo River in the Northern Province.

MAQOMA (1798–1873). Xhosa chief, half-brother of Sandile and heir to the Rharhabe paramountcy. He was expelled from the fertile Kat River valley, the site of the later Kat River Settlement,* in 1828 and subsequently played a leading role in opposing colonial expansion into Xhosa land during the frontier wars of 1834–1835 and 1850–1853. After the cattle-killing,* he was exiled on Robben Island,* where he died. [T. Stapleton, *Maqoma* (Johannesburg, 1994); N. Mostert, *Frontiers* (London, 1992)]

MARKS, Samuel (1843–1920). Wealthy and influential Transvaal industrialist. Marks arrived in South Africa in 1868, and with his cousin and business partner, Isaac Lewis, earned his first fortune on the diamond fields.* They launched a major business enterprise called Lewis & Marks during the gold rush in Barberton in 1885. Marks then moved to Pretoria, where he built a splendid house to the east of the city at Zwartkoppies. He formed close ties with the government of Paul Kruger* and founded numerous industries on the Witwatersrand. His financial and industrial interests included coal, forestry, land, liquor, glassworks, food-processing, brickworks and tanning. [R. Mendelsohn, *Sammy Marks* (Cape Town, 1991)]

MASS DEMOCRATIC MOVEMENT (MDM). After the apartheid government restricted the United Democratic Front (UDF)* and other organizations in 1988, the MDM emerged as an even broader, but also looser, resistance front to apartheid, made up of UDF and ANC supporters, and with close links to the Congress of South African Trade Unions.* It had no permanent structure, which prevented the government from banning it.

MATANZIMA, Kaiser (1915–). Bantustan leader. He studied at Fort Hare* University with Nelson Mandela.* He became a chief in the St Marks district of Transkei.* He was appointed by the government as paramount chief of Emigrant Thembuland, with a status equal to that of King Sabata Dalindyebo of Thembuland. Believing that Verwoerd's policy of 'separate development' was in the best interests of his people, he became head of the Transkei government in 1963 and led his country to 'independence' in 1976. He later became Transkei president. Authoritarian in manner, he was despised by many blacks as a collaborator. [B. Streek and R. Wicksteed, *Render Unto Kaiser* (Johannesburg, 1981); R. Southall, *South Africa's Transkei* (London, 1982)]

MATTHEWS, Zachariah Keodirelang (1901–1968). Educationist, academic and political leader. The first African to obtain a BA degree (from the University of South Africa), Matthews became the first African principal of Adams College in Natal in 1925, then a lecturer in social anthropology at the South African Native College at Fort Hare* in 1936. Appointed professor and head of African Studies there in 1945, he was thereafter increasingly drawn into political activity on the Natives Representative Council (NRC) and in the African National Congress. He resigned from the NRC in protest at government policy in 1950, and was involved in preparations for the Defiance Campaign* and the drafting of the Freedom Charter. After he was acquitted during the Treason trial* in April 1959, he left the country and spent his remaining years in Botswana, Switzerland and the United States. His autobiography, *Freedom for My People*, won international acclaim. [Z.K. Matthews, *Freedom for My People* (Cape Town, 1981)]

MBEKI, Govan Archibald (1910–). Activist and intellectual. Born and educated in the Transkei,* he attended mission schools before graduating from the University of Fort Hare* in 1937. After being dismissed as a teacher for his political activities, he ran a Transkeian trading store and edited the *Territorial Magazine*. He returned to teaching in the 1950s, but was again dismissed. He then edited *New Age* in Port Elizabeth. As leader of the ANC in the eastern Cape, he helped build up the organization there. Secretary of the High Command of Umkhonto weSizwe,* he was arrested at Lilliesleaf farm, Rivonia,* and sentenced to life imprisonment. He was released in November 1987. With the establishment of the new order in 1994, he became Deputy Speaker of the Senate, retiring in 1997.

MBEKI, Thabo (1942–). Born in the Transkei, son of veteran activist Govan Mbeki,* he joined the ANC Youth League* in 1956, and after being detained in 1962 left the country. He studied economics at the University of Sussex and then worked in the ANC office in London, undergoing a brief period of military training in the Soviet Union. In 1984 he became the ANC's director of information and publicity, and in 1989 head of the ANC's department of international affairs. He was the leading member of the ANC team which held a series of meetings with a group of South Africans in England in 1988; he also met South African intelligence officers in Switzerland in September 1989. After his return to South Africa, he rose through the ANC ranks and was made Deputy President in the Government of National Unity*; with the sidelining of Cyril Ramaphosa,* he emerged as the only successor to Nelson Mandela. Charming in public, he also gained a reputation for being ruthless and tough in behind-the-scenes negotiations. By 1997 he was effectively ruling the country and in December that year he took over from Mandela as president of the ANC at the Mafikeng conference.

MERRIMAN, John Xavier (1841–1926). Cape politician, who served in the first cabinet of the self-governing Cape under John Charles Molteno, and under Cecil Rhodes* from 1890 to 1893. He became Prime Minister of the Cape from 1908 to 1910. As a 'Cape liberal', he stood against the polarization of southern African politics, and condemned the Jameson Raid* and the South African War.* He worked towards the rapid restoration of self-government in the defeated republics, and played a prominent role in the National Convention* of 1908–1909. Believed by some to be an ideal first Prime Minister of the new Union, he was not chosen because of his Cape background, and instead became an elder statesman in retirement. [P. Lewsen, *John X. Merriman* (Johannesburg, 1982)]

MEYER, Roelf (1947–). He rose from a humble background to become chair of the Afrikaanse Studentebond and the Ruiterwag (a junior Broederbond),* a National Party (NP) member of parliament, and member of P.W. Botha's cabinet. In the late 1980s he came to see the need for fundamental reform and backed F.W. de Klerk* when he decided to negotiate with the African National Congress. From 1992 he played a key role as the chief government negotiator, and his special relationship with Cyril Ramaphosa* helped prevent the negotiations from breaking down completely at a number of points. He was accused by others in the NP of selling out the interests of the Afrikaners, but he believed that majority rule was inevitable and that it was in the interests of the governing party and group to work for that end, not oppose it. [P. Waldmeir, *Anatomy of a Miracle* (London, 1997)]

MFECANE. Zulu term meaning 'the crushing'; the Sotho used the term *difaqane* or *lifaqane*, meaning 'hammering' or 'forced migration'. From the 1920s the word has been used by historians to describe the period of crisis and revolutionary change among African peoples in the Natal and Zululand region and on the highveld interior during the second and third decades of the 19th century.

Many historical works have portrayed the period as one of enormous destruction and violent upheaval, caused by the rise of the Zulu kingdom* under Shaka,* which set in motion a chain of warfare and raiding across the entire southern African interior. Fierce competition between northern Nguni societies resulted in the flight of defeated groups out of Natal and Zululand west across the Drakensberg and south into the Transkei. This disrupted long-established settlement patterns in these regions, provoking intense conflict for a number of years. Some parts of the country were depopulated, while others saw the emergence of new states, such as those of the Ndebele under Mzilikazi* or of the southern Sotho under Moshoeshoe.* The apparent depopulation of the interior made it easier for the migrant white farmers of the Great Trek* to move into the areas which became the Transvaal and the Orange Free State during the 1830s.

In the 1960s the historian John Omer-Cooper attempted to emphasize the Mfecane period as one of positive state-building rather than gratuitous destruction. During the late 1980s, Julian Cobbing, lecturer in history at Rhodes University, questioned the entire notion of the Mfecane. He argued that historians, in their desire to legitimize white conquest of the interior, had deliberately exaggerated the ferocity and devastation of the period; that where disruption had occurred, particular causes should be found rather than a general apportioning of blame to the Shakan state; and that in any case Shaka's kingdom could not have been single-handedly responsible for the events attributed to it, especially as it was neither as large nor as dominant as it was commonly made out to be. Cobbing argued that the Zulu state and others in the interior were defensive formations, constituted as protection against the influence of commercial capitalists who were encircling the region. Slave trading from Delagoa Bay, as well as from the Cape frontier regions, was far more pervasive than has commonly been accepted; white traders and their agents, such as Griqua raiders, were responsible for disrupting settlements in the interior in their desire to capture labour for the Cape. The motor for the disruption is thus to be found within white colonial society and its need for labour to ensure its continued commercial success.

Cobbing's theories have come under considerable scrutiny: the accuracy of his reading of many of the sources, particularly missionary accounts, has been challenged, and numerous questions of detail have been raised by those sceptical of his arguments. Answers remain elusive on many points because of the inconclusive nature of the evidence. [J. Omer-Cooper, *The Zulu Aftermath* (London, 1966); C. Hamilton, ed., *The Mfecane Aftermath* (Johannesburg, 1995)]

MFENGU (Fingo). Some dispute surrounds the origins of Mfengu people in the eastern Cape during the 1820s. It is usually accepted that they comprised the impoverished and scattered remnants of various Nguni groups (including the Hlubi, Zizi, Bhaca and Bhele) fleeing the disruption of the Mfecane further north. They apparently repeated the simple request 'siyamfenguze' ('we seek work'), and formed a client relationship with the Gcaleka Xhosa,* who employed them to look after herds of cattle, from about 1823. They also proved to be successful traders. The pioneering Wesleyan missionary John Ayliff (1797–1862) saw the Mfengu as potential converts, speaking of their 'slave' status among the Xhosa, and during the frontier war of 1834–1835 he persuaded them to seek the protection of the colonial authorities. After the war, some 16,000 Mfengu were placed on former Xhosa land east of the Fish River as a buffer between the Xhosa and the colonists; their acceptance of this land was regarded by the Xhosa as an act of ingratitude and treachery.

The Mfengu became successful agriculturists; many were prosperous independent peasant farmers, while others were sought after by colonists because of their reputation as loyal servants. Many were quick to accept Christianity and Western education. They fought on the side of the colonists during the frontier wars of 1846–1847, 1850–1853 and 1877–1878, and received further grants of land seized from the defeated Xhosa. After the cattle-killing,* from which many Mfengu prospered, the portion of Xhosa territory allocated to them became known as 'Fingoland', which itself became a springboard for further migration into the Transkei and East Griqualand area in the 1870s and 1880s. [L. Switzer, *Power and Resistance* (Madison, 1993)]

MIGRANCY. The movement of Africans to work for temporary periods became systematic state policy as the mining economy required large numbers of workers. Africans often did not wish to leave their homes in the rural areas permanently, and white governments did not want them settling permanently in so-called white areas. As time passed, however, the economy required more settled labour, especially for manufacturing industry, and urbanization increased, but migrant labour continued to be very important into the late 1990s. [A. Jeeves, *Migrant Labour in South Africa's Mining Economy* (Kingston, 1985); J. Crush et al., *South Africa's Labor Empire* (Cape Town, 1991)]

MILNER, Alfred (1854–1925). Governor of the Cape and High Commissioner of South Africa from 1897 to 1905. An ardent imperialist and doctrinaire social engineer, he aimed to create a self-governing white dominion in which a well-controlled African labour force would ensure the efficient functioning of the country's mines. He viewed the Transvaal as an obstacle to the attainment of his objectives, and used Uitlander grievances against the government of Kruger,* forcing matters until the South African War* broke out.

After the war, Milner administered the conquered republics, with the aid of a group of young men known as the Kindergarten,* and attempted to promote rapid economic growth, particularly the expansion of mining production, and to encourage large-scale British immigration so as to weaken Afrikaner power. He was not successful in either; the mining industry took some years to recover, immigration from Britain was not large enough to achieve his goals, and he alienated Afrikaners through his anglicization endeavours. [C. Headlam, ed., *The Milner Papers* (London, 1931, 1933); G. le May, *British Supremacy in South Africa* (Oxford, 1965); D. Denoon, *A Grand Illusion* (London, 1973)]

MISSIONARIES. The first European missionary sent to work among the indigenous people of the Cape was the Moravian evangelist George Schmidt (1709–1785), who founded the Genadendal mission in 1737. He returned to Europe in 1744, and it was not until the 1790s that mission work was resumed, at Genadendal and elsewhere. The late-18th-century evangelical revival in Europe saw the founding of a number of mission societies, and the 19th century was the primary period of mission activity in southern Africa.

In the first half of the 19th century, the London Missionary Society* (LMS) had more missionaries in the field, and over a wider area, than any other missionary group. The LMS did little work among the settler population, preferring to concentrate its energies on the frontier areas, and beyond them. In the east, the Bethelsdorp mission of Johannes van der Kemp* was regarded with considerable hostility by white farmers, who feared the loss of Khoikhoi labour, while in the north the Kuruman mission of Robert Moffat* became the centre of enormous missionary work. As superintendent of the LMS between the 1820s and 1840s, John Philip* played a central role in colonial developments. Most LMS stations in the colony were gradually incorporated into the Congregational Church.

The other major Protestant missionary society active in South Africa in the early 19th century was the Wesleyan Methodist Missionary Society. William Shaw (1798–1872) established a chain of six missions stretching from the colonial eastern frontier to Port Natal. The Wesleyans also did pioneering work among the Sotho. Other missionary bodies active in South Africa included the Glasgow Society, which in 1824 founded Lovedale, the leading missionary educational institution in the Cape; the Berlin Missionary Society, which worked in the eastern Cape before turning its attention to Natal and the Transvaal; the Rhenish Missionary Society, which operated missions in the western Cape and Namaqualand; and the Paris Evangelical Missionary Society, with eleven missions in Basutoland by 1850. In Natal, the most successful of the missions were those of the American Board, which experienced considerable growth among the Zulu, and which founded Adams College in 1853; here numbers of Natal's African elite were educated until its closure by the National Party government in 1956.

The major churches became involved in mission work only in the latter half of the 19th century. Anglicans* began mission work in the eastern Cape during the 1850s; the Dutch Reformed Churches* started in the 1860s; while the Roman Catholic Church's* mission activities only gained momentum at the beginning of the 20th century.

Missionaries occupy a controversial place in South African history. Many of them were viewed by colonists as enemies of the colonial order, intruders who were too sympathetic towards people of colour, a view which long lingered. They have also been portrayed as agents of colonial expansion who undermined African societies, convinced as most were of their superior culture and the benefits of colonial rule. Many, particularly those on the frontier, acted as intermediaries between African chiefs and the colonial government. Some African societies viewed them as agents of disruption, disease and drought, and missionary intolerance of African customs aroused much hostility to their work. Mission success before 1850 was fairly limited, confined mainly to uprooted and severely unsettled communities; only in the second half of the century did they make significant numbers of conversions. Missionaries were not always able to dictate events; and they were frequently used by African leaders to their own advantage. While some missionaries did attempt to limit the excesses of settler expansion, others, often divided among themselves over strategies and by rivalries for conversion, advocated the conquest of African societies in the interests of the extension of Christianity. [H. Bredekamp and R. Ross, eds., *Missions and Christianity in South African History* (Johannesburg, 1995); R. Elphick and T.R.H. Davenport eds., *Christianity in South Africa* (Cape Town, 1997)]

MOFFAT, Robert (1795–1883). Missionary of the London Missionary Society (LMS),* whose work among the Tlhaping people at Kuruman mission between 1824 and 1870 brought him considerable renown. An able linguist, Moffat was responsible for Tswana becoming the first written African language in South Africa, and also for translating the Bible into Setswana. Kuruman, perhaps the most successful of all the LMS missions, became an important base for further mission work and exploration deeper into the interior, some of which was undertaken by Moffat's son-in-law, David Livingstone.

MOROKA II (c.1795–1880). Chief of the Rolong from 1830 until 1880. A Sotho-speaking community, the Rolong established their capital at Thaba Nchu, in what is now the Free State, in 1833 after moving from the western Transvaal, where they were threatened by the westward expansion of the Ndebele.* Moroka assisted the Voortrekkers* against the Ndebele, and subsequently aided the British against the southern Sotho.

MOSHOESHOE (c.1786–1870). Leader of the main group of southern Sotho. The son of a minor Sotho ruler in the upper Caledon valley, he based himself at an impregnable mountain fortress, Thaba Bosiu (the 'mountain of the night'), in 1824, and from there launched cattle raids, particularly on the Thembu (see XHOSA) south of the Drakensberg. He recruited followers by loaning cattle and winning a reputation for tolerance and magnanimity towards his enemies, and succeeded in uniting disparate Sotho groups into a federal state under his authority.

After 1848 he had to preserve his state in the face of new pressures. In 1843 the British had recognized that his territory extended well to the west of the Caledon River; but their attempts to restrict his lands after the proclamation of the Orange River Sovereignty* in 1848 caused him to lose faith in British promises. During the 1850s, the Boers of the Orange Free State began to encroach on his land, and an inconclusive war was fought between the two sides in 1858. A further conflict with the Boers in 1865–1866 left the Sotho in a serious plight, and forced Moshoeshoe to seek British protection. In March 1868, Basutoland* was annexed as a British colony, but Moshoeshoe lost the fertile lands west of the Caledon in the following year when the boundary was demarcated by the British High Commissioner and the government of the Orange Free State. [P. Sanders, *Moshoeshoe* (London, 1975); L. Thompson, *Survival in Two Worlds* (Oxford, 1975); E. Eldredge, *A South African Kingdom* (Cambridge, 1993)]

MPANDE (1798–1872). Zulu* king from 1840, Mpande was the half-brother of Dingane,* and the father of Cetshwayo,* who was *de facto* ruler long before his formal succession. Mpande forged an alliance with the Voortrekkers* at the end of the 1830s, and defeated Dingane in 1840. He succeeded in maintaining Zulu independence until his death, avoiding direct confrontation with the growing colony of Natal south of the Zulu kingdom, and alternately dealing with the British and the Boers to prevent any erosion of his authority.

MPUMALANGA ('where the sun rises'). Province created in April 1994, from part of the former Transvaal and incorporating the bantustan of KaNgwane. Its first premier was Mathews Phosa. Initially called Eastern Transvaal, it was renamed in 1995. Beset by a series of scandals in its early years, it hoped to profit greatly by the development of the 'Maputo corridor', a Rl billion project to open a new road link from the Rand to the harbour of Maputo.

MRS PLES. Name given to the cranium of a female of the species *Plesianthropus transvaalensis* (later classified as *Australopithecus africanus*), discovered by Robert Broom and J.T. Robinson at Sterkfontein near Johannesburg in 1947. Mrs Ples was related to the Taung child, though of a different subspecies, and was dated to 2.5 million years before the present. The discovery provided further evidence that the earliest hominids lived in southern Africa.

MUJAJI (c.1800–1895). Ruler of the Lovedu people in the north-eastern Transvaal, popularly known as the 'Rain Queen'. She claimed tribute from many peoples surrounding her chiefdom during the latter part of the 19th century because of her position in the rain cult and her powers over rainfall. Since her reign, the Lovedu have always had a female ruler.

MULTI-PARTY NEGOTIATING FORUM. A continuation, in effect, of the Convention for a Democratic South Africa,* it drew up the interim constitution of 1993 and provisions for the transition to the new order. Meeting at the World Trade Centre at Kempton Park, outside Johannesburg, from April 1993, it completed the draft of the interim constitution in November. The National Party (NP) negotiating team under Roelf Meyer* agreed to the establishment for a five-year term of a Government of National Unity,* in which the NP had no veto over decisions. The NP also backed down over federalism and agreed to a two-thirds majority requirement for the passage of the final constitution by the Constitutional Assembly* and a 60% majority in a referendum if deadlock was reached in the Assembly. The African National Congress negotiating team was ably led by Cyril Ramaphosa.* [S. Friedman and D. Atkinson, eds., *The Small Miracle* (Johannesburg, 1994)]

MUSLIMS. See ISLAM

MZILIKAZI (c.1795–1868). Leader of the Ndebele* state from its inception in the 1820s. The son of the chief of the Khumalo chiefdom among the northern Nguni, Mzilikazi rose to prominence during the conflict between the Zulu* and the Ndwandwe. A most effective military commander, he switched allegiance from the Ndwandwe ruler Zwide* to the Zulu leader Shaka* in about 1819. He alienated Shaka by refusing to surrender captured cattle in 1821, and fled north the following year with about 300 followers. With this nucleus, he created in the 1820s a new state north of the Vaal River, which he moved progressively further west, to escape possible Zulu retaliation. This state grew into a large polity, which by the mid-1830s embraced much of what became the southern and western Transvaal. The Voortrekkers posed a new threat from the south from 1836, and after the defeat they inflicted on his army at Vegkop,* he withdrew northwards, and re-established his kingdom north of the Limpopo River* in what became known as Matabeleland. He remained ruler there until his death in 1868, when power passed to his son Lobengula. [K. Rasmussen, *Migrant Kingdom* (London, 1978)]

NAMIBIA. South Africa conquered German South West Africa (SWA) during World War I, and the territory was granted to it as a C-class mandate by the League of Nations* in 1920. South Africa extended the system of reserves introduced by the Germans, and permitted whites from the Union to settle there. Smuts ordered resistance by the Bondelswartz people in 1922 to be suppressed harshly. When the League dissolved during World War II, Smuts hoped to be able to annex the territory, and formally applied to the newly established United Nations (UN)* in 1946 to do so, but his request was refused, largely on the grounds that the indigenous people had not been adequately consulted. The UN instead asked South Africa to place the territory under the UN's trusteeship system, which provided for eventual independence for such territories. When South Africa refused, a long-drawn-out legal battle began, in the course of which the International Court of Justice at The Hague handed down a series of judgments on the status of South West Africa. In 1966 the court decided that it had no legal standing in a case which turned on whether South Africa was governing the territory in the spirit of the mandate. This led directly to the beginning of armed conflict in the north of South West Africa, in which at first the South African Police sought to combat guerrilla insurgents of the South West African People's Organization (SWAPO). In October 1966 the UN General Assembly unilaterally terminated the mandate, a decision which was, a few years later, ratified by the Security Council. In 1971 the ratification was in turn given legal validity by the International Court. In the same year a general strike of Namibian workers posed a new threat to South African rule in the territory.

In the face of these developments, the South African government decided to abandon its policy of seeking to incorporate the territory to a greater extent into its own administration, as a *de facto* fifth province. Instead it determined that the territory should remain as one entity, despite the fact that it had begun to apply there a bantustan policy on the South African model, and should be led towards self-government and independence under a black-led government that would be friendly to South Africa. An ethnically based advisory council was established, and then in 1975 a conference of ethnic representatives was brought together in the Turnhalle building in Windhoek. By that time the South African government feared that once Angola was independent, the People's Liberation Army of Namibia (PLAN), SWAPO's armed wing, would be able to operate from southern Angola* and so pose a much greater threat to the South African army defending northern Namibia. A small South African expeditionary force moved towards the Angolan capital in October 1975 to try to prevent the pro-SWAPO MPLA from taking power in Luanda, but in the face of the arrival of Cuban troops and the failure of support from the West, the South African force had to withdraw and SWAPO was able to establish itself in part of southern Angola.

In 1977, when it seemed that the Turnhalle might produce an 'internal settlement', in terms of which the South African government would give independence to a local client group, a so-called Western Contact Group was established, consisting of the five Western countries then members of the UN Security Council, to press for a form of independence that would mesh with the UN demand for a transfer of power to the people of the territory (UN Security Council resolution 385 of 1976). By April 1978 a formula had been worked out providing for joint UN–South African administration during a transition period in which the UN would provide a monitoring team and a force to keep the peace. The South African government accepted this plan in April 1978, probably without any serious intention of ever implementing it.

Numerous reasons were advanced in the years following by South African government spokesmen why the plan (embodied in UN Security Council resolution 435) could not be implemented: the alleged partiality of the UN; the composition of the UNTAG force that would enter the territory during the transitional phase; the monitoring and location of SWAPO's military bases; and, from 1981, the presence of Cuban forces in Angola. From northern Namibia the South African forces – (from 1980) together with South West African forces under South African command – launched raids against SWAPO bases in southern Angola. Brutal repression was used in northern Namibia to try to destroy SWAPO, while at the same time the Democratic Turnhalle Alliance and other groupings were built up in an attempt to form an anti-SWAPO front.

It was events in southern Angola which did most to force the South African government to implement resolution 435. By early 1988 the South African forces had had to intervene twice to save South Africa's ally, UNITA, from annihilation by the Angolan army. After the second of these, the South African-led forces moved close to Cuito Cuanavale* and there a military stalemate ensued, owing to the arrival of large numbers of Cuban troops to aid the Angolan army. By May 1988 the Cubans had also moved closer to the Namibian border, and the threat of a major war with Cuba loomed. A negotiated settlement was the only way out, and this meant the implementation of resolution 435.

As a result of an agreement signed in December 1988 between South Africa, Angola and Cuba, the date for implementation was fixed for 1 April 1989. After an initial crisis, caused by a SWAPO armed incursion into the north of the territory, the plan was carried out as envisaged in 1978, and in November 1989 the electorate of Namibia chose a Constituent Assembly in which SWAPO won 41 of the 72 seats. SWAPO then agreed to abide by the constitutional principles it had agreed to in 1982, a liberal constitution was approved unanimously in remarkably short time, and on 21 March 1990, in a moving ceremony attended by De Klerk* and the recently released Mandela,* the South African administration came to an end and the territory finally became independent.

The Western Contact Group had accepted that Walvis Bay,* Namibia's main port, would not be included in the negotiations and that its status would be decided after Namibian independence. While it controlled the port, South Africa dominated the new nation economically. After discussions between the two governments, a joint administration was set up over the Walvis Bay enclave, and it was formally incorporated into Namibia at the end of February 1994. After Mandela took office as South African President he announced that Namibia's debt* to South Africa would be cancelled; after lengthy negotiations this debt, amounting to over R1 billion, was written off in 1997. [G. Leistner and P. Esterhuysen, *Namibia 1990* (Pretoria, 1991); R. Dreyer, *Namibia and Southern Africa* (London, 1994); D. Herbstein and J. Evenson, *The Devils are Amongst Us* (London, 1989); L. Cliffe et al., *The Transition to Independence in Namibia* (Boulder, 1994)]

NATAL. Territory lying between the Drakensberg and the Indian Ocean, Natal was given its name by the first European to pass by its shores, the Portuguese explorer Vasco da Gama,* at the end of the 15th century. By that time, it had been inhabited for centuries by San hunter-gatherers and by Nguni-speaking farmers. Towards the end of the 18th century, considerable struggle for hegemony occurred among various chiefdoms north of the Thukela River, and resulted in the emergence of the Zulu kingdom* under Shaka* at the beginning of the 19th century.

The first white settlers established a trading post at Port Natal, later Durban,* in 1824, but the first large group of whites to enter Natal were Voortrekkers, who crossed the Drakensberg in 1837. By 1839, some 6000 trekkers were living in the Republic of Natalia situated south of the Thukela River. In 1843 Britain annexed the area, largely for strategic reasons, to prevent any hostile power from gaining a foothold on the southern African coast. Most of the trekkers left for the highveld, and were replaced by immigrants from Britain, the first large group of 5000 arriving between 1849 and 1852. By the mid-1850s, there were still fewer than 10,000 whites; these were greatly outnumbered by over 100,000 Africans, who were placed in reserves administered by Theophilus Shepstone* through a system of paternalism and indirect rule.

Natal was an autonomous district of the Cape Colony until 1856, when it was given its own Legislative Council. Although Natal's franchise* was theoretically non-racial, like that of the Cape, in practice it was closer to that of the trekker republics: the Exemption and Native Franchise Laws of 1865 required Africans to obtain exemption from customary law before qualifying for the vote, an exemption which was extremely difficult to obtain. After the Langalibalele Rebellion* in 1873, an attempt was made to reduce Natal to crown colony status, in part so that Natal could lend its support to the confederation scheme of Lord Carnarvon.* In reaction, a movement grew for responsible government, which was finally achieved in 1893. In 1897, Zululand was incorporated into Natal (the Zulu kingdom having been annexed by the British in 1887 after the Anglo-Zulu War* of 1879 and the subsequent civil war).

By the end of the 19th century, Natal's economy and political order were firmly in white hands. From 1860, indentured Indian labourers arrived in Natal, and the sugar plantations on which they worked became the mainstay of the economy. Other significant economic activities were agriculture, pastoral farming, timber plantations and coal mining. White dominance, though established, was insecure, as evidenced by the poor handling by the authorities of the Bambatha Rebellion* of 1906, which helped to propel Natal into the Union* of South Africa in 1910. Within the Union, Natal's English-speaking whites feared Afrikaner domination, and occasionally spoke of secession. During the 20th century, Natal's white politicians were frequently preoccupied with attempts to secure further provincial rights rather than with broader issues.

During the 1970s, over forty separate pieces of land were excised from the province to constitute the bantustan of KwaZulu.* Many thousands of people living on white farms were forced to move into KwaZulu, which included the major black townships on the outskirts of Durban, where most of the inhabitants worked. KwaZulu politics was dominated by Mangosuthu Buthelezi,* its chief minister (from 1977). He rejected full independence for KwaZulu, to the annoyance of the National Party government, although relations between the two sides warmed during the 1980s as Buthelezi became involved in a struggle against the United Democratic Front* and rejected economic sanctions against South Africa.

Buthelezi tended to view the regional economy of the KwaZulu-Natal area as inextricably linked, arguing that it should be governed as such. During the 1990s, secessionist talk was again aired as a viable option for the region, as Buthelezi and his supporters adopted increasingly strident positions against the major thrust of South African politics and against the negotiations for a new national constitution and democratic elections. A low-key and violent civil war, which began in about 1986 and grew in intensity during the 1990s, polarized the region: many commentators saw it as the product of Buthelezi's Inkatha Freedom Party and the ANC competing for political dominance. In 1994, the region was again united as the province of KwaZulu-Natal, one of the nine provinces of the country. [A. Duminy and B. Guest, *Natal and Zululand from the Earliest Times to 1910* (Pietermaritzburg, 1989); B. Kline, *The Genesis of Apartheid* (Lanham, 1988); B. Guest and J. Sellers, eds., *Enterprise and Exploitation in a Victorian Colony; Receded Tides of Empire* (Pietermaritzburg, 1985, 1994); A. Jeffrey, *The Natal Story* (Johannesburg, 1997)]

NATIONAL CONVENTION. The body which drafted the constitution of the Union* of South Africa. It assembled in Durban on 12 October 1908, precisely nine years after the outbreak of the South African War.* Thirty white delegates from the four colonies participated, the numbers being roughly proportionate to the white populations: twelve from the Cape, eight from the Transvaal, and five each from Natal and the Orange River Colony. The National Convention convened in Cape Town in February 1909 and finalized its business in Bloemfontein in May 1909. Its decisions were enshrined in the South Africa Bill, which was passed by both houses of the British parliament. As the South Africa Act, it received royal assent on 20 September 1909. The most contentious issues confronting the National Convention were those of the franchise* and the national capital. Compromise was reached on both. Existing franchise arrangements in each colony were to continue, but only whites were entitled to serve in the new Union parliament. Cape Town was to be the seat of parliament, Pretoria the administrative capital, and Bloemfontein the seat of the Appellate Division of the Supreme Court.

A South African Native Convention (SANC) also met in 1908–1909 in response to the drive by whites to unify South Africa. The SANC was unable to prevent the inauguration of the Union on 31 May 1910. It was a forerunner of the South African Native National Congress of 1912, later the African National Congress.* [L. Thompson, *The Unification of South Africa* (Oxford, 1960); A. Odendaal, *Vukani Bantu!* (Cape Town, 1988)]

NATIONAL PEACE ACCORD. Signed in Johannesburg on 14 September 1991, its 29 signatories included the De Klerk* government, the African National Congress, the Inkatha Freedom Party and trade unions. It was drawn up to combat the escalating level of political violence in the country, and to create a suitable climate for negotiation. It laid down codes of conduct, provided for the establishment of local committees to resolve political disputes, and obliged all parties to refrain from violence for political ends. Its provisions were often blatantly ignored, and violence continued at a high level, but many of its local dispute resolution committees were effective, and its monitors facilitated the work of peace monitors from the United Nations,* the European Community and the Commonwealth.*

NATIONAL SECURITY MANAGEMENT SYSTEM. See STATE SECURITY COUNCIL

NATIONAL UNION OF SOUTH AFRICAN STUDENTS (NUSAS) (1924–1991). Formed initially to represent students from English- and Afrikaans-speaking universities, it shifted in its politics to the left after World War II, and in the late 1950s strongly opposed the government's policy of segregating tertiary education. From 1959, when the universities were segregated, NUSAS opposed apartheid in general. Some leading figures in NUSAS were involved in the African Resistance Movement and arrested in 1964. John Vorster,* Minister of Justice, had by then come to regard NUSAS as dangerously subversive. Though infiltrated by police spies, it nevertheless carried on its opposition to apartheid and helped radicalise thousands of students on those English-medium campuses on which it was able to operate. State harassment continued: after the Schlebusch Commission of 1972 investigated its activities, eight of its leaders were banned for five years.

By then most of its black members had left to join the South African Students' Organization,* founded by Steve Biko,* but NUSAS continued to work closely with black students in anti-apartheid work in the 1980s. In 1989 it decided to link up with the black-dominated South African National Students' Congress, formed from the Azanian Students' Organization. The two bodies merged in 1991: NUSAS dissolved itself and a new student body, the South African Students' Congress Organization, was launched.

NDEBELE STATE. Powerful, centralized state created during in the mid-1820s in the Transvaal by Mzilikazi.* By the early 1830s it embraced much of the area between the Limpopo, Vaal, Crocodile and Molopo rivers, and had perhaps 80,000 subjects, the majority of whom were Sotho-speakers absorbed through conquest or marriage. The capital moved several times, from close to the Vaal River, to north of present-day Pretoria, to the Marico area in the present North-West Province. Regiments were stationed both at the capital and at far-flung military outposts.

In 1832 the Zulu ruler Dingane* sent a raiding army to the highveld in an attempt to reduce Ndebele power, but it was repulsed. Challenged by Griqua* raiders and then by Voortrekkers* from the south and south-west in the mid-1830s, Mzilikazi decided to withdraw, and in 1838 moved north across the Limpopo River. He re-created his state in what became known as Matabeleland in south-western Zimbabwe. [K. Rasmussen, *Migrant Kingdom* (Cape Town, 1975)]

NDZUNDZA NDEBELE. Inhabitants of part of what later became the Transvaal long before the arrival there of the Ndebele of Mzilikazi,* the Ndzundza Ndebele clashed with invaders from KwaZulu in the 1820s, and then in the 1830s and 1840s regrouped under Mabhogo in an area round the capital Erholweni on the upper Steelpoort River. Less powerful than the Pedi to the north, they came into conflict with the Voortrekkers over issues of land and labour. A sub-group, the Kekana, were almost entirely wiped out when the trekkers laid siege to a cave in the Waterberg in which they had taken refuge in 1854. They nevertheless numbered about 10,000 by the 1860s, and in 1879 they helped the British conquer the Pedi.* Then in 1882 Erholweni was besieged by the Boers; in the following year their ruler surrendered and their land was seized and distributed to whites.

Under white rule, the Ndebele struggled to find a new identity: the most striking form this took was the colourful decorations they painted on the walls of their mud homesteads. In the 1970s and early 1980s the government created a new bantustan, known as KwaNdebele, but the offer of 'independence' made to it was refused. The struggle to create the bantustan led to much violence between them and neighbouring people.

NGQIKA (c.1775–1829). Chief of the Rharhabe, or western Xhosa,* from 1786, whose lengthy and bitter rivalry with Ndlambe, his uncle, was finally resolved in 1818–1819. Ngqika was defeated by the combined forces of Ndlambe and Hintsa* at the Battle of Amalinde in 1818, after which he enlisted colonial assistance, which was readily given, for the Cape Colony was keen to establish its dominance on the frontier. Ndlambe was defeated by Cape forces in 1819, and the Cape then recognized Ngqika as paramount chief. But the colonial authorities forced Ngqika to surrender the land between the Kei and Keiskamma rivers, comprising much of the Rharhabe land, as a neutral zone between the Xhosa and white settlers. This lost Ngqika the support of many of his followers, and he died an outcast and an alcoholic in 1829. [J. Peires, *The House of Phalo* (Johannesburg, 1981); N. Mostert, *Frontiers* (London, 1992)]

NGUNI. Linguistic term for a group of south-east Bantu languages, spoken by people living along the coastal belt from Zululand and Swaziland in the north to the Ciskei region in the eastern Cape in the south. The Nguni languages are commonly divided into a northern and southern group: the northern languages include Zulu and Swazi, while the southern, or Cape, Nguni embrace those spoken by Xhosa, Thembu, Mpondo and Mpondomise.

Compared with the Sotho* languages, Nguni languages are distinguished by the number of clicking sounds, an indication of close interaction with Khoisan people over centuries. Extensive intermarriage between Nguni and Khoisan people is further suggested by physical appearance and the incorporation of Khoisan religious and medical ideas into Nguni culture. Nguni-speakers were mixed farmers, practising both agriculture and pastoralism; cattle ownership played a particularly important part in their economies. From the 15th and 16th centuries, chiefdoms were relatively autonomous, and communities within them were usually small in scale. Segmentation and secession from chiefdoms were conspicuous features of southern Nguni society; political unity seldom occurred.

NONGQAWUSE (1841–1898). Xhosa prophetess. As an adolescent in 1856, she reputedly had a vision of her ancestors in a pool of water advising the Xhosa to slaughter their cattle. This action would ensure the re-establishment of bonds with the supernatural world and the victory of the Xhosa over the evil forces currently afflicting them: colonial military supremacy, the alienation of their land, the breakdown of traditional custom, as well as the cattle lung-sickness of 1855–1856. Nongqawuse's guardian and uncle, Mhlakaza, was able to convince Sarili of the validity of the prophecy, and he ordered subordinate chiefs, as well as those living under colonial rule in British Kaffraria, to slaughter their cattle, with disastrous results. [J. Peires, *The Dead Will Arise* (Johannesburg, 1989)]

NORTHERN CAPE. New province created in 1994 out of what had been the Cape Province and parts of the Bophuthatswana* bantustan.

NORTHERN PROVINCE. New province created in April 1994 with the transition to democratic rule. Initially called Northern Transvaal, it changed its name in 1995. In the April 1994 election the African National Congress won a large majority in the provincial legislature, and Ngoako Ramathlodi became the first provincial premier. The inhabitants of Bushbuckridge protested that they did not wish to belong to the poorer Northern Province but instead to Mpumalanga*; an administrative compromise in 1997 ended the protest.

NORTH-WEST. Province created in April 1994 from what had previously been part of the Transvaal, the Cape and the bantustan of Bophuthatswana.* The town of Mmabatho/Mafeking,* later called Mafikeng, was chosen as its capital and Popo Molefe of the ANC became the first provincial premier. To the surprise of many, the province's white right-wingers did not use force, as they had threatened, to oppose the new order.

NTSIKANA (c.1760–1820). Xhosa* prophet, hymn-writer and mystic. Ntsikana was converted to Christianity* as a result of the preaching of Johannes van der Kemp* of the London Missionary Society.* He was an adviser to Ngqika,* and was tolerant of the presence of whites on the western borders of the Xhosa chiefdom. Ntsikana was greatly respected for his prophetic abilities and his skill as a composer of hymns.

NUCLEAR WEAPONS. In 1993 President De Klerk* made public the information that since the late 1970s, at a time when the government felt threatened by the Cuban presence in Angola* and the critical attitude of its Western allies, South Africa had, as many long suspected, been developing nuclear weapons. Six such weapons had been built. De Klerk announced that he had ended the programme, and the weapons had been destroyed. His announcement opened the way for South Africa to sign the Nuclear Non-Proliferation Treaty and win international credit for being the first country in the world to destroy its nuclear stockpile.

O

OIL SUPPLY. The oil-price hikes of 1973, consequent on the formation of OPEC (the Organization of Oil Exporting Countries), showed up South Africa's vulnerability and led to the expansion of the production of oil from coal, which had been started in 1955. Then in 1979 the apartheid regime suffered a severe blow when its close ally, the Shah of Iran, was overthrown, for Iranian oil had accounted for almost 90% of South African requirements, and the Khomeini regime immediately cut off supplies. Local production at SASOL (South African Coal, Oil and Gas Corporation) was again stepped up, but the main plant was damaged when limpet mines planted by Umkhonto weSizwe* operatives exploded in 1980. Large quantities of oil were bought to be stored, in mine shafts and in a giant underground storage facility built near Saldanha on the west coast. Because leading multinational oil companies continued to operate in South Africa, and oil could be bought on the spot market at relatively high prices, the regime was able in these ways to circumvent the United Nations embargo against the supply of oil to South Africa, but at vast cost. The search for oil offshore also absorbed great amounts of money, and no suitable finds were made, though a large gas field was discovered off Mossel Bay, and R12 billion was spent in the 1980s to exploit it, making the Mossgas project the largest of P.W. Botha's many white elephants. After the transition to democratic rule began in the 1990s, the selling-off of oil stocks brought in revenue for development. [A. Klinghoffer, *Oiling the Wheels of Apartheid* (Boulder, 1989); R. Hengeveld and J. Rodenburg, *Embargo* (Amsterdam, 1995)]

OORLAM (Malay, 'those who are clever'). Term widely used in the 19th century to refer to a range of mixed groups of Khoikhoi, Bastards and Afrikaners, renowned for their mastery of firearms and horses. Oorlam groups usually spoke or understood Dutch, as some of their members were born among the Dutch colonists in the Cape, with whom they maintained ties. They lived in the Cape interior, along the Orange River and northern frontier, and in Namibia, and they were often feared by indigenous groups for the terror they inflicted through their weaponry.

OPPENHEIMER, Ernest (1880–1957). Entrepreneur and founder of South Africa's largest multinational company, the Anglo American Corporation. Oppenheimer arrived in South Africa in 1902 as the representative of a London-based diamond company, and soon became involved in amalgamating various diamond interests in South Africa and South West Africa. In the depression of the 1930s, he exploited the diamond monopoly of De Beers to keep the diamond industry profitable, and then oversaw the opening up of new gold mines in the Orange Free State after World War II. [T. Gregory, *Ernest Oppenheimer and the Economic Development of Southern Africa* (Cape Town, 1962); E. Jessup, *Ernest Oppenheimer* (London, 1979)]

OPPENHEIMER, Harry (1908–). Son of Ernest Oppenheimer,* he succeeded his father as chairman of the Anglo American Corporation and De Beers Consolidated

Mines. He served as United Party member of parliament for Kimberley from 1948 until 1958, and was a founder member and substantial funder of the Progressive Party.* He retired as head of Anglo American in 1982 and as head of De Beers in 1984.

ORANGE FREE STATE. The territory between the Orange and Vaal rivers was named the Orange Free State in 1854, when the British formally recognized the independence of white farmers in the area in terms of the Bloemfontein Convention. The region had, however, been settled by Bantu-speakers for at least eight centuries prior to this, as the hundreds of stone ruins in the northern parts attest. At the beginning of the 19th century, Sotho-speakers lived across virtually the entire region. During the Mfecane* of the 1820s, the region experienced considerable turmoil, and two major states emerged on either side of the Caledon River valley: that of Moshoeshoe* east of the river and the Tlokoa state of Sekonyela (c.1804–1856) to the west. The two rivals clashed finally in 1853, and Moshoeshoe's forces forced most of Sekonyela's followers to flee south of the Orange.

White Voortrekkers* passed through the region during the 1830s, en route to the areas across the Vaal River and the Drakensberg; many returned to settle as farmers in the region after the British annexation of Natal* in 1843. Some began to infiltrate the land of the Griqua* around Philippolis in the south, provoking tension and the subsequent proclamation of British sovereignty in the area. The Orange River Sovereignty* lasted from 1848 until 1854, when the British recognized its independence. A republican constitution, partly modelled on that of the United States, was drawn up, granting the franchise only to white males who had registered for military service.

The Griqua in the south surrendered their land rights to whites in 1861, and moved across the Drakensberg. War broke out in 1858 in the east, as a result of rivalry between white farmers and the Sotho under Moshoeshoe for control of the fertile lands of the Caledon River valley. Conflict again began in 1865, as whites staked further claims in the region, but ended when Britain, fearing that the Orange Free State was seeking a route to the sea, annexed Basutoland* in 1868. In 1884, Thaba Nchu, the largest African settlement in the region, was incorporated into the Orange Free State, thereby finalizing white monopoly of land ownership. The census of 1890 revealed that 77,000 whites and 128,000 Africans resided in what was an overwhelmingly rural and agricultural society. About 15,000 white commercial farmers controlled the land. Blacks were prevented by law from acquiring land, and most entered sharecropping arrangements with white farmers, or became squatters and labourers.

Initially close economic ties with the Cape were forged, with wool as the main export. Orange Free State farmers were slow to respond to the growing demand for agricultural produce from the diamond fields* during the 1870s, partly because transportation was extremely undeveloped. Between 1880 and 1891, however, agricultural production doubled, much of it coming from the land in the east conquered from the Sotho. Orange Free State claims to the Kimberley diamond fields failed, but £90,000 was paid in compensation by the British. After the discovery of gold* on the Witwatersrand in 1886, the Orange Free State moved into the

Transvaal's orbit, weakening ties with the Cape. A growing feeling that Afrikaners should stand together against the British was boosted by the Jameson Raid,* after which the Free State entered an alliance with the Transvaal that took it into the South African War* in 1899. The war brought great conflict and devastation. The capital of Bloemfontein was occupied by the British army in March 1900, and the area became the Orange River Colony. It was incorporated as a province into the Union of South Africa in 1910, reverting to the name Orange Free State; Bloemfontein became the country's judicial capital.

The practice of sharecropping on farms spread rapidly after the South African War, with Africans commonly giving half their crops to white landowners in return for seed and use of the land. Sharecropping was increasingly attacked by white farmers who wished to commercialize, and who argued that the practice left them without adequate labour and undermined proper master–servant relations. After the passage of the Natives Land Act of 1913, many Africans were ejected from white-owned farms. Commercial maize farms in the north and north-east, in what became known as South Africa's 'maize triangle', formed the heart of the regional economy. After World War II, the opening of the goldfields brought much new wealth to the north of the province. The region was renamed the Free State after the democratic national elections of 1994, when a strong African National Congress-led provincial government under Patrick Lekota assumed control of the territory, now one of South Africa's nine provinces. [K. Schoeman, *Bibliography of the Orange Free State until 31 May 1910* (Cape Town, 1984); T. Keegan, *Rural Transformation in Industrializing South Africa* (Johannesburg, 1987); C. Murray, *Black Mountain* (Edinburgh, 1992)]

ORANGE RIVER. The longest of South Africa's rivers, it stretches some 1200 miles from its source in Lesotho to the Atlantic Ocean. It is also the least navigable major river, parts of it becoming a mere chain of pools in the dry winter months. It has nonetheless served as an important source of water for various peoples for at least 2000 years. It was known to the Nama and Korana,* who lived along its banks from early in the Christian era, as the Gariep (Great) River, and was named 'Orange River' by an employee of the Dutch East India Company in 1779 for the Dutch prince of the House of Orange. In the mid-20th century a vast scheme was undertaken to dam the Orange, and divert some of its waters to the eastern Cape.

Individual white trekboers began to cross the Orange from the 1760s, and they were followed by missionaries and traders. It became the northern boundary of the Cape in stages (1835, 1847). In 1868, war broke out along the middle Orange River between Korana pastoralists living in loosely organized bands and white farmers encroaching on their land from the south. Conflict again occurred in 1878–1879, during which white farmers supported by Cape mounted forces suppressed Korana resistance with great brutality. From 1880, with its annexation of Griqualand West, the Cape gained considerable territory north of the Orange, and extended its area of influence yet further when it annexed British Bechuanaland in 1895. As the result of an agreement with the Germans, the border with South West Africa ran along the northern bank of the river. [A. Smith, ed., *Einiqualand* (Cape Town, 1995)]

ORANGE RIVER SOVEREIGNTY (1848–1854). In February 1848, Sir Harry Smith,* Governor of the Cape and High Commissioner for South Africa, proclaimed British sovereignty over the land between the Orange River* and its major tributary, the Vaal River. Smith wished to create stability on the northern border of the Cape, where Griqua* and white farmers had clashed for some years. Frequent disputes between white farmers and the Sotho people under Moshoeshoe* in the region wearied the British, as did the administrative burden and expense of running the territory. In 1854 the Sovereignty was ended when Britain formally recognized the independence of the white colonists in terms of the Bloemfontein Convention.

ORDINANCE 50 (1828). Legislation promulgated by the Cape authorities which removed legal inequalities suffered by 'Hottentots and other free persons of colour'. It guaranteed the legal right of Khoisan people to own land, lifted restrictions on their freedom of movement by removing the requirement that they carry passes, and stressed the need for employers to give service contracts to their labourers.

Its origins lie in part in pressure from humanitarians such as John Philip,* who used his influence with prominent British politicians to achieve the extension of legal equality between Khoisan and whites. For their part Cape officials wished to create a freer labour market and foster the emergence of a Khoisan or Coloured elite. Apart from the establishment of the Kat River Settlement,* however, virtually nothing was done to enable Coloured people to escape their inferior and servile position. Though Ordinance 50 had little effect on master–servant relations, particularly in the frontier districts where distances rendered the legislation ineffective, white farmers in general felt that the Ordinance removed controls over vagrancy, and it was thus a source of considerable grievance against the British and Cape authorities during the 1830s. [T. Keegan, *Colonial South Africa and the Origins of the Racial Order* (Cape Town, 1996)]

OSSEWA-BRANDWAG (Afrikaans, 'oxwagon-sentinel'). What was originally a cultural organization became, in the early years of World War II, a paramilitary body propagating national socialist ideas. It embarked on sabotage against the war effort, but D.F. Malan,* leader of the Purified National Party, was able to prevent it from dominating or splitting the Afrikaner nationalist movement. [P. Furlong, *Between Crown and Swastika* (Johannesburg, 1991)]

P

PACT GOVERNMENT (1924–1933). In the 1924 election campaign, J.B.M. Hertzog,* leader of the National Party, entered a pact with the white Labour Party, and once the election was won, the two parties formed a coalition government. The pact gradually fell apart, and was finally destroyed by the Depression and Hertzog's decision to remain on the gold standard.

PAN AFRICANIST CONGRESS OF AZANIA (PAC). In the 1940s a small group of men within the African National Congress (ANC) began calling themselves Africanists. Led by Anton Lembede* until his death in 1947, this group included Robert Mangaliso Sobukwe,* Potlako Leballo, A.P. Mda and others who became increasingly unhappy with ANC policy in the 1950s. They opposed the multi-racialism of the Congress Alliance,* fearing that leadership of the struggle for liberation would be taken over by white and Indian communists, and they rejected the Freedom Charter, particularly those sections which guaranteed minority interests, as well as its declaration that South Africa belongs to all who live in it, black and white. They believed in the slogan 'Africa for the Africans', and although their definition of Africans could include whites, they saw most whites as settlers without valid claim to the land they owned.

The Africanists believed that the fostering of a racially assertive nationalism was necessary in order to mobilize the masses, and advocated a militant strategy of mass action, involving boycotts, strikes, civil disobedience and non-cooperation, and taking advantage of opportunities presented by popular protests. They identified their struggle for freedom with that of blacks throughout the African continent, spoke of seeking a United States of Africa, and were inspired by the socialist, anti-imperialist leadership of Kwame Nkrumah of Ghana and Tom Mboya of Kenya. In 1958 they broke away from the ANC and in April the following year they formally established the PAC. Sobukwe, the leading theoretician among them and a lecturer at the University of the Witwatersrand, was elected its president. The new organization stood for government of the country by Africans for Africans, and the establishment of an Africanist social democracy.

One of the PAC's first acts was organizing the anti-pass law campaign of March 1960. Within hours of the launch of the campaign, the Sharpeville massacre* occurred. The PAC was then banned on 8 April 1960. Some of its members formed Poqo (meaning 'pure') to promote change by violence, but harsh repression and lack of leadership brought the organization to the brink of disintegration by the end of the 1960s. Internecine rivalries continued among the exiled leadership, based at Dar es Salaam in Tanzania. In the mid-1960s the PAC absorbed members of the Coloured People's Congress who rejected the ANC's approach as reformist. For a time, the controversial Potlako Leballo, who had taken over the leadership when Sobukwe was jailed, hoped to wage an armed struggle from Lesotho, and he worked closely with the Lesotho Liberation Army. He was effectively sidelined at a conference in Arusha in 1978, and a rival, David Sibeko, was shot by members of the PAC's armed wing, the Azanian People's Liberation Army (APLA), in Dar es Salaam. John Pokela then became leader, but proved weak and ineffective. The PAC in exile failed to win the international support given to the ANC, and APLA achieved little before the 1990s.

When unbanned in February 1990, the PAC continued to refuse to suspend its armed struggle. In 1993 APLA conducted a number of terrorist attacks aimed at white civilians. Members of a church congregation were fired upon in Kenilworth in Cape Town, and shots were fired into a pub in the Cape Town suburb of Observatory. Though the party finally decided to participate in the democratic election of April 1994, many of its members did not support that decision and in the election it received only 1.8% of the total vote. At the end of 1996, the lacklustre Clarence Makwetu, whose support came mainly from the Eastern Cape, was replaced as leader by the former head of the Methodist Church, Stanley Mogoba, and it seemed possible that the PAC might revive itself. In 1997 one of its parliamentarians, Patricia de Lille, read out a list of ANC leaders who the PAC claimed had worked for the apartheid regime as spies. [G. Gerhart, *Black Power* (Berkeley, 1979); B. Pogrund, *Sobukwe and Apartheid* (Johannesburg, 1990)]

PASS LAWS. Laws designed to control the movement of blacks; these achieved special notoriety during the apartheid era. Their origins lay in the early 18th-century Cape: slaves were required to carry passes from 1709. Such a requirement was extended to Khoikhoi labourers by the end of the century, tying them to the farms. These early provisions were consolidated by the new British administration in 1809, but the Khoikhoi were freed from them by Ordinance 50* of 1828. From the mid-19th century Africans entering the Cape Colony from the east were required to carry passes.

With the growth of the country's first industrial centre at Kimberley in the 1870s, a more rigid pass system was introduced by a Griqualand West proclamation of 1872. Though it made no direct mention of race, this served both to control the flow of African labour to the diamond fields and to regiment the African workers there. In 1895 the Transvaal enacted similar, more overtly racial legislation: Africans were liable for arrest and imprisonment if they failed to carry passes indicating their employment or authorizing them to seek employment. Pass laws were also used to try to stem the high rate of desertion among African workers on the gold mines (in 1910, 15% of all workers deserted). Shortly after Union,* the Native Labour Regulation Act of 1911 required all male African workers, including foreigners, to carry passes. The pass system helped to keep labour cheap by directing labour where employers required it.

In 1952, the most comprehensive legislation yet was enacted: all Africans over the age of 16 were compelled to produce a pass (renamed a reference book) on request by any member of the police or any administrative official at any time. The pass carried personal data and details of employment. Parallel to the main police force and law courts, a special police and court system emerged to enforce the pass laws. Persons appearing before these courts, which came to be known as commissioners' courts, were deemed guilty until they proved their innocence; the vast majority of cases under the pass laws were undefended, and were often dealt with at over thirty cases per hour. About 500,000 Africans were arrested each year during the 1960s and 1970s, and in the early 1980s many of these, instead of being tried and imprisoned, were deported to 'independent' bantustans, in terms of an Act of 1972 allowing for the summary deportation of foreigners. But by the early 1980s, attempts to enforce the pass laws and control the urbanization of Africans were collapsing and in 1986 the government repealed the pass laws. By then an estimated 15–20 million people had been arrested, fined, imprisoned or deported in terms of these laws since the beginning of the century. For protest against the pass laws see ANTI-PASS CAMPAIGNS. [D. Hindson, *Pass Controls and the Urban African Proletariat in South Africa* (Johannesburg, 1987); I. Evans, *Bureaucracy and Race* (Berkeley, 1997)]

PEDI. In the mid-17th century, a Kgatla group called the Pedi moved from the region around modern Pretoria to the Steelpoort River valley, where they gained control of trade routes running from the interior to the Mozambique coast, and established their supremacy over other Sotho-speakers in the area. By the beginning of the 19th century, they had built up considerable power under Thulare (*c.*1780–1820). Pedi power was severely disrupted during the Mfecane,* as well as by internal succession disputes. Their influence was stabilized under Sekwati (*c.*1780–1861), who attracted refugees to a new capital called Phiring, situated in a good defensive position between the Steelpoort and Olifants rivers. Sekwati managed to forge friendly ties with the Zulu,* but relations with the Swazi remained tense. During the 1840s and 1850s, he also had to deal with hostile Voortrekkers* who were encroaching on his territory; their capital at Lydenburg was later subsumed within the South African Republic.* Sekwati's successor, Sekhukhune, initially consolidated the power of the Pedi, but years of drought and a series of attacks from the South African Republic and the Swazi chiefdom weakened the Pedi during the 1870s. In 1879, the British broke Pedi power and ended their independence; the Transvaal government then expropriated much of their land and forced many to work as apprentices on white-owned farms.

In the 1950s a Pedi migrant workers' organsation (Sebatakgomo) tried to oust chiefs, headmen and others who accepted Bantu authorities and rural betterment programmes. In 1958 a major protest took place in Sekhukhuneland in which those who sought to defend the chieftainship were challenged by the new forces. Conflict broke out again in 1986 in what had by then become the bantustan of Lebowa. Members of the United Democratic Front and the underground African National Congress were involved in this youth revolt. [P. Delius, *The Land Belongs to Us* (Johannesburg, 1983) and *Lion Among the Cattle* (Johannesburg, 1997)]

PHILIP, John (1777–1851). Congregational minister from Aberdeen, Scotland, who arrived at the Cape in 1819, and became the influential superintendent of the London Missionary Society (LMS)* until his resignation in 1849. He consolidated and expanded the work of the LMS, and campaigned for full legal equality for the colonial Khoikhoi. A vigorous polemicist, he published his *Researches in South Africa* in 1828 in England, having returned there to use his influence to lobby British politicians and philanthropists. His lobbying resulted in the recommendation of the

House of Commons that free people of colour should enjoy equal status with whites, and the subsequent passage of Ordinance 50* at the Cape. Philip was also responsible for preventing the implementation of a draft vagrancy law at the Cape in 1834, which would have reimposed many former restrictions on the Khoikhoi. During the 1830s and 1840s, he worked hard to persuade the Cape government to develop a new approach to the frontier through a system of treaties with African and Griqua leaders. He approved the extension of British authority, but envisaged that Christianized Coloureds and Africans, retaining possession of their land, would live harmoniously with the British on both sides of the colonial borders.

Philip's campaigns and writings alienated white settlers, who demonised him as an 'interfering cleric'. Much historical writing, particularly in the settler and Afrikaner traditions, similarly vilified him, but two classic books by the historian W.M. Macmillan in the 1920s, based on Philip's papers, confirmed his stature. [A. Ross, *John Philip* (Aberdeen, 1986)]

PIETERMARITZBURG. Named after the Voortrekker* leaders Piet Retief* and Gerrit Maritz, it was founded in 1838 as the capital and seat of government of the Boer Republic of Natalia. In the decade after the British annexation in 1843, the immigration of English-speakers was encouraged, and a significant proportion of them settled in Pietermaritzburg, which became capital of the crown colony of Natal* in 1856. It enjoyed considerable commercial prosperity in the 19th century because of its geographical situation between the interior of southern Africa and the coastal port of Durban.* Its economic importance declined markedly in relation to that of Durban during the 20th century, but it remained the provincial capital and seat of the Natal division of the Supreme Court. From 1994 it was capital of KwaZulu-Natal, one of South Africa's nine provinces in the new democratic dispensation. [J. Laband and R. Haswell, *Pietermaritzburg* (Pietermaritzburg, 1988)]

PLAATJE, Solomon Tshekisho (1876–1932). Linguist, writer, journalist and politician. Despite a lack of formal education, he mastered eight languages, worked as an interpreter and magistrate's clerk in Mafeking* during the South African War,* and subsequently became editor of three newspapers, including the English–Tswana *Bechuana Gazette*. He was a founder of the South African Native National Congress (later the African National Congress), and served as its first general secretary. He spent several years campaigning against the Natives Land Act of 1913, and his closely researched and powerful attack on the Act, *Native Life in South Africa*, was published in 1916. His novel *Mhudi*, written in about 1917, also dealt with dispossession; when it appeared in 1930 it was the first novel in English to be published by a black South African. [B. Willan, *Sol. T. Plaatje* (London, 1984)]

POLICE. The South African Police (SAP) was formed in 1913 out of various colonial and city police forces which had existed prior to Union. The colonial police model, in which policing was centralized under state control in order to maintain the authority of the government and police were regularly called upon to exercise paramilitary duties, heavily influenced the structure and organization of the SAP. Another force, the South African Mounted Rifles, was simultaneously established alongside the SAP; although intended as a regular military force, its duties in peacetime chiefly comprised policing among blacks in the rural areas. This body was disbanded in 1920, and its members and areas of concern were incorporated into the SAP.

Throughout the 20th century, and particularly during the years of apartheid, the SAP portrayed itself as an independent servant of the law, whose duties involved the maintenance of law and order, the protection of life and property, and the investigation and prevention of crime. The police motto, 'Servamus et servimus' ('We protect and we serve'), was central to the creation of an official image of a civil police force above political manipulation and control. In reality, however, the political, legal and social circumstances of South Africa ensured that the SAP played a central role in the maintenance of white political power. Its regulation of the edifice of segregationist and apartheid laws undermined the public image of the SAP as an apolitical non-partisan body; rather, it was a key institution of the state which operated to maintain state authority. Given the nature of police activities during the 1970s and 1980s, it is not surprising that critics of apartheid referred with increasing frequency to South Africa as a 'police state'.

The SAP consisted of almost 6000 members in 1913, just under half of whom were black; in 1972, it totalled just over 32,000 people, with the same proportion of black recruits. There were only 20 black commissioned officers out of almost 1800 in 1972, the year in which women were first recruited into the SAP. The ratio of police per thousand head of population barely changed between 1913 and the mid-1970s; it was only after the Soweto uprising* of 1976 that the SAP's ranks were significantly boosted, as the state was obliged to rely more heavily on the SAP to enforce social control. The SAP nonetheless experienced considerable difficulty in countering opposition to the state and, despite ever-greater allocations in the national budget, remained under-resourced and unsophisticated, to the extent that in 1984 the state was obliged to begin using the South African Defence Force and citizen reserve forces to police the townships and counter mass opposition to apartheid.

Despite criticisms of the SAP for its inefficiency, some sections operated with considerable effectiveness. Most notable was the Special Branch, established in 1960 to counter sabotage and other activities subversive of the state. The security police were granted greatly enhanced powers by B.J. Vorster,* Minister of Justice in the early 1960s, and gained notoriety because of their pursuit and torture of opponents of apartheid. The underground South African Communist Party* was infiltrated, and in the 1970s Craig Williamson, a police spy who had been a student leader at the University of the Witwatersrand, became assistant director of the International University Exchange Fund in Geneva, where he gathered information on anti-apartheid activities. From 1963 to the early 1980s a number of political activists, held under detention-without-trial provisions, died while in police custody. In the mid-1980s some members of the security police abducted and assassinated anti-apartheid activists.

In 1969 the government created a Bureau of State Security, popularly known as BOSS even after the name was changed to the National Intelligence Service. It gathered intelligence and undertook covert operations, the budget for which was greatly increased in the mid-1970s. It clashed with the Military Intelligence section of the South African Defence Force on a number of occasions in the 1970s, but until the uncovering of the Information scandal* revealed something of BOSS's role and power, Military Intelligence was subordinated to it.

Widely despised and enormously controversial as the SAP was for its role during the 1970s and 1980s, its reform posed difficult problems during the period of transformation in the 1990s. Steps were taken in 1995 and 1996 to demilitarize the SAP, with military ranks, for example, being replaced by civilian ones. More intractable problems involved the racial composition of the force (mainly in regard to the lack of senior black appointments), the allocation of resources, the provision of adequate training, and the boosting of police morale, as well as widespread public perceptions of the inefficiency and inability of the SAP to cope with mainstream policing tasks such as the combating of crime. [G. Cawthra, *Policing South Africa* (Cape Town, 1993); J. Brewer, *Black and Blue* (Oxford, 1994); J. Pauw, *In the Heart of the Whore* (Halfway House, 1991)]

POLITICAL VIOLENCE. Political violence has taken many forms in South African history, but in the early 1990s politically related violence reached new proportions. Unlike the Soweto and township revolts of 1976–1977 and 1984–1987, the violence of the late 1980s and early 1990s was more random and sporadic, involving the occasional massacre, attacks on commuters in trains, and a large number of individual shootings and murders. Beginning in Natal, where it became a kind of low-intensity civil war between United Democratic Front and Inkatha supporters, this violence moved to the Witwatersrand in mid-1990. In each year in the early 1990s, on average almost 2000 people were killed, though such statistics must be viewed with caution.

There was no doubt that criminal elements participated in the violence, and some of what was called political violence was the product of an environment in which law and order had broken down and the African National Congress had called for the townships to be made 'ungovernable'. In Natal especially, local warlords sought to retain control of their areas, and one instance of violence often provoked another, producing a cycle of violence. But much of the violence was also deliberately fomented by members of the security forces. In the early 1990s it flared up when negotiations reached sensitive phases, and was clearly designed to throw those negotiations off track. Details of who was responsible emerged slowly. In 1989 Dirk Coetzee, former head of the police's Vlakplaas base outside Pretoria, told the newspaper *Vrye Weekblad* of assassinations and other 'dirty tricks' carried out by the police in the 1980s. A commission headed by Judge Louis Harms heard disclosures about the activities of the Civil Co-Operation Bureau in 1990, and the Commission of Enquiry Regarding the Prevention of Public Violence and Intimidation (the Goldstone Commission) uncovered evidence for covert operations conducted by a body linked to Military Intelligence. In 1996 General Magnus Malan, the former Minister of Defence, and others went on trial for the training of an Inkatha hit-squad, but they were acquitted. It was the Truth and Reconciliation Commission which did most to uncover information concerning some of the killings in the period to 1994. After the April 1994 election, political violence subsided except in KwaZulu-Natal,* where it continued at a high level for another eighteen months.

PONDOLAND REVOLT (1960–1961). Perhaps the most important of a series of rural revolts that occurred in the late 1950s and early 1960s The Xhosa people of Pondoland resented the interference of the state in their affairs, and an anti-dipping rebellion culminated in a revolt, during which the police opened fire on protesters at Ngquza Hill. The government declared a state of emergency through Proclamation 400, and as a result thousands of men and women went to jail for indefinite periods. About twenty people from Eastern Pondoland were sentenced to death for the role they played during the revolt.

PORT ELIZABETH. Coastal city in the eastern Cape, founded in 1820, and named after the wife of Sir Rufane Donkin, then Acting Governor of the Cape. The place where the British settlers of 1820 landed, it developed as the major port in the eastern Cape, second only to Cape Town in size, and the chief outlet for the export of wool. During the 20th century, it became an important industrial and commercial centre, a major base for South Africa's automobile industry, but with the collapse of this industry unemployment soared in the city. [J. Kirk, *Making a Voice* (Boulder, 1998); J. Robinson, *The Power of Apartheid* (London, 1997)]

POTCHEFSTROOM. Founded in 1838 by the Voortrekker leader Andries Pretorius, it was the capital of the Transvaal until 1860, when it was superseded as the centre of government by the newly founded and more centrally situated Pretoria. It then remained an important educational and ecclesiastical centre for Afrikaners. It is today situated in the North-West Province.

PRESS. In the first decades of the 19th century, the only regular publication at the Cape was the *Cape Town Gazette and African Advertiser*. The first newspaper, the *South African Commercial Advertiser*, appeared in 1824, but was closed by Governor Somerset. It resumed publication in 1828 with the promise of freedom to publish subject only to the law of libel. Thereafter, a number of English and Dutch newspapers appeared, including the bilingual *De Zuid–Afrikaan* (1830) based in Cape Town and the *Graham's Town Journal* (1831) in the eastern Cape.

Many leading English-language newspapers were established in the second half of the 19th century. The formation of the Argus Printing and Publishing Company in 1866 began the era of managerial newspapers. The two leading newspapers in the Argus stable were the *Cape Argus* (first published in 1857) and the *Star* (1889) in Johannesburg. The *Rand Daily Mail* (1902) and the *Sunday Times* (1906), both Johannesburg-based, became part of the South African Associated Newspapers (SAAN) group in 1955. Other important newspapers established towards the end of the 19th century were the country's first daily, the *Cape Times* (1876), and the *Natal Witness* (1881). The first Afrikaans-language newspaper, *Die Patriot* (1876), aimed to promote nascent Afrikaner culture and the Afrikaans language. In 1915, Nasionale Pers was established, and began to publish the Cape Town-based *De Burger*, a mouthpiece of the National Party; the first editor was D.F. Malan. The

National Party later acquired another voice in the Transvaal, in the form of *Die Transvaler* (1937), edited by H.F. Verwoerd.

The first journals aimed at a black readership emerged from the missions of the eastern Cape in the mid-19th century, and appeared in both English and Xhosa. An independent black-controlled press began with the establishment in King William's Town in 1884 of *Imvo Zabantsundu* ('Opinions of the People'),* under the editorship of J.T. Jabavu. Another prominent newspaper was *Ilanga lase Natal* (1903), founded by J.L. Dube. *Indian Opinion* (1903), a weekly founded by Mohandas Gandhi in 1903 to serve an Indian readership, remained financially independent, but most of the black press was taken over from the 1920s by white business interests, who were attracted by the market it served, as well as by some concern about the potential consequences of independent black journalism.

During the apartheid era, newspapers and magazines had to cope with increasing numbers of laws affecting press freedom. The most prominent newspaper to cease publication in the 1950s was *the Guardian*, an organ of the Communist Party, which was first banned in 1950, but emerged sporadically under different names until 1963. The *World*, a newspaper which had over 150,000 black readers, was banned in 1977, and the *Post*, which took its place, was closed in 1981. By this time, over a hundred laws and regulations restricted press freedom, particularly in the reporting of matters concerning the military, the police, the prisons, black politics (particularly exile politics) and issues affecting 'national security'. Some English-speaking newspapers, of which the *Rand Daily Mail* was the most prominent, were outspoken critics of government policy, but the closure of this newspaper by the management of SAAN in 1985, on the grounds that it was no longer commercially viable, provoked considerable controversy, and its owners stood accused of capitulating to government pressure and fears about the consequences of editorial independence. An independent newspaper, the *Weekly Mail* (1985), founded by ex-*Rand Daily Mail* journalists, managed to survive as the flagship publication of an embattled alternative press during the late 1980s. Many of the draconian laws governing freedom of the press were withdrawn or were disregarded by the authorities after 1990. Faced with increasing competition from other media, the press underwent major changes, with the Argus Group becoming Independent Newspaper Holdings, and the SAAN group Times Media Ltd. [E. Potter, *The Press as Opposition* (London, 1975); L. Switzer, ed., *South Africa's Alternative Press* (New York, 1997)]

PRETORIA. Now in Gauteng province,* Pretoria was founded in 1855 by Marthinus Pretorius, son of the Voortrekker leader Andries Pretorius, after whom it is named. It became the capital of the Transvaal in 1860, and the administrative capital of the Union of South Africa in 1910. As headquarters of numerous government departments and South Africa's civil service, it became the political heart of the country, although from 1910 the national parliament sat in Cape Town. After 1948, when the government fell under the control of Afrikaner nationalists,* the term 'Pretoria' became synonymous with the South African government and apartheid, but it was here, on 10 May 1994, at the Union Buildings, that Nelson Mandela was sworn in as South Africa's first democratic President.

PRETORIA MINUTE (6 August 1990). This agreement between the government and the African National Congress (ANC) stated: 'In the interest of moving as speedily as possible towards a negotiated political settlement and in the context of the agreement reached, the ANC announced that it was now suspending all armed actions with immediate effect. As a result of this, no further armed actions and related activities by the ANC and its military wing Umkhonto weSizwe (MK) will take place.' This major concession by the ANC did not win any major immediate reward, but was an essential preliminary to formal negotiations. The ANC subsequently made it clear that MK had not disbanded, and refused to disclose the whereabouts of its arms caches.

PRINGLE, Thomas (1789–1834). Scottish-born librarian, journalist and poet who settled in Cape Town in 1820. He published and edited the *South African Journal* and the *South African Commercial Advertiser* during the 1820s, and clashed with Governor Somerset over issues relating to freedom of the fledgling Cape press. He is also recognized for his poetry, in particular his *African Sketches* (1834).

PROGRESSIVE PARTY. In 1959 eleven liberal MPs from the United Party (UP) broke with that party over its refusal to challenge more effectively the apartheid policies of the National Party government. They then established the Progressive Party. Though it rejected all forms of racial discrimination, it decided in 1968, in the face of new legislation barring mixed-race political parties, to carry on as a whites-only party, effectively ditching its few black members. Initially, like the Liberal Party before it, it advocated a qualified franchise, on the recommendation of a commission under the chairmanship of a lawyer and former MP, Donald Molteno (1908–1972).

Helen Suzman (1917–), a doughty fighter for human rights, was for thirteen years the only Progressive member of parliament. From 1974 its parliamentary strength began to grow, helped by the disintegration of the UP. In 1975 it amalgamated with the small Reform Party, and after it was joined by a further breakaway from the UP, it was renamed the Progressive Federal Party (PFP). After the general election of 1977 it became the official parliamentary opposition. Under the influence of the charismatic Frederik van Zyl Slabbert (1942–), a former Professor of Sociology at the University of Stellenbosch, who was returned for the Rondebosch constituency in 1974, it adopted universal suffrage as its policy and in 1979 Slabbert took over as leader. In February 1986, however, angered by the refusal of P.W. Botha to give ground, Slabbert suddenly announced that he was leaving the tricameral parliament, because he had come to realise it was incapable of fundamental change. The loss of Slabbert and Alex Boraine (1931–) weakened the party, which in 1987 lost its position as official opposition to the right-wing Conservative Party. Early in 1989 the PFP merged with other parties to the left of the government to form the Democratic Party. [H. Suzman, *In No Uncertain Terms* (Johannesburg, 1993); J. Strangeways-Booth, *A Cricket in the Thorn Tree* (Johannesburg, 1976); R. Swart, *Progressive Odyssey* (Cape Town, 1991)]

q

QWAQWA (formerly Witzieshoek). A bantustan created in 1974 for the southern Sotho from a reserve in the Orange Free State which had originally been granted by President Brand* to a southern Sotho group headed by a relative of Moshoeshoe.* It bordered Lesotho. As squatters were evicted in the Orange Free State with the implementation of the Natives Land Act, the population increased, but the land was mountainous and barren, and most men had to work as migrants. Discontent grew until in early 1950 a series of skirmishes, later called a 'rebellion', took place. The reserve housed 20,000 people in 1960, but there were 300,000 in the bantustan by 1980 and well over a million by 1990, as those classified Sotho were forcibly relocated there. Most lived in the capital, Phuthaditjhaba, and their main income was the remittances of migrant labourers working on the Witwatersrand or in the Free State. From April 1994 the area again fell under the Free State administration.

RACIAL INEQUALITY. South Africa remained throughout the 20th century one of the most unequal societies on earth. In 1995, the poorest 40% of households earned less than 6% of total income, while the richest 10% earned more than half the total income. This inequality was largely related to race. Africans made up 76% of the population, but the African share of income amounted to only 29% of the total. Whites, who made up less than 13% of the population, received 58.5% of total income. Per capita, whites earned 9.5 times the income of blacks and lived, on average, 11.5 years longer. In 1992, the average monthly income per head was R1572 for whites, R523 for Indians, R325 for Coloureds, and R165 for Africans.

By the 1950s white poverty had largely been eliminated, and only in the 1990s did it again emerge as a noticeable phenomenon. In the 1990s, the gap between white and black narrowed, but the gap between a new black elite and the African poor widened. Though class became more important than race, the threat of race conflict remained because of the close correlation between race and class.

RACIAL SEGREGATION. While some historians trace the origins of racial segregation to the first white settlers, others have highlighted the importance of ideas that came from Britain in the 19th century, or have pointed to Shepstone* in Natal as the first to put segregationist policies into practice. Most scholars now agree that an ideology of racial separation did not develop until the early 20th century, that a full-scale set of segregationist policies was not implemented until after Union,* and that apartheid was a more developed and comprehensively applied form of the racial segregation already in place before 1948. [G. Fredrickson, *White Supremacy* (New York, 1981); J. Cell, *The Highest Stage of White Supremacy* (Cambridge, 1982); S. Dubow, *Racial Segregation and the Origins of Apartheid* (London, 1989); W. Beinart and S. Dubow, eds., *Segregation and Apartheid* (London, 1985)]

RACISM. The Europeans who settled at the Cape in the 17th century, like those who went to other parts of the world, looked down upon the indigenous people as inferior, heathen and 'barbarous'. Scholars have suggested that because the Dutch, and the British settlers who followed them, came from a Protestant, bourgeois and northern European background, they were more racially prejudiced than southern Europeans would have been. At the Cape the Dutch found people – Khokhoi and San – whom they regarded as among the lowest forms of human life, and sometimes as not truly human at all. Though cohabitation between whites and people of colour frequently took place in the Dutch period, there were few mixed marriages, and the offspring of mixed unions joined the 'non-white' groups. Racial prejudice imported from Europe was reinforced by the system of racially based slavery at the Cape and by the conflict between white and black on the eastern frontier. The weight which some writers once attached to the Calvinism of the Dutch as a cause of racism can be discounted.

Though racially prejudiced, the early white settlers did not develop a systematic racial ideology. This emerged as the social order was challenged by the ideas of British humanitarians in the early 19th century. Racism was then used to justify dispossession of blacks, and their subordination and oppression. With the creation of an industrial society, first at Kimberley and then on the Rand, a vast array of discriminatory measures came into being to provide a cheap African labour force, and these were buttressed by a racist ideology. In the 20th century racism was perhaps most blatantly expressed by those whites who were threatened by African competition for jobs in the urban areas.

By the late 1970s Afrikaner leaders had to some extent dropped their ideological commitment to racial discrimination, because the co-optation of some blacks (especially Coloureds and Indians) was seen as necessary for the continued maintenance of white supremacy. Conservative Afrikaners, and perhaps a majority of the white electorate, remained firmly committed to racist beliefs. With the collapse of apartheid and the transition to democracy blatant white racism largely went underground, and the extent to which racist beliefs and practices continued became more difficult to assess. It did seem, however, that the advent of African majority rule made anti-African racism in the Coloured community, especially in the Western Cape, more overt. [T. Keegan, *Colonial South Africa and the Origins of the Racial Order* (Cape Town, 1996); N. Worden, *The Making of Modern South Africa* (Oxford, 1994); S. Dubow, *Illicit Union* (Johannesburg, 1995)]

RAILWAYS. Construction of the country's first railway, which linked Cape Town to Stellenbosch and Wellington, began in 1859, and in 1860 a line of two miles was opened in Durban. After 1870, with the growth of Kimberley,* major construction began. Because of the distance from the coast to the diamond fields, and the absence of intermediate traffic, the new lines were state ventures. Competition between the coastal towns for the interior trade led to the building of separate lines from Cape Town, Port Elizabeth and East London to the diamond fields. After the discovery of gold in the Transvaal in 1886, both the Cape and Natal extended their lines to the Witwatersrand. The link with the Cape was completed in 1892, that with Natal in 1895. The Transvaal government was keen to develop a rail link with the non-British port of Delagoa Bay, and although the Netherlands–South African Railway Company responsible for construction experienced financial difficulties, the line was completed in 1894. In the same year, a line from the Cape which bypassed the Transvaal and headed for Central Africa through Bechuanaland had reached Mafeking. By the end of the century, a considerable portion of the country's present rail network had been completed.

After the South African War,* a single central South African Railways was established (1903); this underpinned the political union of the country in 1910, and provided an essential infrastructure for the later development of manufacturing industry. [O. Nock, *Railways of Southern Africa* (London, 1971)]

RAMAPHOSA, Cyril (1953–). A Black Consciousness* supporter in the 1970s, and a lawyer by training, he was imprisoned a number of times, and on one occasion spent seventeen months in solitary confinement. In 1982 he became the first general secretary of the National Union of Mineworkers. He took the union into the charterist Congress of South African Trade Unions* in 1985, and called his members out on strike in 1985 and 1987. In the union, he learnt how to cut a deal, which was useful when in the early 1990s, following his election as secretary general of the African National Congress (ANC) in July 1991, he became the ANC's chief negotiator at the Convention for a Democratic South Africa* and then the Multi-Party Negotiating Forum.* He and Roelf Meyer,* who became the chief negotiator for the National Party (NP) in 1992, established a bond of trust, which began, it is said, when the two men were trout fishing in August 1991 and Ramaphosa removed a fishhook embedded in Meyer's finger. He and Meyer met over forty times between June and September 1992 in an effort to get their parties talking again when negotiations threatened to break down. He remained the chief ANC negotiator until the agreement on the interim constitution was reached in November 1993, and then became head of the Constitutional Assembly* in 1994, and continued in that post until the successful completion of the final constitution. In 1997 he moved into the business world, taking a top post in the leading black empowerment consortium, New Africa Investments. [P. Waldmeir, *Anatomy of a Miracle* (London, 1997)]

RAMPHELE, Mamphela (1947–). While training as a medical doctor at the University of Natal, she worked closely with Steve Biko.* She later bore his son after he was murdered by the security police. One of the first Black Consciousness* activists to be detained, she was banished to a remote part of the northern Transvaal, where she started the Ithuseng health clinic. After her banning order was lifted, she moved to Cape Town, first to help with the Carnegie enquiry into the roots of poverty (she became co-author, with Francis Wilson, of the final report, entitled *Uprooting Poverty* (Cape Town, 1989)), and then as a researcher at the University of Cape Town. There she gained a doctorate in anthropology and was appointed a Deputy Vice-Chancellor. In 1995 she was elected the university's Vice-Chancellor. [M. Ramphele, *Mamphela Ramphele: A Life* (Cape Town, 1995)]

RANDLORDS. Men of diverse class and national origins who made fortunes from their control of the gold mines of the Witwatersrand. By the mid-1890s, some of them believed that their collective interests were being thwarted by the Transvaal government. They resented its failure to provide an adequate and stable labour force, as well as its monopolistic control of dynamite, its concessions to the Netherlands–South African Railway Company, and its sales of liquor to African labourers.

Writing in 1900, J.A. Hobson blamed the Randlords for both the Jameson Raid* and the South African War.* But while many Randlords aligned themselves with British imperial objectives, some supported Kruger,* and most did not want the mines disrupted by conflict. The view that the Randlords determined British policy and exerted major influence on Sir Alfred Milner* between 1895 and 1899 is now discredited. That the interests of the Randlords came largely to coincide with those of British imperial policy-makers did not mean that the mining magnates were able to dictate imperial policy. [G. Wheatcroft, *The Randlords* (Johannesburg, 1986); I. Smith, *The Origins of the South African War* (London, 1996); M. Fraser and

A. Jeeves, eds., *All That Glittered* (Cape Town, 1977)]

RAND REVOLT (1922). A rebellion of white miners and others against the government of Jan Smuts.* It began as a strike on the coal and gold mines, at a time of depression, against the relaxation of the job colour bar that would have given jobs to blacks instead of whites. The strike escalated into a large-scale uprising, and Smuts used the full might of the state to suppress it. About 200 people were killed. The brutal way in which the revolt was put down was a factor in Smuts's defeat in the 1924 election. [F.R. Johnstone, *Race, Class and Gold* (London, 1976); D. Yudelman, *The Emergence of Modern South Africa* (Cape Town, 1983)]

RECONSTRUCTION AND DEVELOPMENT PROGRAMME (RDP). The major policy initiative of the Government of National Unity created in 1994, the RDP emerged from discussion documents put together by the Congress of South African Trade Unions.* The African National Congress then advocated such a programme as part of its election manifesto for the April 1994 election. Accepted by all parties in parliament in 1994, the RDP was an integrated, socio-economic plan to meet basic needs and develop potential, and a vision for the fundamental restructuring of society. A separate ministry was set up under Jay Naidoo, and in the first year free health care was provided for children and pregnant mothers and school meals at primary schools, while electrification and provision of water advanced rapidly. Major delivery problems were soon experienced, and there was much criticism of unnecessary bureaucracy. In 1996 Naidoo's separate ministry was done away with, and responsibility for co-ordinating RDP spending shifted to Deputy President Mbeki's office. This went with a new recognition of the importance of economic growth for the achievement of the RDP's goals. The government's Growth and Employment policy (GEAR), with its emphasis on fiscal discipline as a way to promote foreign investment, then became the main focus of government rather than the RDP itself.

RECORD OF UNDERSTANDING (26 September 1992). Perhaps the most important single turning-point in the transition period after 1990, this agreement between the De Klerk government and the African National Congress (ANC) followed the Bisho massacre* and enabled negotiations to be resumed. One of the pre-conditions which the ANC set for such an agreement was the release of political prisoners, including three who had been convicted of murder. De Klerk balked especially at the release of Robert McBride, whose bomb placed in Magoo's bar had killed three people on the Durban beachfront, but he agreed to it in the interests of further negotiation. The agreement was angrily repudiated by Mangosuthu Buthelezi,* who was annoyed at the way he had been sidelined, and at the provisions providing for the fencing of hostels and a ban on the carrying of 'traditional' weapons in public, both of which seemed aimed at the Inkatha Freedom Party. [A. Sparks, *Tomorrow is Another Country* (Sandton, 1994); P. Waldmeir, *Anatomy of a Miracle* (London, 1997)]

REITZ, Francis William (1844–1934). A lawyer by training, Reitz was President of the

Orange Free State from 1889 until 1895, when he moved to the Transvaal to serve as a judge and as State Secretary to Paul Kruger's government. He was the first president of the Senate of the Union of South Africa.

REPUBLIC. Jan Smuts* had accepted South Africa's position as a dominion in the Empire, then the Commonwealth, and realised that many English-speaking South Africans had deep ties with Britain and other parts of the Empire/Commonwealth. During World War II, some Afrikaners, H.F. Verwoerd* among them, advocated the establishment of a Boer republic which would be Christian-National in character and in which English would only be a second language. After the war, realising that achieving such a republic was impractical, republicans argued for a 'democratic' republic in which English-speakers would have full rights. After being elected in 1948, D.F. Malan's priority was to consolidate the National Party (NP) in power. He said that a republic would only come about after a referendum of whites, and throughout the 1950s the NP had too precarious a hold on power for them to risk a referendum defeat. In January 1960 Verwoerd announced in parliament that the time to establish a republic had arrived. The republic would be democratic and Christian, and the equality of the two official languages would remain. There would be no drastic constitutional change: the Governor-General would be replaced by a state president, chosen by parliament, who would be the constitutional head of state and above politics. Verwoerd deliberately played down the changes that a republic would bring in order to gain votes in the referendum on the issue. He accepted the idea that the new republic would be in the Commonweatlth, though he preferred one outside that body.

Verwoerd gained support from his forthright reply to Macmillan's wind of change* speech, from the way the Sharpeville* crisis was handled, and by the fact that he survived an assassination attempt at the Rand Easter Show in April: some attributed his remarkable recovery, after he was shot in the face by a deranged farmer, David Pratt, to divine providence. The chaos which erupted when the Belgian Congo obtained its independence at the end of June, encouraged whites to support the strong South African Prime Minister. In the referendum campaign held in October 1960, Verwoerd appealed to English-speaking whites to support a republic as a way to bring about white unity; the NP warned that the chaos of the Congo would come to South Africa if it did not become a republic. Of the whites who participated in the referendum, 52% voted for a republic, a majority of 74,580 votes. Verwoerd had all along said that a simple majority would be sufficient. Few English-speakers voted for the republic, fearing that it might mean leaving the Commonwealth and cause South Africa to become isolated in the world. Some in Natal spoke of secession, but, as in 1909, that was a pipe-dream.

Verwoerd had promised to do everything he could to retain South Africa's membership of the Commonwealth but when he attended a meeting of Commonwealth Prime Ministers in London in March, he came under pressure over his government's apartheid policies. When it seemed that South Africa's application to remain in the Commonwealth as a republic might be rejected, he withdrew it. He said: 'No self-respecting member of any voluntary organisation could, in view of ... the degree of interference shown in what are South Africa's domestic affairs, be expected to wish to retain membership in what is now becoming a pressure group.' He predicted the break-up of the Commonwealth. On his return to South Africa, his supporters welcomed him back and proclaimed that his journey had ended in triumph, and that providence had produced a 'miracle'. The Republic came into being on Union Day, 31 May 1961, with C.R. Swart, a former Minister of Justice, the first President. [B. Liebenberg and B. Spies, eds., *South Africa in the 20th Century* (Pretoria, 1993)]

RESERVES. As whites conquered more and more territory in the 19th century, small portions were set aside for various black groups. In Natal, Theophilus Shepstone* was the first to implement a comprehensive reserve policy. Reserves in Natal and elsewhere became reservoirs of labour, from which migrant labourers went off to the white cities and farms to work. In the 1950s and after, the reserves were incorporated into the bantustan policy of the apartheid regime. [D. Welsh, *The Roots of Segregation* (Cape Town, 1971)]

RETIEF, Pieter (1780–1838). Voortrekker* leader and martyr. An unsuccessful businessman in Grahamstown,* he left the Cape Colony in 1837 and became leader of the trekkers, advising them to move into Natal. Offered land there by Dingane,* the Zulu king, he and his party were being entertained at the Zulu capital when the king suddenly ordered that the white visitors be killed. Other trekkers avenged Retief's death at the Battle of Blood River.*

RHARHABE (c.1722–1782). Xhosa* leader. Son of the paramount chief Phalo, he lost a dispute for succession with his brother Gcaleka during the 1770s, and moved to the west of the Kei River with his followers, where he consolidated his power. This rift among the Xhosa people weakened them as whites began to encroach upon their land towards the end of the 18th century. [J. Peires, *The House of Phalo* (Johannesburg, 1981)]

RHODES, Cecil John (1853–1902). Imperialist, mining magnate and politician. The son of an English parson, he arrived in Natal in 1870, to join his brother Herbert on a cotton farm, but moved to Kimberley* at the end of 1871, where he began to work as a speculative digger on the diamond fields. He built his initial wealth through a pumping contract for the removal of water from submerged claims, some of which he was then able to buy. With the goal of controlling the entire production of diamonds at Kimberley, he established in 1880 the De Beers Mining Company, which owned 90 claims to the De Beers mine, and by 1887 had secured ownership of the entire De Beers mine. In 1888 he formed De Beers Consolidated Mines, which had the monopoly he desired and which brought him vast profits. The same year, he acquired an important stake in the gold mines of the Witwatersrand, and by 1895 his Consolidated Gold Fields of South Africa Company had become an even larger source of income than De Beers, though he was personally less involved in its operation.

Rhodes used his base in Kimberley to further a political career: from 1880, when Griqualand West was incorporated into the Cape, until his death, he served as a Cape parliamentarian, and devoted much of his time to attempting to limit

Transvaal influence in the subcontinent. He secured an alliance with Jan Hofmeyr's Afrikaner Bond,* and was thus able to become Prime Minister of the Cape in 1890 with the backing of Cape agrarian interests as well as his traditional mining allies. As Prime Minister, he was responsible for the passage of the Glen Grey Act* (1894), designed in part to provide labour for the mines, as well as the take-over of Pondoland, the last independent area between the Cape and Natal, which completed the annexation of the Transkeian territories by the Cape. In 1895 he plotted to overthrow the Transvaal government, but the failure of the Jameson Raid* forced him to resign as Prime Minister, and alienated him from much of his former Cape Afrikaner support. Though he retained English-speaking support in the Cape, his political career was effectively over, particularly as his health deteriorated after 1897.

From the late 1880s much of his time was occupied with promoting white settlement in the area north of the Transvaal, which was to bear his name for over eighty years. His chief instrument in settling what became known as Rhodesia was his British South Africa Company.* [J. Flint, *Cecil Rhodes* (Boston, 1974); R. Rotberg, *The Founder* (Johannesburg, 1988); A. Davidson, *Cecil Rhodes and His Time* (Moscow, 1988)]

RIVONIA TRIAL (1963–1964). Trial in Pretoria of the High Command of Umkhonto weSizwe,* those who were arrested at Lilliesleaf farm in Rivonia, outside Johannesburg, along with Nelson Mandela,* who was already in jail when the others were arrested. Charged with high treason, they faced a possible death sentence, but in the event eight were found guilty of sabotage and sentenced to life imprisonment. The black prisoners were taken from the courtroom to Robben Island. In his famous statement from the dock, Mandela spoke of being prepared to die for 'the ideal of a democratic and free society'. [J. Joffe, *The Rivonia Story* (Bellville, 1995)]

ROAD TO THE NORTH. Also called the 'missionaries' road', this was the corridor linking the Cape to Central Africa through the territory annexed by Britain as Bechuanaland in 1885. It lay on the outer western limits of pastoral farming, just within the rainfall belt averaging 15 inches or more per year; further west lay the Kalahari Desert. Transvaal farmers moved into the area during the 1880s, when two small republics, Stellaland and Goshen, were formed on the western border of the Transvaal. Cecil Rhodes* feared that, were the Transvaal to secure a hold over the road, further British expansion would be checked, the route used by migrant labourers to Kimberley would be threatened, and territory that might include undiscovered diamonds would be lost to his control. British officials were persuaded that the Transvaal's westward expansion should be halted in order to prevent a possible link-up with the territory that Germany had acquired in South West Africa in 1884. A British protectorate was thus established in Bechuanaland in 1885. During the 1890s, Rhodes built a railway along the route from Kimberley to the north, skirting the Transvaal. [A. Agar-Hamilton, *The Road to the North* (London, 1937); P. Maylam, *Rhodes, the Tswana and the British* (Westport, 1980)]

ROBBEN ISLAND. Flat island guarding the entrance to Table Bay, known especially as a political prison – South Africa's Alcatraz – which housed Nelson Mandela* and others. Before 1652 it was used as a place to leave letters, and occasionally as a prison for sailors; during Dutch and British rule it continued to be used as a prison for both criminals and political prisoners, housing, among others, a number of leading Xhosa chiefs in the 1860s. After 1846, however, it was used mainly to accommodate chronic sick, those who were insane and lepers, until 1931. During World War II, troops were stationed there, and it was used by the South African Navy until 1961. Then for thirty years it housed political prisoners. A brutal 'hell-hole', it was also a 'university', where the prisoners taught each other and their warders. After a hunger strike by prisoners in 1966, conditions began to improve. African National Congress (ANC) and Pan Africanist Congress prisoners were able to discuss ideology and policy, and a number of those who arrived after 1976 on the Island as Black Consciousness* supporters left as ANC supporters. In 1982 Mandela and a few of his colleagues were moved from Robben Island to Pollsmoor prison on the mainland. The last criminal prisoners left in 1996, and the island then became a heritage site, visited by tourists in large numbers. It was presented as both a symbol of oppression, and one of resistance to oppression. [H. Deacon, ed., *The Island* (Cape Town, 1996); C. Smith, *Robben Island* (Cape Town, 1997)]

ROCK ART. Southern Africa is perhaps the richest storehouse of prehistoric art in the world; on the eastern slopes of the Drakensberg* alone, there are over 30,000 individual paintings. Most paintings on rock are to be found either in the mountainous regions of the south-western and eastern Cape, or in the Drakensberg; engravings are more common in the central interior plateau, on rocks and boulders of various sizes in the open veld. The oldest known painting (from a site in Namibia) dates from about 26,000 years ago; the earliest engraving is about 10,000 years old. The most recent paintings date from the mid-to-late 19th century. Subject matter varies greatly, and a multiplicity of human activities are depicted, as well as animal characterizations and geometric patterns. Later paintings reveal a greater range of colours, more detail and a wider variety of subject matter than earlier ones.

This rock art, distinguished by its quantity, excellence and detail, provides an indispensable record of San* life and history, and particularly religious belief. It was once believed to comprise mere artistic representations of the immediate environment, but scholars have now shown that it is closely associated with the trance experiences of shamans, or medicine people, who were the bridge between the physical and spiritual worlds. They played a central role in using spiritual power to resolve social conflict, cure the sick, and control rain and the movement of game. Their insights into the spiritual realm were painted or engraved for members of the hunting communities to see, giving people visual reminders of the power that linked people, animals and the environment, particularly during times of change and stress. [D. Lewis-Williams, *Discovering Southern African Rock Art* (Cape Town, 1990); T. Dowson, *Rock Engravings of Southern Africa* (Johannesburg, 1992); T. Dowson and D. Lewis-Williams, eds., *Contested Images* (Johannesburg, 1994)]

ROLONG. Tswana-speaking* Sotho group, whose name is derived from the legendary chief Morolong. In the early 18th century, under their powerful ruler Tau, the Rolong dominated the northern Cape and south-western Transvaal regions. Their power was built through alliances with other groups, exploitation of herding and hunting opportunities, and the creation of extensive trading networks, which stretched as far as present-day Namibia. They built large stone-walled towns, including Taung, their capital, and Dithakong, later a centre of Tlhaping power. After Tau's death, Rolong power was eclipsed: they split into four groups, all of which experienced disruption during the 1820s. Many sought refuge at Thaba Nchu, on land which was to become part of the eastern Orange Free State.

ROMAN CATHOLIC CHURCH. Catholics were prohibited from public worship at the Cape until the Church Ordinance of 1804, which established religious toleration. The authorities remained ambivalent towards Roman Catholicism, however, even after the appointment in 1837 of the first Vicar Apostolic for South Africa, Father Raymund Griffith. The spread of Catholicism was slow in the face of Protestant hostility; in particular, mission work among Africans was delayed until the late 19th century because of Protestant opposition. The most famous Catholic mission centre, Mariannhill, outside Durban, was founded in 1882 by contemplative Trappist monks, who later established daughter houses throughout Natal.

During the 20th century, Catholicism experienced significant growth, both among whites and Africans, despite the antagonism of the Dutch Reformed Church* and the National Party government. The hierarchy of the church was often cautious in its confrontation with state authorities during the apartheid era, although from 1952 the South African Catholic Bishops' Conference was critical of apartheid policies. From the 1970s protests grew stronger, and the Catholic Church took the lead among the churches in opening schools to children of all races despite laws forbidding this.

By the 1980s the Roman Catholic Church had over 2.5 million adherents, making it the largest single Christian denomination in the country (although it was the third-largest Christian grouping after the African independent churches and the Dutch Reformed Churches). Over 80% of the church's total membership comprised black people. [W. Brown, *The Catholic Church in South Africa* (London, 1960); A.Prior, ed., *Catholics in Apartheid Society* (Cape Town, 1982)]

RUBICON SPEECH (15 August 1985). Major reforms were widely expected in the speech which President P.W. Botha* was to make to the Natal congress of the National Party in Durban, and Botha himself spoke of his speech as 'crossing the Rubicon'. But the address as delivered ruled out significant concessions to South Africa's black population and Botha explicitly rejected demands that apartheid be abandoned. Dashing hopes, the speech led directly to the imposition of economic sanctions,* and there was an immediate flight of capital from the country. Foreign banks, led by Chase Manhattan, refused to roll over their loans. The rand fell sharply in value. The country had to wait until 2 February 1990 for the speech which did mark a major change of direction, and hence a real 'crossing of the Rubicon': that given by F.W. de Klerk unbanning the African National Congress and other organizations. [P. Waldmeir, *Anatomy of a Miracle* (London, 1997)]

147

SAN. The earliest people who lived in southern Africa were hunter-gatherers. They were widely dispersed across the subcontinent, in a variety of habitats, with the probable exception of areas that were thickly forested. The lifestyle has often been characterized as precarious, but it was probably relatively stable and secure. Hunter-gatherers had an extensive and profound knowledge of their immediate environment, which they systematically exploited for their survival. They utilized an enormous number of plants (probably over 60% of their diet was gathered) as well as game, smaller animals and some insects. They lived in small, loosely knit bands, based on the family unit, which facilitated nomadic behaviour. During the 18th and 19th centuries, however, they were mercilessly hunted down by white settlers, and large numbers were exterminated. As they came under pressure, they retreated to the deserts and the mountains. From the Drakensberg in particular, they launched raids on cattle-keeping people and their stock in the 19th century, before being overpowered and eliminated. Those who survived were increasingly threatened by new forms of economic activity, and only in the remoteness of the deserts on the fringes of South Africa have a small number of people been able to sustain a mainly hunter-gatherer way of life.

The word 'San', used by Khoikhoi herders at the Cape to describe their hunter-gatherer neighbours, was probably never used by the hunter-gatherers to describe themselves, for they had no need to distinguish themselves from pastoralists or agriculturists. 'Sa', 'to inhabit', probably implied a recognition of the San as the original inhabitants of the land. As 'sab' means 'bush', it is possible that 'San' was translated literally as 'Bushman'. In the 1650s, the Dutch settlers at the Cape heard the term 'Sonqua', which probably meant 'poor people', used by herders to describe hunter-gatherer groups who lived without domesticated animals in the mountains to the north of Table Bay. By the 1680s, colonists spoke of 'Bosjesmanne' or variants, later 'Boesmanne' and 'Bushmen', a term frequently used, in a derogatory sense, to describe any marginal community, including dispossessed herders and even runaway slaves.

The word 'San' came into use again during the 1960s, when historians, anthropologists and ethnographers wanted an alternative to the belittling 'Bushman'. Recently, it has been recognized that 'San' barely differs from 'Bushman', in that it is probably no more than a translation, and was most likely as disparaging; hence the word 'Bushman' has come back into usage. [H. Deacon, *Where Hunters Gathered* (Cape Town, 1976); R. Elphick, *Khoikhoi and the Founding of White South Africa* (Johannesburg, 1985); R. Gordon, *The Bushman Myth* (Boulder, 1992); P. Skotnes, ed., *Miscast* (Cape Town, 1996)]

SANCTIONS. Many different kinds of sanctions were imposed on the country under the apartheid regime between 1960 and 1990. Among the most important were the mandatory arms embargo* of November 1977, the financial sanctions that followed P.W. Botha's Rubicon speech* in August 1985, and those in the United States

Comprehensive Anti-Apartheid Act (CAAA) of 1986, passed over the veto of President Ronald Reagan. There was a lively debate within South Africa on the efficacy of sanctions: Desmond Tutu,* Archbishop of Cape Town, was a leading proponent of sanctions, as an alternative to violence, while Helen Suzman of the Progressive Party* and Mangosuthu Buthelezi* of Inkatha, among others, argued that sanctions would only strengthen white resolve not to change, and would hurt the poor and create further unemployment. There is no doubt that the sanctions imposed did help persuade the government to accept the need to negotiate with the African National Congress, but their precise role in bringing about negotiations remains open to debate.

From 1990 the ANC used the removal of sanctions as a way of keeping pressure on the De Klerk government, arguing that there should be no lifting of sanctions until change was 'irreversible'. But there was a gradual relaxation of sanctions: the CAAA was terminated in July 1991 after President Bush agreed that the De Klerk government had met the conditions laid down in the law. Nevertheless 139 state and local sanctions remained in place in the United States. Then in November 1993 President Clinton removed further sanctions, including the ban on the United States voting for an International Monetary Fund loan for South Africa. Other sanctions, including the United Nations arms embargo, were not lifted until after the election of the democratic government in April 1994. [M. Lipton, *Sanctions and South Africa* (London, 1988); *South Africa: The Sanctions Report* (London, 1988); M. Orkin, ed., *Sanctions Against Apartheid* (Cape Town, 1989)]

SANDILE (1820–1878). Son of Ngqika,* and chief of the Rharhabe Xhosa* from 1840. His position was eroded by the frontier wars of 1846–1847 and 1850–1853, and most particularly by the cattle-killing* of 1856–1857, when he accepted the prophecies and ordered his people to slaughter their cattle. He died during the last frontier war of 1878–1879, while resisting British forces in the Ciskei.* [J. Meintjes, *Sandile* (Cape Town, 1971); N. Mostert, *Frontiers* (London, 1992)]

SARILI (*c.*1814–1892). Son of Hintsa,* paramount chief of the Xhosa* from 1835, and head of the Gcaleka Xhosa. Despite a treaty of friendship with the Cape in 1844, he was forced by the colonial authorities to pay reparations after the frontier war of 1846–1847. Cape forces then expelled him from much of his land east of the Kei River after the cattle-killing,* and he and his followers clashed several times thereafter with the Mfengu* who were settled on what had been his land. After the frontier war of 1878–1879, he lost what remained of his power. Forced to flee north to Bomvanaland in the Transkei, he died there in exile. [N. Mostert, *Frontiers* (London, 1992)]

SCHOOL PEOPLE. Xhosa* who accepted Christianity and attended mission schools were named 'school people', in contrast to 'red' people, who continued to practise traditional customs. The cleavage between the two groups dates back to the mid-19th century, and ran deep within the traumatized Xhosa society from the time of the cattle-killing and the success of missionaries in its aftermath. [L. Switzer, *Power and Resistance* (Madison, 1993)]

SCHREINER, Olive (1855–1920). Novelist, political writer and feminist. Her novel *The Story of an African Farm* (1883), written while she was a governess on Karoo farms, won her fame in Europe and the United States. An eloquent opponent of Cecil Rhodes's* imperial ambitions, and of British imperialism, she was an early advocate of equal rights for women, and her *Woman and Labour* (1911) formed a powerful feminist tract. [R. First and A. Scott, *Olive Schreiner* (London, 1980); K. Schoeman, *Olive Schreiner* (Johannesburg, 1991); K. Schoeman, *Only an Anguish to Live Here* (Cape Town, 1992)]

SECURITY POLICE. See POLICE

SEKHUKHUNE (*c.*1810–1882). Paramount chief of the Pedi* from 1861. For most of his period of leadership, he was engaged in a struggle with the Boers of the Transvaal to retain his land and independence. After the British annexation of the Transvaal in 1877, Pedi power was finally broken by British forces and their allies in 1879, and he was taken prisoner.

SEME, Pixley kaIsaka (1881–1951). Lawyer and founder of the South African Native National Congress (SANNC), later the African National Congress (ANC). After legal studies in the United States and Britain, Seme returned to South Africa convinced of the need for Africans to unite, in the face of the newly created Union. He therefore called the founding meeting of SANNC at Bloemfontein in January 1912, and became the new organization's first treasurer. A conservative and ambiguous figure, he sought to avoid conflict with the authorities and stayed out of the limelight during the 1920s. He became president of the ANC in 1930, but was a weak leader, and did nothing to reverse the decline in the organization's fortunes. He remained an elder statesman of African politics, however, and one of those he helped was Anton Lembede.* [R. Rive and T. Couzens, *Seme* (Johannesburg, 1991)]

SEPARATE DEVELOPMENT. See APARTHEID, BANTUSTAN POLICY

SHAKA kaSenzangakhona (*c.*1787–1828), creator of the Zulu kingdom.* Between *c.*1810 and *c.*1816 he was a tributary chief and military commander in the Mthethwa confederacy, during which time he built up a formidable fighting force by equipping his followers with a short stabbing spear and a large shield to make close fighting possible. After Dingiswayo, leader of the Mthethwa, was defeated by the Ndwandwe under Zwide,* Shaka then routed Zwide at Gqokoli Hill in *c.*1819. He then consolidated his power, bringing all northern Nguni people living between the Pongola and Thukela rivers within his control. His militarized and centralized state was the greatest power in south-east Africa during the 1820s; it was surrounded by vassal communities in varying degrees of subordination, who paid him tribute. Shaka was murdered by his half-brother Dingane in 1828.

Shaka's personality and life have been the subject of considerable historical and popular writing. He has been portrayed as a ruthless villain and a violent psychopath, as well as a brilliant strategist, visionary and statesman. His symbolic importance is frequently recalled in speeches by Mangosuthu Buthelezi* and other

Zulus. [S. Taylor, *Shaka's Children* (London, 1994); D. Golan, *Inventing Shaka* (Boulder, 1994); C. Hamilton, *Terrific Majesty* (Cape Town, 1998)]

SHARPEVILLE MASSACRE (21 March 1960). Nervous police, faced with a crowd of unarmed anti-pass campaigners of the Pan Africanist Congress (PAC), panicked and opened fire, and 69 people died, many of them shot in the back. In the crisis that followed, the African National Congress and the PAC were banned, and the decision was taken to launch the armed struggle. But the crisis of legitimacy for the regime passed, and apartheid was applied with new determination and far greater repression in the 1960s. The massacre opened a new era, however, and remained symbolically important: it was therefore appropriate that Nelson Mandela* went to Sharpeville on 10 December 1996 to pay tribute to those who had died and to announce the signing of South Africa's new democratic constitution. [T. Lodge, *Black Politics in South Africa since 1945* (Johannesburg, 1983)]

SHEPSTONE, Theophilus (1817–1893). Colonial administrator and Secretary for Native Affairs in Natal from 1856 to 1876. He believed that Africans should be governed separately and coerced two-thirds of Natal's African inhabitants into reserves* (locations), where they were ruled either through their traditional authorities or by appointed chiefs loyal to him. Customary law was recognized, but the Governor, as 'supreme chief', was given extensive powers, which were exercised by Shepstone on his behalf. Some of the origins of later segregationist practices lie in the system Shepstone elaborated in Natal.

In 1877 Shepstone was sent by Carnarvon to annex the Transvaal, and he then administered that territory for two years. He urged Sir Bartle Frere* to deal with the Zulu, and so helped to precipitate the Anglo-Zulu War* of 1879. He retired in 1880, but remained influential in directing policy towards Africans in Natal for another decade. [D. Welsh, *The Roots of Segregation* (Cape Town, 1971); B. Kline, *The Genesis of Apartheid* (Lanham, 1988)]

SIMON'S TOWN. South Africa's principal naval base, a safe anchorage on the eastern side of the Cape Peninsula, 30 miles south of Cape Town. From 1743, the Dutch East India Company made it their official winter base, because of the damage that winter storms in Table Bay caused shipping. British forces landed in Simon's Town when they captured the Cape in June 1795. It became the headquarters of the British South Atlantic Naval Squadron in 1814, and it remained an important naval base during the 19th century, being used chiefly to protect the Cape sea route. The South African government took over the land defences of the port from the British in 1921. Simon's Town served as a base for Allied vessels operating in the South Atlantic and Indian oceans during World War II. In 1957, Britain handed over control of the port to the South African authorities, and it became the headquarters of the South African Navy. The terms of the Simon's Town agreement gave Britain the right to use the base in peacetime and in war, whether or not South Africa was also at war. The agreement was suspended during the 1960s by Britain in protest at South Africa's racial policies.

SISA (a Bantu word; also *mafisa*; *ngoma*). Among both Nguni and Sotho, *sisa* was the practice of loaning out cattle. The cattle themselves, or their milk, could be claimed at any time, for the person entrusted with the cattle had the use of them but did not obtain ownership. It was a way of acquiring dependants. Moshoeshoe* of Lesotho in particular used it extensively in the aftermath of the Mfecane* to build up a large following.

SISULU, Walter Max Ulyate (1912–) A trade unionist, he joined the African National Congress (ANC) in 1940, opposed black involvement in World War II, became a member of the Transvaal executive of the ANC and a founder member of the ANC Youth League.* He was arrested and banned under the Suppression of Communism Act. After a tour of Eastern bloc countries, Israel, China and Great Britain, his views were modified and he came to support the multi-racial Congress Alliance.* One of the leading Rivonia* trialists, he was sent to Robben Island* in 1964, and released in October 1989, after which he was active as an elder statesman in the ANC.

SLAGTER'S NEK REBELLION. A rebellion in 1815 of white frontier farmers against the British authorities in the eastern Cape. It followed the refusal of Frederik Bezuidenhout to appear before a tribunal investigating charges of his ill-treatment of a Khoikhoi servant. Bezuidenhout was shot dead while resisting arrest; the subsequent rebellion was put down by British and Khoikhoi soldiers at Slagter's Nek, and the leaders were executed. The event was long commemorated by Afrikaner nationalists as an example of British oppression. [L. Thompson, *The Political Mythology of Apartheid* (New Haven, 1985)]

SLAVERY. Slaves were introduced by Van Riebeeck,* the first commander at the Cape. Slave labour was to form the backbone of the Cape economy for a century and a half, and so played a major role in shaping Cape society. Initially, imports of slaves were sporadic. Some slaves came from Angola, Mozambique and Madagascar, but most slaves were imported from Asia. From about 1720, the number of slaves at the Cape exceeded that of white colonists. Slaves were employed mainly on the arable farms of the south-western Cape; although some pastoral trekboer* farmers in the interior owned slaves, they more commonly used Khoisan labour. Slaves were also employed by the Dutch East India Company* itself on public works projects and on its farms. In Cape Town, semi-skilled slaves were to be found working as artisans. Most settlers came to associate slaves with menial and manual labour, and thus a close correlation developed at the Cape between class and race. Slave manumission rates at the Cape were extremely low, and the free black* community in Cape Town remained small.

Cape slavery has often been described as 'mild', mainly because of some contemporary observations and a largely uncritical historiography before the 1970s. In reality, conditions for many slaves were as harsh as in any other slave society, even though the Cape lacked large plantations such as those in North America. Company laws and the direct supervision of masters kept slaves firmly in check; physical punishment was frequent; freedom of movement and association was

152

strictly curtailed; and the theoretical right of slaves to seek the protection of the courts could seldom be claimed in practice. Many slaves were incorporated into the paternalistic households of the farmers, which either prevented them from questioning their last or made them unwilling to do so. Apart from two small slave rebellions, in 1808 and 1825, slave resistance tended to take individual forms. Numerous escapes occurred, and some slaves fled to the frontier areas, where towards the end of the 18th century they linked up with Oorlam and Griqua groups. Covert joined a community of escaped slaves which existed at Hanglip on False Bay for almost a century. Other forms of resistance, such as inefficient work and damage to the property of owners, regularly occurred.

Because slaves came from many places, spoke different languages, were scattered widely on farms, and few were Cape-born until the 19th century, a strongly distinctive slave culture, similar to that in North America, did not emerge. Slaves nonetheless contributed to a broader popular culture that emerged at the Cape out of the mix of indigenous and settler communities. Slave languages fed into the creole which later became Afrikaans.* There was a thriving Muslim community comprising mostly slaves in Cape Town, particularly after the end of the 18th century.

In 1808, the slave trade was abolished. Humanitarian campaigns in Britain and the Cape became more vociferous in their protests against the continuing enslavement of people, and economic shifts in the colony during the 1820s also resulted in growing doubts about the desirability of slave labour. Wine farming experienced a decline, while wool production was far less dependent on slaves. Farmers and merchants in the eastern Cape began to argue that a cheaper and more mobile labour force was required. The British parliament abolished slavery in 1834, but provided for a four-year apprenticeship period until 1838, the year of final emancipation for the Cape's 36,000 slaves. Most of the former slaves remained on the farms as labourers, although some settled on mission stations or moved to towns. The legacy of slavery lasted, both in the frontier districts, where it set the pattern for labour relations, and in the interior, where indentured labour was commonly practised (see APPRENTICESHIP). [N. Worden, *Slavery in Dutch South Africa* (Cambridge, 1985); R. Ross, *Cape of Torments* (London, 1983); R. Shell, *Children of Bondage* (Johannesburg, 1994); R. Watson, *The Slave Question* (Johannesburg, 1990)]

SLOVO, Joe (1926–1995). African National Congress (ANC) and communist activist. Born in Lithuania, he was brought up in Johannesburg, where he became a lawyer and member of the Communist Party. He married Ruth First in 1949, helped draft the Freedom Charter of 1955, was one of the founders of Umkhonto weSizwe (MK),* and fled the country before the Rivonia* arrests. In exile, he helped draft the ANC's strategy document of 1969 and emerged as the organization's main theoretician. He was also the mastermind behind some of MK's main operations while he was based at Maputo, Mozambique, between 1977 and 1984. He rose to become general secretary of the South African Communist Party in 1986 and commander of MK in 1987. Though in his work *Has Socialism Failed?* (1989) he admitted the errors of Stalinism, he continued to believe in the socialist dream. He returned to the country in 1990 and became a key figure in the negotiations which followed. He adopted a pragmatic position, and the 'sunset clauses' which he advocated led to the ANC accepting a form of power-sharing with the NP. In the Government of National Unity,* which came into office after the first democratic election, he served as Minister of Housing until his death. [J. Slovo, *Slovo: The Unfinished Autobiography* (Randburg, 1995)]

SMALLPOX. The virulent form introduced from abroad after white settlement played a major role in destroying Khoikhoi* societies. Epidemics in the early 18th century, in particular, caused enormous loss of life. A less virulent form, *variola minor*, commonly known as 'amaas', existed amongst African societies as an endemic form of the disease, and protected Africans from the more virulent forms introduced by white settlers.

SMITH, Sir Henry (Harry) George Wakelyn (1787–1860). Egocentric and bombastic British Governor of the Cape and High Commissioner from 1847 to 1852. He extended British rule northwards to the Vaal River and east to the Kei. He led the colony into war with the Xhosa* in 1850 and, largely as a result, was recalled in 1852. [A. Harington, *Sir Harry Smith* (Cape Town, 1980)]

SMUTS, Jan Christiaan (1870–1950). Soldier, intellectual and statesman, Smuts was Prime Minister of South Africa from 1919 to 1924 and from 1939 to 1948. He grew up on a farm north of Cape Town, read law at Cambridge University and was appointed State Attorney of the Transvaal in 1898. During the South African War* he acquired fame as a commando leader. A minister in the Transvaal government from 1907, he played an important role in the making of Union.* A member of the first Union government, he served during World War I* in East Africa and was a member of the Imperial war cabinet. Louis Botha's right-hand man, he succeeded him as Prime Minister in 1919.

His first term as Prime Minister ended when he lost the 1924 election to Hertzog,* but as a result of the depression crisis he became Deputy Prime Minister under Hertzog in 1933 and Prime Minister again when Hertzog wished to remain neutral in World War II.* During the war, Smuts served as adviser to Churchill. His activities as international statesman – he helped found both the League of Nations* and the United Nations* – led him to neglect his domestic constituency, and in 1948 he lost the general election to the National Party under D.F. Malan* and became leader of the parliamentary opposition until his death. For all his intellectual brilliance, Smuts failed to recognize the injustice of racial segregation and so did little to wean the white electorate from racism. Among his many intellectual interests was philosophy; he published *Holism and Evolution* in 1926. [W. Hancock, *Smuts* (Cambridge, 1962, 1968); K. Ingham, *Jan Christiaan Smuts* (Johannesburg, 1986); T. Cameron, *Jan Smuts* (Cape Town, 1994)]

SOBUKWE, Robert Mangaliso (1924–1978). A modest but charismatic man who became a student leader at the University of Fort Hare,* where he was active in African National Congress (ANC) politics. He then taught, becoming lecturer in

African languages at the University of the Witwatersrand in 1954. He came increasingly to question ANC strategy, believing its involvement with non-Africans, especially communists in the Congress of Democrats, weakened it. In 1958 he urged those who thought as he did – they were known as Africanists – to break away. In 1959 he was elected first president of the newly formed Pan Africanist Congress (PAC)* of Azania. He gave up his lecturing post to lead the mass protest of the PAC against the pass laws in March 1960. Arrested and imprisoned on Robben Island,* he was detained there, under special legislation, for another six years after serving his sentence. On his release, he was allowed to settle in Kimberley, where despite being under severe restrictions he opened a law practice. His funeral in Graaff-Reinet, the place of his birth, was disrupted when some members of the PAC threatened Mangosuthu Buthelezi,* whom they regarded as a sell-out because he worked within the bantustan system. [B. Pogrund, Sobukwe and Apartheid (Johannesburg, 1990)]

SOGA, Tiyo (1829–1871). Xhosa missionary, writer, linguist and composer. He trained as a missionary in Scotland between 1846 and 1848, and was the first Xhosa Christian minister of religion, after he was ordained in the Presbyterian Church in 1856. He married a Scottish woman, Janet Burnside, and had seven children, in whom he instilled pride in their African heritage. He translated the four gospels and Bunyan's Pilgrim's Progress into Xhosa, and wrote several hymns before his death at the age of 42. [D. Williams, Umfundisi (Lovedale, 1978)]

SOMERSET, Lord Charles Henry (1767–1831). Governor of the Cape from 1814 until 1826. Conservative and autocratic, with a military background and aristocratic connections, his name is associated with his attacks on the fledgling colonial press during the 1820s. He adopted a firm frontier policy against the Xhosa,* attempting to enforce a 'neutral territory' between white and black, and encouraging the settlement of some 5000 English-speaking immigrants to close the frontier against Xhosa intrusion. He sponsored the establishment of several colonial institutions, such as the South African Public Library and the South African Museum, and also strove to improve agricultural practices and livestock farming.

SOTHO (or Sesotho). The name used by linguists to apply to a sub-group of Bantu languages spoken by Africans on the highveld. This sub-group is usually divided into three sub-clusters: the northern Sotho lived in what became known as the Transvaal and included, in the north-east, the Pedi*; the western Sotho or Tswana*; and the southern Sotho, some of whom became known as the BaSotho.

The southern Sotho trace their origins to the 15th and 16th centuries, when their ancestors settled south of the Vaal River, mostly in small villages, in contrast to the much larger settlements to be found among the Tswana. The most prominent chiefdoms in the region were the Fokeng, Kwena, Tlokoa and Phuting. In the 1820s during the Mfecane,* the southern Sotho were attacked by Nguni-speaking refugees from across the Drakensberg, and the area experienced considerable upheaval. Thereafter, Moshoeshoe* was able to establish hegemony in the region. By the late 1830s he had attracted a large number of followers through offering protection to displaced people at his secure mountain base of Thaba Bosiu, building up his cattle herds, and showing tolerance to his enemies. Moshoeshoe was obliged to spend much of his time after the 1830s defending his land from British and Boer claims, alternately using military and diplomatic means in attempting to secure his chiefdom. In 1868, he was forced to give up valuable land to the Orange Free State.* His core territory became the British colony of Basutoland.*

SOUTH AFRICAN COMMUNIST PARTY (SACP). The legal life of the Communist Party* ended in 1950, with the passage of the Suppression of Communism Act, under which it would have been declared unlawful. The underground SACP was born in 1953, though its newspaper, the *Guardian* (also published under other names), continued until finally extinguished in 1963. Many members of the CP were active in the Congress of Democrats, formed as part of the Congress Alliance* in the 1950s. In the early 1960s the security police infiltrated the leadership of the underground SACP and a number of its officials were tried and convicted, the most notable being Bram Fischer.*

In exile, leading members of the tightly knit party, which continued to adopt a strongly pro-Soviet line, served on the executive of Umkhonto weSizwe (MK) and helped co-ordinate the military strategy of the African National Congress (ANC). Its members participated in MK structures. At the Morogoro conference of 1969 the SACP backed the 'Strategy and Tactics' document which endorsed the struggle for a national democratic revolution. From its exile base in London, the party published the *African Communist*. In June 1989 its congress in Havana, Cuba, accepted the idea of a negotiated settlement, and adopted a new policy entitled 'The Path to Power'. South Africa, the party had long argued, represented colonialism of a special type, in that colony and metropolis were one, and revolution in such a territory must unite class and national forces. Though the SACP had long taken a firmly Stalinist line, in 1989 Joe Slovo,* its leading theoretician, began a self-critical evaluation in *Has Socialism Failed?*

The party was unbanned by F.W. de Klerk* in February 1990. In July that year it launched itself openly in South Africa, though it did not reveal the names of all its members. Some SACP members played an important role in the negotiations which followed, in which it endorsed a liberal multi-party democracy as a first step to the goal of socialism. In 1992 it supported mass action to get the negotiations restarted. Its tripartite alliance with the ANC and the Congress of South African Trade Unions* tended to blur its independent role, and the assassination of its general secretary, Chris Hani,* in April 1993 deprived it of its most charismatic figure. Up to half the members of the ANC's National Executive Committee were thought to be members of the SACP. In the April 1994 election the party did not put up candidates, but supported ANC ones. There was speculation that after the 1999 election it might establish its independence of the ANC. [S. Clingman, *Bram Fischer* (Cape Town, 1998)]

SOUTH AFRICAN CONGRESS OF TRADE UNIONS (SACTU). Founded in 1955 by people critical of the decision by the Trade Union Congress of South Africa* to restrict its membership to registered (non-African) unions. SACTU joined the

Congress Alliance* as its trade-union wing. By 1961 it claimed 46 affiliated unions and 53,000 members, the vast majority of whom were Africans. In the aftermath of the Sharpeville massacre,* its leadership was banned and it was driven underground. [K. Luckhardt and B. Wall, *Organise or Starve* (London, 1980)]

SOUTH AFRICAN DEFENCE FORCE. See DEFENCE FORCE

SOUTH AFRICAN INSTITUTE OF RACE RELATIONS (SAIRR). A liberal research body, concerned with improving black–white relations, it was founded in 1929 by a small group of intellectuals led by J.D. Rheinallt-Jones. The Institute acted as a critical pressure group on the government, and though accused by the National Party government after 1948 of acting in an unpatriotic manner, it continued to collect and publish material on the effects of segregation and discrimination. Its single most influential publication was its annual *Survey of Race Relations*. In the early 1990s, no longer the target of government attack, it came under criticism from the left for its links with Inkatha and because it seemed to blame the ANC for the continuing violence. [E. Hellmann and J. Lever, *Conflict and Progress* (Johannesburg, 1979); P. Rich, *Hope and Despair* (London, 1993)]

SOUTH AFRICAN PARTY (SAP) (1911–1934). Established in November 1911, after the achievement of Union,* through the amalgamation of various parties represented in the cabinet of Louis Botha.* This included the Afrikaner Bond* in the Cape, and Het Volk* in the Transvaal. Under Botha and Jan Smuts,* the SAP stood for 'conciliation' between Afrikaners and English-speakers on the basis of a common loyalty to South Africa. After the breakaway of Hertzog* and the formation of his National Party, the SAP found itself increasingly reliant on the jingoistic Unionist Party, and an informal alliance led to the SAP absorbing the Unionists in 1920. After winning 79 seats in the 1921 general election, the SAP grew increasingly unpopular, not least because of Smuts's brutal suppression of the Rand Revolt*. It lost power to the Pact* in 1924. By then it had been depicted as the party of mining capital, with Smuts as the lackey of Hoggenheimer (i.e. Jewish capitalism) and the tool of British imperialism. Many Afrikaners remained *bloedsappe* ('blood South African Party men', i.e. those with a hereditary loyalty to Botha and Smuts). The policy of conciliation took on new life when, at a time of economic crisis, Hertzog in 1933 agreed to form a coalition with the SAP. This led to fusion with Hertzog's party the following year, and the formation of the United Party.*

SOUTH AFRICAN REPUBLIC (SAR). State which emerged after the independence of the trekkers north of the Vaal River was recognised by Britain in the Sand River Convention of 1852. Also known as the Transvaal, it was politically divided initially, but gradually unity was achieved among the various trekker communities and it claimed the entire territory from the Vaal to the Limpopo River. The constitution of 1860 reserved citizenship, the ownership of land and the franchise for whites. The SAR lost its independence when annexed by Britain in 1877, and regained it in 1881 after the Battle of Majuba.* It was conquered by Britain during the South African War* in 1900 and became the crown colony of the Transvaal.

157

SOUTH AFRICAN STUDENTS' ORGANIZATION (SASO). Steve Biko* saw that the few African students active in the National Union of South African Students* largely left it to white students to articulate black grievances, and so decided in 1968 to form an all-black student organization. SASO was inaugurated at a conference at Turfloop, the campus of the University of the North, in 1969, with Biko as its president. Biko argued that blacks should work on their own, not under the guidance of white liberals. While critics called SASO racist, the apartheid government tolerated its strong rhetoric for a time, probably because it was all-black. It won strong support on the African campuses and also among Indian students at the University of Durban-Westville and Coloured students at the University of the Western Cape. It helped establish in 1972 the Black People's Convention (BPC), an umbrella political movement based on the Black Consciousness* philosophy, and called for various campus boycotts. From 1973 its leaders began to be banned and detained without trial, and in 1975 some were charged under the Terrorism Act. SASO remained active, however, working closely with the BPC, until October 1977, when both organizations were banned.*

SOUTH AFRICAN WAR (1899–1902). The most costly war fought by the British between 1815 and 1914, popularly known as the Anglo-Boer War, but known to Afrikaner nationalists as the Second War of Independence. For much of the 20th century, its causes were generally sought in Britain's political and strategic objectives: the need to maintain political dominance in the region in order to protect its sea route to India, and its anxiety about the ambitions of other foreign imperialist competitors, particularly Germany, in the subcontinent. In the 1970s, historians began to explore the economic circumstances of the war, returning to examine the argument, first advanced by J.A. Hobson (1858–1940) at the time of the war, that it was fought primarily for economic reasons.

The gold mines of the Witwatersrand had by the mid-1890s become the world's largest single producer of gold, responsible for almost one-quarter of the world's supply. An efficient gold-mining industry was essential to Britain, with London the financial capital of the world. Mine-owners and the British shared a common frustration with the Transvaal government of Paul Kruger,* which they perceived to be backward, ill-prepared and unwilling to develop the mines. The abortive Jameson Raid* aroused the worst fears of the Transvaal about the converging interests of British imperialists and the mining magnates; these were deepened by the later demands of Sir Alfred Milner, the British High Commissioner, regarding political reform in the Transvaal. In October 1899, the Transvaal and the Orange Free State declared war to preserve their independence.

The British expected a rapid and easy war, predicting a victory before Christmas; instead, they suffered a succession of severe defeats during December 1899, particularly in Natal. Reinforcements and more competent command in the form of Lord Roberts (1832–1914) and Lord Kitchener (1850–1916) slowly reversed the tide in 1900. The Boers suffered a significant defeat at Paardeberg in February 1900, and by June 1900 both Bloemfontein and Pretoria had fallen to British forces, and Boer field armies were disintegrating. The war, however, was far from over. Boer commandos* resorted to guerrilla warfare, which proved highly effective in disrupting enemy supply lines and preventing the consolidation of British military power. In turn, Kitchener ordered a scorched earth strategy, burning farms and destroying crops and livestock in an attempt to deny the commandos the means to continue the war. A vast network of blockhouses connected by barbed-wire barricades was created, and civilians were interned in concentration camps.* The growing difficulties faced by commandos and the civilian suffering gradually wore down Boer resistance; some 14,000 guerrillas (dubbed *hensoppers*, or 'hands-uppers') surrendered to the British, while over 5000 impoverished landless Boers joined the British forces as scouts to play an active role against their former comrades.

In May 1902, the war ended with the Treaty of Vereeniging,* in which the Boers formally surrendered their independence in return for the promise of large-scale British assistance for the reconstruction of the shattered republics. Britain employed some 450,000 soldiers during the war, against 88,000 Boer fighters. Over 100,000 African and Coloured South Africans became directly involved in the military conflict, approximately one-third of whom were armed and saw active service, thus giving the lie to the 'white man's war'. Altogether 22,000 British troops and 7000 Boer soldiers lost their lives, in addition to 28,000 Boer civilians and perhaps 20,000 Africans. Given the splits within Boer society between the *hensoppers* and the *bittereinders* (the 'bitter-enders' or diehards), as well as black involvement on both sides, the war can to some extent be considered as a civil war.

Although Britain had asserted its imperial superiority, the securing of its long-term interests depended on the reconciliation of the white inhabitants of the defeated republics and the colonists of the Cape and Natal. To this end, African hopes of greater civil and political rights and economic opportunities were sacrificed, leaving a residue of deep bitterness among those who had supported the British cause against the Boers. [P. Warwick, ed., *The South African War* (London, 1980); P. Warwick, *Black People in the South African War* (Johannesburg, 1983); I. Smith, *The Origins of the South African War* (London, 1996); J. Krikler, *Revolution from Above, Revolution from Below* (Oxford, 1993)]

SOUTH WEST AFRICA. See NAMIBIA

SOWETO (acronym formed from 'South-Western Townships'). A vast, sprawling African residential area south-west of Johannesburg. There were no houses for tens of thousands of Africans who went to Johannesburg to work during World War II and most joined the squatter population, living in shanties on the outskirts of the city. After the war, together with the bulk of the remainder of Johannesburg's African population, they were gradually provided with houses in the 28 townships eventually grouped into Soweto. Africans living in the suburb of Sophiatown, much closer to the city centre, were forced out and relocated to Soweto in the mid-1950s, losing their freehold titles, as also were many from Alexandra township, to the north of the city centre, in the 1970s.

The Soweto houses were mostly four-room 'matchboxes', with no electricity, ceilings or running water. The miles and miles of identical houses were laid out to make control by the authorities as easy as possible. As in other African townships, the spartan conditions were partly a product of an unwillingness to spend more money, but also partly the result of a belief that better conditions might encourage permanent residence and should not be provided for that reason. From 1955 an attempt was made to zone individual townships on an ethnic basis – Nguni, Sotho or 'other' – and Zulu male migrants lived separately in hostels, but most of Soweto remained polyglot. As many of its residents were there illegally, its exact population was never known, but in the mid-1970s it was probably over one million. Soweto had no industries, and a quarter of a million of its people travelled each day to work on the single railway which ran into Johannesburg. The poverty and dreariness of the place attracted adverse publicity during the Soweto uprising,* and this led the government to announce plans to provide electricity and entertainment and sporting facilities.

Initially run by the Johannesburg City Council's Non-European Affairs Department, Soweto was taken over by the West Rand Administration Board, a nominated government body, in 1973. Residents of Soweto had served on an Advisory Board, which was replaced by an Urban Council in 1968; this in turn became a Community Council in 1978. Elections to these bodies consistently produced minuscule polls, for the vast majority of Sowetans rejected them as powerless institutions of the oppressors. After the transition to democracy, it was proposed that Soweto be incorporated in a mega-city that included the rest of Johannesburg.

SOWETO UPRISING (1976–1977). Often viewed as the event which signalled the end of apartheid, this revolt began on 16 June 1976 as a protest by schoolchildren in Soweto township south of Johannesburg against the government's insistence that Afrikaans be used as a medium of instruction in schools. Hector Petersen was the first martyr of the revolt, which soon spread from Soweto across the country. The African National Congress was caught off guard when the revolt began, but tried to capitalize on it. Ideas of Black Consciousness* were undoubtedly important in flaming the resistance and spreading it. Before the revolt was suppressed, at least 600 people, and probably many more, most of them teenagers, had been shot by the security forces. Thousands of others fled abroad, and there joined the liberation struggle. The harsh measures taken to suppress the uprising aroused much international condemnation, and created a crisis of legitimacy for the apartheid regime that led eventually to the negotiated settlement of the 1990s. [J. Kane-Berman, Soweto (Johannesburg, 1978); B. Hirson, Year of Fire, Year of Ash (London, 1979); R. Price, The Apartheid State in Crisis (Berkeley, 1991)]

SPORT AND SPORT BOYCOTTS. Modern sport – with its emphasis on physical prowess, self-discipline, individual and collective effort, as well as team competitions, carrying the various communal identities of local district, province and nation – was brought to South Africa in the 19th century by British immigrants. Sport and British cultural values were closely intertwined, and the development of sport reflected the emerging colonial society and its social structures. Although the first recorded cricket match was played in Cape Town in 1808, cricket clubs were slow to form in the Cape before the 1870s. Port Elizabeth saw the establishment of both the first cricket club for whites in 1843 and that for blacks in 1869. Cricket took root in English-speaking public schools and in mission schools in the Cape; by the 1870s, the game was popular throughout the Cape and Natal, although no official leagues or competitions took place. In 1888, the first tour by an English team saw South Africa join England and Australia as a recognized contestant in international cricket, and further impetus was given to the game in 1890, when Sir Donald Currie donated a trophy, called the Currie Cup, to promote first-class competitive cricket, between the colonies and the republics.

The first rugby match was played in Cape Town in 1862, after which rugby began to spread in schools. During the decade from 1875 organized sport developed rapidly: the first rugby, football, athletics, tennis, golf, horse-racing and cycling clubs were formed and regular competitions began. From the late 1880s, national associations began to be established, as the mineral and industrial transformation of South African began. In 1891 the South African Rugby Board was founded to ensure uniformity in rules and to organize tournaments and overseas visits; in that year, the first tour by a British team took place. A trophy donated by Sir Donald Currie, which was first competed for in 1892, became the premier interprovincial award. In 1892, the South African Football Association (SAFA) was formed to control the sport. At the same time, black sportsmen also began to initiate moves to co-ordinate competition on a national level: the South African Coloured Rugby Board was formed in 1896, and the South African Coloured Cricket Board in 1902; black rugby players competed for the Rhodes Cup from 1897 and cricket players for the Barnato trophy from 1898, for the mining magnates Cecil Rhodes and Barney Barnato were persuaded to donate trophies similar to the Currie Cup. At the beginning of the 20th century, cricket was the most popular sport among the small black middle class, and competition between black and white cricket (as well as rugby) teams occurred regularly, particularly in the Cape.

After 1910, however, with the intensification of racism and segregation that occurred as the century progressed, contests between black and white teams declined, along with the assimilationist ideals of the black middle class. The powerful mining industry began to control the development of black sport, and cricket went into decline in favour of working-class mass sports, in particular soccer, boxing and athletics. Cricket tended to be associated in popular discourse as the sport of English-speaking whites, while rugby came to be dominated by Afrikaners. After 1948, the apartheid policies of the National Party stretched, not surprisingly, to the sporting arena. In 1955, the government published its official sports policy based on racial differentiation: each race was to have its own sports amenities, controlling bodies, emblems, and local and international competitions. By the end of the 1950s, this official policy of sport apartheid was making its influence felt in almost every sporting code. Between 1959 and 1962, several black federations, in cricket, football, tennis and athletics, made a transition towards non-racialism; in 1962, the most influential of these, the South African Non-Racial Olympic Committee (SANROC), was formed. Under the leadership of Sam Ramsamy it established itself in exile in London in 1966, and led campaigns to isolate South Africa on the sportsfield.

The international boycott of South African sport, although unevenly applied, increasingly made an impact on the white establishment. South Africa was expelled from international football in 1964, from the Olympic Games in 1966 and the Olympic movement in 1969, and from international cricket in 1970; many other sportspersons experienced various degrees of difficulty in playing sport abroad. The unyielding attitude of the government was symbolized most clearly in its refusal to grant permission to Basil D'Oliveira, a Coloured cricketer of South African birth, to participate in a cricket test series between England and South Africa in 1966. This was the same year in which a Department of Sport and Recreation was established to influence the practice of sport in the country.

In 1973, the South African Council of Sport (SACOS) was formed within the country, and, together with SANROC, campaigned for the complete isolation of South African sport, using the slogan 'no normal sport in an abnormal society'. Considerable division occurred even within government circles about the respective paths of complete international isolation and limited reform to permit some international competition. A policy of 'multinationalism' was introduced in 1976, which rapidly gave way in 1979 to 'sports autonomy', whereby the government, in a vain attempt to 'depoliticize' sport, began to remove restrictions on the practice and organization of sport, and allowed individual sports bodies to choose for themselves their structures. During the 1980s, the sports boycott was applied with considerable effectiveness, with only rugby and some individual sportspeople succeeding in evading isolation to any significant degree. Opponents of international tours argued that sport should rather be developed in disadvantaged communities. The hostility of anti-apartheid campaigners towards international competition was most obviously seen in the difficulties which the athlete Zola Budd faced in 1984–1986. She managed to run in British colours in controversial circumstances. In 1990 a tour of rebel English cricketers had to be cancelled.

Campaigners had long argued that the use of sport in isolating white South Africa was an extremely effective psychological weapon in the broader anti-apartheid struggle, and the termination of the rebel cricket tour was a significant landmark in popular domestic opposition to apartheid. In November 1990, a broad coalition of opposition sporting organizations decided in Harare that the sports boycott should remain in place until the scrapping of apartheid. An interim body, the National Olympic Committee of South Africa (NOCSA), under the leadership of Ramsamy, managed the process towards the readmission of South Africa to international competition; in July 1991, the International Olympic Committee recognized NOCSA as the sole controlling body for Olympic sport in South Africa, and readmitted the country to the Olympic Games. The isolation of cricket ended in October 1991, with a short tour of the national team to India, and an invitation to the World Cup in Australia in March 1992. South African sportspeople then performed with credit in international competition: the country reached the semi-finals of the cricket World Cup in 1992, was victorious in the rugby World Cup in 1995, and in the soccer Africa Cup of Nations in 1996; at the 1996 Olympics, Josiah Thugwane won the gold medal in the men's marathon.

These successes have not disguised considerable challenges facing many sports in the post-apartheid era: the allocation of resources, vastly diverse facilities, and the virtual absence of Africans in many national teams are among the major issues which confront sporting bodies. In 1998 there was a crisis in rugby, when those who controlled that sport tried to have the President's decision to appoint a commission of inquiry into the sport overturned. In 1991, a government survey revealed that soccer was the most popular sport played in South Africa, followed by netball, cricket, squash, rugby, golf, tennis, athletics, bowls and hockey. Soccer attracted the most spectators, followed by boxing, tennis, athletics, rugby, golf and cricket. [R. Lapchick, *The Politics of Race and International Sport* (Westport, 1975); R. Archer and A. Bouillon, *The South African Game* (London, 1982); G. Jarvie, *Class, Race and Sport in South Africa's Political Economy* (Boston, 1985); A. Grundlingh et al., *Beyond the Tryline* (Johannesburg, 1995); J. Nauright, *Sport, Cultures and Identities in South Africa* (Cape Town, 1998)]

SQUATTERS. Term used both for Africans who lived on white-owned rural land and for those who lived in informal or irregular settlements in towns. For much of the 20th century, attempts were made to remove rural squatters, many of whom moved to the cities and became urban squatters. The shacks of urban squatters were frequently bulldozed in the 1970s, but by the mid-1980s the government began to tolerate squatting in limited urban areas.

STATE ENTERPRISES. Though critical of socialism, the National Party government, which ruled from 1948, controlled over 50% of fixed assets in the country, including the oil-from-coal industry, Sasol; the steel-producing company, Iscor (founded in 1928); the electricity-supplier, Escom (founded in 1922); the telephone company which became known as Telkom; the arms-manufacturing companies Armscor and Denel; South African Airways; and many others. In the 1950s and 1960s, control of state enterprises was a way to provide jobs for poor Afrikaners and raise them to the middle class. The African National Congress, which had believed in nationalization, on coming to office moved towards privatization, despite some opposition from the trade unions. This new policy began to take off in 1997, when Telkom obtained a foreign strategic equity partner, and it was announced that all of South African Airways would be sold off. [N. Clark, *Manufacturing Apartheid* (New Haven, 1994)]

STATE SECURITY COUNCIL (SSC). Established as a permanent cabinet committee in 1972, the SSC was at first little more than an advisory body on intelligence matters, but after P.W. Botha took over as Prime Minister in 1978, it became a major policy-making body, which met just before cabinet and took decisions which cabinet then rubber-stamped. Its operational arm was the secret National Security Management System (NSMS): a network of Joint Management Centres brought together members of the security forces and others, and co-ordinated the implementation of SSC policies on the ground. Certain townships were identified as target areas for upgrading, but above all the emphasis was on control and security. In November 1989 De Klerk* abolished the NSMS and effectively returned power to the cabinet. The working of the SSC became known in detail in 1997–1998 when the Truth and Reconciliation Commission,* which had gained access to its minutes, held a series of hearings relating to its activities.

STAYAWAYS. The stayaway, which involved a general withdrawal of labour, not over a workplace dispute but for political purposes, emerged as a tactic of black resistance in December 1949, when it was one of the forms of action listed in the Programme of Action adopted by the African National Congress (ANC). The first stayaway organized by the ANC took place on the Witwatersrand on 1 May 1950 as a protest against unjust laws, and was followed by a national stayaway on 26 June of that year. The tactic was used, with varying degrees of success, in 1957, 1958, 1960, 1961, 1976 and 1977. In the most successful, 500,000 workers stayed away from work for three days in 1976 during the Soweto uprising.*

STEYN, Marthinus Theunis (1857–1916). Attorney-General, President of the Orange Free State,* and Afrikaner nationalist. He attempted to promote co-operation between the Boer republics and the Cape, but was strongly alienated by the imperial ambitions of Sir Alfred Milner* and Joseph Chamberlain.* He lent military and guerrilla support to the Transvaal during the South African War,* and remained a convinced Afrikaner nationalist until his death.

STOCKENSTRÖM, Andries (1792–1864). Administrator on the Cape eastern frontier, in the roles of landdrost of Graaff-Reinet (1815–1828), Commissioner-General for the Eastern Province (1828–1833) and Lieutenant-Governor of the Eastern Districts (1836–1839). He was independent-minded and rejected several key aspects of British frontier policy. He tried to reduce the incursions mounted by whites on Xhosa land and livestock, supported Ordinance 50 of 1828,* and helped to establish the Kat River Settlement* in 1829. When he gave evidence to the Select Committee of the British House of Commons on the treatment of Aborigines in 1835, the colonists regarded his criticisms of them as betrayal. He returned to be a much-reviled Lieutenant-Governor of the Eastern Districts from 1836. He remained critical of British policy after his dismissal in 1839, arguing for a reduced British role in southern African affairs and advocating representative government for the Cape.

He played a key role in the frontier war of 1846–1847. After the introduction of representative government in 1853, Stockenström gave up retirement on his farm near the modern town of Bedford and served as a member of the Legislative Council for the eastern districts from 1854 until 1856. In the 19th-century Cape no one had greater breadth of vision; none gained the respect of a wider constituency, black as well as white. [N. Mostert, *Frontiers* (London, 1992)]

STONE AGE. The term used by archaeologists to describe the period in southern Africa from about 2.5 million years ago, when hominids first began to shape stone tools, until about 2000 years ago, when iron-using agriculturists first settled in southern Africa. The Stone Age is separated into Earlier, Middle and Later periods, the division between the Earlier and Middle period occurring about 150,000 years ago, and that between the Middle and Later periods dating from about 30,000 years ago. Through time, tools became more varied and sophisticated, increasingly designed for more specific tasks, and smaller in size. Hunter-gatherers and Khoikhoi herders, who did not smelt metals, continued to belong, technologically, to the Stone Age.

STRIJDOM, Johannes Gerhardus (1893–1958). National Party leader and Prime Minister from 1956 to 1958. A dour man, nicknamed 'The Lion of the North', he interpreted apartheid as mere *baasskap*, or domination by whites. A lawyer and farmer, he found himself, when he supported D.F. Malan* in his refusal to enter fusion,* the sole NP member of parliament in the Transvaal. He was chosen NP leader, and therefore Prime Minister, on Malan's retirement in 1954 because he was leader in the Transvaal and had built up the party there. As Prime Minister he pushed through the removal of the Coloureds from the common voters' roll (see FRANCHISE). [D. O'Meara, *Forty Lost Years* (Johannesburg, 1996)]

STRIKES. Perhaps the earliest strike to be recorded is that by Coloured boatmen and stevedores at the Cape Town harbour in 1854. They struck for an increase in wages to help compensate for a higher bread price. African workers in Port Elizabeth harbour struck in 1856. In the Cape Town docks African and Coloured workers sometimes joined in strikes together, but cross-ethnic strike action was relatively rare.

The period 1907–1922 was one of great militancy among labour on the Witwatersrand, marked by a series of major strikes on the mines. The first such strike by white miners took place in 1907 when the mine-owners instructed miners to supervise three instead of two drills. More than 4000 struck and the army was called in. Afrikaners were hired to take the place of strikers, and the strike was broken. In 1913 some 19,000 white miners went on strike over union bargaining rights. Again, strong-arm tactics were used by both soldiers and the police against the strikers. Louis Botha* and Jan Smuts* intervened and an agreement was reached. Following the strike, the Riotous Assemblies Act (1914) was passed to give the government the power to ban outdoor meetings and picketing. Massive force was used against another strike in 1914 and the strike leaders were deported. The most important strike by whites took place in 1922. Faced with a crisis of profitability in the coal and gold mines, the owners cut wages in the coal mines and announced that they would do the same for the gold mines, and also allow Africans to take over semi-skilled jobs from whites. First the coal miners struck, then there was a general strike of 20,000 white workers on the gold mines. An armed revolt followed, put down by the army. White labour was cowed, and then co-opted through the Industrial Conciliation Act (1924).

The first strike by Africans on the gold mines took place in 1896. In 1913 some 9000 African workers on four gold mines struck, and the army was called in to force them back to work. A subsequent commission of inquiry produced certain improvements in compound and work conditions. In 1918 the Johannesburg sanitation workers struck; arrested for breaking their contracts, the strikers were sentenced to two months' hard labour. Then in 1920, at a time of rapid inflation and severe drought in the rural areas, some 71,000 migrant workers on twenty-one gold mines struck for higher wages. Again the army was called in, and one by one the compounds were forced to resume work. Some working conditions were improved, but the pass laws were also tightened up.

Massive strike action by Africans began again during World War II, when labour was in short supply. In 1942 some 8000 workers in various Witwatersrand industries went out on strike. A war measure then outlawed strikes by Africans and provided severe penalties for strike action. After the war, under the auspices of the African Mine Workers' Union, formed in 1941, over 60,000 workers on nineteen mines went on strike. The 1946 strike was forcibly broken up by the police; twelve miners were killed. One of the consequences was closer relations between the African trade union movement and the African National Congress.

An Act of 1953 made strikes by Africans illegal, and in the repressive post-Sharpeville* decade black labour was largely docile. But from 1973 there was a dramatic change, which in part followed a successful strike by Ovambo workers in Namibia the previous year. Early in 1973, seemingly spontaneously, strikes spread from brickmakers to textile and other workers in Durban; over a two-month period more than 61,000 workers were involved, and in most cases they were able to extract increased wages. The government's first response was to try to encourage the creation of liaison committees, but by the mid-1970s, as major strike action continued, it was clear that such committees were no substitute for representative and recognized trade unions. Though Africans were allowed to form and join registered unions in 1979, strike action continued at roughly the 1973 level as South Africa entered the 1980s. Consumer boycotts organized by community associations often supported strikers. [D. MacShane et al., *Power* (Nottingham, 1984); J. Baskin, *Striking Back* (Johannesburg, 1991)]

SWAZILAND. The Swazi state was constructed at the beginning of the 19th century, when Sobhuza I fled north of the Pongola River after defeat in battle by Zwide of the Ndwandwe in 1815. Sobhuza established his base at Elangeni, and won the allegiance of both Nguni- and Sotho-speakers, some of whom lived south and west of the boundaries of modern Swaziland. He managed to avoid conflict with both Shaka* and Dingane* of the Zulu kingdom.* His son Mswati II was thus able to inherit an important chiefdom on Sobhuza's death in 1838. During the mid-1840s Mswati, faced with continuing threats from the Zulu in the south, entered into treaties with the Voortrekkers in the eastern Transvaal. After his death in 1865, the Transvaal claimed virtually all the territory of the Swazi chiefdom. The present western boundaries were demarcated by the British during their occupation of the Transvaal after 1877; as a result many Swazi people were left within the Transvaal. When gold was discovered in the north-west of Swaziland in 1879, the mineral and land concessions which white prospectors obtained weakened the chiefdom. The Transvaal took over the administration of the territory in 1895, to be succeeded by Britain during the South African War.* By this time, only 38% of the land remained in Swazi hands, the rest having passed into the control of individual whites.

Swaziland became a High Commission territory in 1907, and remained under British rule until it was granted independence in 1968. A KaNgwane* bantustan was created by the South African government for the 500,000 Swazi living within South Africa. Considerable tension existed during the 1970s and 1980s between the South African and Swaziland governments over the fact that African National Congress and Pan Africanist Congress refugees sought shelter in the country, which some used as a base to launch guerrilla attacks on South Africa. A secret non-aggression pact was signed between the two countries in 1982. Negotiations between the two for the interchange of territory, allowing KaNgwane to be incorporated into Swaziland, and Swaziland to obtain access to the Indian Ocean, were not concluded. [P. Bonner, *Kings, Commoners, and Concessionaires* (Johannesburg, 1983); J. Crush, *The Struggle for Swazi Labor* (Kingston, 1987); R. Lewin, *When the Sleeping Grass Awakens* (Johannesburg, 1997)]

t

TAMBO, Oliver Reginald (1917–1993), President of the African National Congress (ANC) from 1967 to 1991. A leading member of the ANC Youth League in the 1940s, Tambo worked with Nelson Mandela* as a lawyer and in politics in the 1950s. When the Sharpeville* crisis broke in 1960, he was instructed to continue the fight in exile. He settled first in London and later in Lusaka, working tirelessly to promote the ANC's cause. He successfully held the organization together so that by the mid-1980s it had gained considerable international recognition. He was initially sceptical when told that Mandela wished to talk to the government, and he authorized a secret operation to send senior cadres back into South Africa to mobilize underground support for the ANC (Operation Vula). He suffered a stroke in 1989, and returned from exile in poor health after the ANC was unbanned. [S. Johns and R. Davis, *Mandela, Tambo and the African National Congress* (New York, 1991); E. Reddy, *Oliver Tambo* (New Delhi, 1991)]

TAUNG SKULL. Professor Raymond Dart of the University of the Witwatersrand caused a furore in the international scientific world when he published his analysis of this fossilized skull in the British scientific journal *Nature* in January 1925. Discovered in lime deposits at Taung in the arid north-west region of South Africa in 1924, it was the skull of a child who had died at about the age of four. It possessed both ape-like and human-like features: the child had walked upright, had human-like teeth, a smooth, vertical forehead, and a small brain with human-like features. From the skull, Dart identified an extinct ape family with human-like characteristics, which he called *Australopithecus africanus*, the 'southern ape-man of Africa'. He suggested that the Taung skull was the link between primates and hominids, and provided evidence that humans originated in Africa. [R. Dart, *Adventures with the Missing Link* (London, 1957)]

THEAL, George McCall (1837–1919). South Africa's first major and most prolific historian. Canadian-born, Theal edited a newspaper in British Kaffraria before he became a teacher at Lovedale in the eastern Cape, where he conducted oral research on the history of the Xhosa and began to write a general history of his adopted country. He was then employed in various capacities in the Cape Native Affairs Department, during which time he produced most of his best-known work, including an eleven-volume *History of South Africa*. He was also given the office of Colonial Historiographer. Among the works he prepared for publication were 36 volumes in a series entitled *Records of the Cape Colony* and an 8-volume series, *Records of South-East Africa*. Though he believed he was objective, he presented a highly selective view of the country's past, and seldom cited sources, making later verification difficult. He became increasingly racist in his writing after he moved to Cape Town. His *History*, enormously influential, did much to underpin a settler view of the country's past, which in turn fed into apartheid ideology. [C. Saunders, *The Making of the South African Past* (Cape Town, 1988)]

THONGA (Tsonga, Tonga), from a root meaning 'east', and therefore 'people from the east'. People who lived in small chiefdoms north of the Zulu in the hinterland of Delagoa Bay. Thonga had hunted for ivory along the Limpopo River from at least the early 18th century, and were the chief middlemen in trade between the Portuguese at Delagoa Bay and both the Nguni and the Sotho. During the Nguni raids of the early 19th century, many Thonga were forced westwards into the Transvaal. One of the earliest African people to participate in migrant labour on an extensive scale, they moved through Zululand into Natal from the 1860s to seek work on the sugar plantations and elsewhere in Natal. The Cape tapped this labour source and imported Thonga labour by sea; at the Cape they were known as 'Mosbiekers' ('from Mozambique'). Large numbers travelled overland to the diamond fields in the 1870s, where they were known as 'Shangaans'.

The Thonga chiefdoms were annexed by the British in 1895 in order to prevent the Transvaal from obtaining access to the sea. Swiss missionaries who worked in the region, particularly the pioneer ethnographer Henri-Alexander Junod (1863–1934), used the term 'Thonga' to include both the people of southern Mozambique and many in the eastern Transvaal. It was, to a considerable extent, the Swiss missionaries who helped construct a Thonga identity, a process carried much further by the South African government during the 1960s and 1970s, when they established a separate bantustan for the Transvaal Thonga, called Gazankulu. [L. Vail, ed., *The Creation of Tribalism in Southern Africa* (London, 1989)]

THULAMELA. Hill-top site near the confluence of the Luvuvhu and Limpopo rivers, in the extreme north of the Kruger National Park. It was excavated in the mid-1990s. The site was inhabited from about the 13th to 16th centuries AD, by people with cultural links with the inhabitants of Mapungubwe* to the west and Great Zimbabwe to the north. The remains of stone-walled domestic and court enclosures, now reconstructed, made up the residence of a ruler of considerable power and wealth, who is assumed to have had 'divine' status.

TLHAPING. The most southerly chiefdom of the Tswana* people. In the 18th century, the Tlhaping lived north of the Orange River, and possessed considerable wealth in the form of livestock. They formed close ties with the Korana* and acted as middlemen in trade between Tswana people to the north of them and Khoikhoi people along the Orange River and in Namibia. Because of their geographical position, they were also the first Tswana to meet whites: a party of travellers and government officials from Cape Town visited their capital, Dithakong, in 1801.

They managed to maintain their power and independence through an alliance with the Griqua* at the beginning of the 19th century. In 1823, Tlhaping aided the Griqua and the missionary Robert Moffat* in repulsing an attack by displaced people at the Battle of Dithakong. The Tlhaping slowly surrendered their land and autonomy to the Cape Colony as the century progressed, a process which accelerated after the discovery of diamonds in the late 1860s. Some Tlhaping rebelled against the Cape in 1878, and others in 1896. Many of them found themselves living in the Bophuthatswana* bantustan in the 1980s. [K. Shillington, *The Colonisation of the Southern Tswana* (Johannesburg, 1985)]

TORCH COMMANDO (TC). Originally the War Veterans' Action Committee, the TC was a quasi-political ex-servicemen's organization which suddenly emerged in opposition to the National Party (NP) government in 1951. In May of that year, it staged a series of spectacular protests, some of which included torch-light processions, against legislation being introduced to remove Coloured voters from the common roll (see FRANCHISE). It opened its membership to non-veterans and had by late 1951 attracted some 120,000 members in 350 branches. There were a few Afrikaners in the leadership, but most of the members were English-speaking whites. Whether Coloureds could become members was never clarified, but they were not welcomed in the organization, which saw itself as white.

Besides opposing the government on the Coloured vote issue, there was no agreement on what the Torch Commando should do. Some members wanted a new National Convention* to revise the constitution; others successfully pushed the Torch Commando into a united front with the United Party and (the white) Labour Party. The National Party (NP) sought to depict the Torch Commando as dangerous and unconstitutional. After the NP won the general election of 1953, some Torch members joined the new Liberal Party,* while others argued that the Torch had failed and should disband. A very small majority of those at its June 1953 congress decided to carry on, but by then the Torch was on its deathbed, and attempts to revive it in 1955 came to nothing.

TOTAL STRATEGY. The 1977 a Defence White Paper advanced the idea that South Africa was faced by a total onslaught against it, instigated by Moscow, and that to meet the challenge a total strategy was called for. When P.W. Botha became Prime Minister in 1978, he promoted the idea so as to justify apartheid, and the use of any means necessary – including destabilization of neighbouring countries – to resist those who sought to overthrow the regime by violence. An elaborate National Security Management System, under the State Security Council,* was put in place to implement the total strategy, and co-ordinate state activities in the interests of defending the country from the 'revolutionary forces' opposed to it. In reality, to the extent that there was a co-ordinated onslaught on the country, it was one directed at apartheid, not a communist-inspired design to control South Africa. [A. Seegers, *The Military in the Making of Modern South Africa* (London, 1996)]

TOWNSHIP REVOLT (1984–1986). An uprising which began in the Vaal Triangle south of Johannesburg in September 1984, as the tricameral* parliament was inaugurated. It was in part a response to the imposition of increased service charges on residents by new township authorities, who were rejected as illegitimate. The revolt soon spread countrywide, and for brief periods some townships were beyond police control. The army was drafted in to aid the police in suppressing the revolt. As a result of harsh repression, including the imposition of a general State of Emergency in 1986, the revolt was brought under control, but by then the apartheid regime was condemned internationally as never before, and widespread sanctions had been imposed against it. More than any other single factor, the revolt led the government to rethink its policies, and open negotiations with the jailed Nelson Mandela [G. Mbeki, *Sunset at Midday* (Braamfontein, 1996); W. Cobbett and

R. Cohen, eds., *Popular Struggles in South Africa* (London, 1988)]

TRADE UNION CONGRESS OF SOUTH AFRICA (TUCSA). Formed in 1954–1955 as a federation of registered trade unions, it was in the early 1980s the largest such body in the country. In 1956 it opposed legislation extending the job colour bar, though it excluded African unions from its membership, and the South African Congress of Trade Unions was set up as a rival body to mobilize the African working class. In 1962 TUCSA decided to allow African unions to affiliate, but under pressure from both the government and white unions those that had joined were forced to withdraw in the late 1960s. From 1974 TUCSA once again allowed African unions to affiliate. Those that did so were mainly unions organized parallel to the registered unions, and under white control. Those on the left criticized TUCSA for its narrow, non-political approach. [J. Lewis, *Industrialisation and Trade Union Organisation in South Africa* (Cambridge, 1984)]

TRADE UNIONS. The earliest unions, formed among white immigrant workers, were craft unions. Cape printers made an attempt to organize in 1838. In 1881 typographical and carpenters' unions were established in Cape Town. Unionism greatly increased with the mineral revolution. An Artisans and Engine Drivers Association came into being on the diamond fields in 1883 and a branch of the British Amalgamated Society of Engineers was formed in 1886, the forerunner of the Amalgamated Engineering Union established in 1920. The Transvaal Miners' Association brought together white miners in 1902, foreshadowing the all-white Mine Workers' Union established in 1913.

As mine-owners sought to lower their labour costs by fragmenting craft operations and substituting semi-skilled or unskilled Africans for whites, white trade unions were increasingly concerned not only to improve the economic position of their members against employers and win union recognition, but also to prevent Africans (or, for a few years, Chinese) from acquiring jobs held by whites. The two decades after the South African War were years of great militancy by the white unions (see STRIKES). After the suppression of the Rand Revolt,* however, trade union membership declined markedly and the state stepped in to control industrial relations through the recognition of non-African unions and the provision of new conciliation machinery.

With more and more Afrikaners joining the urban working class, the Afrikaner Broederbond* played a crucial role in detaching them from English-controlled unions, or wresting control of unions from English-speaking cliques. In 1933, for example, a new railwaymen's union was set up for Afrikaners. After a long battle, control of the powerful white Mine Workers' Union passed into Afrikaner hands.

The first African trade unions of any significance were formed at the end of World War I.* The Industrial Workers of Africa emerged out of classes run for Africans by the International Socialist League in Johannesburg in 1917. Its slogan was *Sifuna zonke* (Zulu, 'We want all'); it was hoped that it would grow into a large union of the unskilled, along the lines of the American union called the Industrial Workers of the World. But the police infiltrated it, and it soon fell apart. The first large general union on the African continent was the Industrial and Commercial

Workers' Union,* formed by Clements Kadalie in 1919.

In the late 1920s and early 1930s, as the ICU collapsed, a number of short-lived industrial unions began to emerge among African workers parallel to unions registered under the Industrial Conciliation Act. Some unions – the Garment Workers' Union, most notably – brought together Afrikaner and Coloured workers. It was not until 1956 that an amendment to the Industrial Conciliation Act prevented any further registration of such unions, but long before that many of them had been hard hit by state action.

During World War II, when the African workforce in industry grew rapidly and labour was in short supply, African unionism entered a militant phase, culminating in the 1946 strike, when the African Mine Workers' Union, formed in 1941, brought out over 60,000 miners. The brutal suppression of the strike was followed by greater co-operation between the African trade union movement and the ANC. Then between 1954 and 1960, some 40 unions affiliated with the South African Congress of Trade Unions,* part of the Congress Alliance.* The 1960s was a decade of repression, with minimal union activity. From the early 1970s, however, young whites, with close links to the universities, helped organize unregistered unions; some of these organizers suffered detentions and bannings as a result. (The sixth trade unionist to die in detention was a young white trade-union leader, Neil Aggett, who died in February 1982.)

Gradually both employers and the state were converted to the belief that the best way to control African unionism was by recognizing it and permitting the registration of African unions. This major step, recommended by the Wiehahn Commission,* was taken in 1979. The new possibility of registration sparked off a fierce debate within the labour movement, with some arguing that because registration meant increased state control, it should therefore be rejected. The Federation of South African Trade Unions (FOSATU) – formally constituted in 1979 though it grew out of attempts to bring together unions formed during the strikes of 1973 and after – sought to create a non-racial labour movement and encouraged the formation and affiliation of broadly based industrial unions. It was prepared to accept registration, so long as its affiliated unions could be non-racial. This was conceded in 1981, and FOSATU made great gains. Of the unregistered unions, the South African Allied Workers' Union grew especially in the eastern Cape and Ciskei, despite great police harassment. In the 1980s union membership increased at an unprecedented rate, and individual unions combined in large organizations, the most important of which was the Congress of South African Trade Unions,* launched in 1985, which later allied itself with the African National Congress. The largest union in COSATU was the National Union of Mineworkers, the successor to the African Mine Workers' Union. [S. Friedman, *Building Tomorrow Today* (Johannesburg, 1987); J. Lewis, *Industrialisation and Trade Union Organisation in South Africa* (Cambridge, 1984); B. Hirson, *Yours for the Union* (London, 1989); E. Katz, *A Trade Union Aristocracy* (Johannesburg, 1976)]

TRANSITIONAL EXECUTIVE COUNCIL (TEC). A key element in the process of transition from apartheid to democratic rule, the TEC was designed by the constitutional negotiators to meet the need for a body to replace the government in the run-up to the April 1994 election. Made up of representatives from the parties in the constitutional negotiations, it was formally constituted by parliament in December 1993 and served as a joint executive; it was thus a precursor of the Government of National Unity.* One of the TRC's seven sub-councils, that on defence, was responsible for establishing the National Peacekeeping Force, which proved a disastrous experiment. The planning which that sub-council did for the creation of a new defence force was much more successful. With the inauguration of a new government after the election, the work of the TEC came to an end. [S.Friedman and D. Atkinson, ed., *The Small Miracle* (Johannesburg, 1994)]

TRANSKEI (the land 'across' the Kei River). Iron Age and probably Bantu-speaking people lived on the Transkei coast by the 7th century AD. From the 16th century, shipwrecked European sailors told of mixed farmers, speaking Nguni languages, in the region. During the 1820s, the small northern chiefdoms in the Transkei were devastated by Zulu* armies. Disruption would probably have been greater had an intrusive group of Ngwane not been defeated at the Battle of Mbholompo in the central Transkei in 1828. Large numbers of refugees from the Mfecane* settled in the Transkei at this time, and European missionary and colonial trading networks from the south began to spread across the Kei.

In the mid-19th century, 'Transkei' usually meant the land immediately east of the Kei, between that river and the Mbashe. From the 1870s it often referred to the entire area from the Kei to the southern border of Natal, and from the Drakensberg to the Indian Ocean. This area, annexed to the Cape Colony in stages between 1879 and 1894, became a separate administrative unit within the colony, one in which a policy of legal differentiation was applied. In the 20th century, it formed the largest African reserve in the country, and the pace-setter in the bantustan scheme of H.F. Verwoerd.* The Transkeian bantustan, with its capital at Umtata, received 'self-government' in 1963 and 'independence', recognized only by South Africa, in 1976. In 1987 its civilian prime minister was overthrown by a military coup; Major-General Bantu Holomisa emerged as the Transkei's last ruler. In April 1994 the bantustan was reincorporated into South Africa, and the Transkei became part of the Eastern Cape province. [W. Beinart and C. Bundy, *Hidden Struggles in Rural South Africa* (Johannesburg, 1987); B. Streek and R. Wicksteed, *Render Unto Kaiser* (Johannesburg, 1981)]

TRANSORANGIA. The area 'across the Orange River'; also known as the TransGariep, from the Korana word for the Orange River, 'Gariep'. A predominantly highveld grassland region, it had been occupied originally by Khoisan hunters and herders, and parts of it were settled by Bantu-speaking pastoralists and agriculturists by AD 1000. During the 17th and 18th centuries, the region experienced considerable conflict between competing Sotho–Tswana* groups, a pattern which intensified in the first half of the 19th century, with the arrival of new people in the region. The Griqua* under Adam Kok* established themselves in the southern parts, while Voortrekkers* settled further north during the 1830s. These groups provided fresh challenges to the Rolong,* Tlokoa and Sotho peoples of the region. By the 1840s prevailing conditions of unrest threatened the northern frontier of the Cape, and persuaded the Governor, George Napier, to try to establish subsidized buffer states as a means of exercising indirect control without heavy military commitment. The strategy failed, and Britain annexed the area between the Orange and Vaal rivers as the Orange River Sovereignty* in 1848. [T. Keegan, *Colonial South Africa and the Origins of the Racial Order* (Cape Town, 1996)]

TRANSVAAL. The land 'across (north of) the Vaal River'. Evidence of pastoral farming and cultivation in parts of the area dates from at least the 5th century AD. Bantu-speaking farmers were scattered across the region from the 10th century; according to tradition, Sotho–Tswana* peoples claim descent from the farmers of the 'Greater Magaliesberg' area in the 13th and 14th centuries. By the 16th and 17th centuries, Sotho–Tswana speakers had dispersed from this relatively densely populated region across most of the trans-Vaal. Large portions of the area were disrupted during the 1820s by the Mfecane.* Mzilikazi* incorporated large numbers of Sotho-speakers into his Ndebele state,* and for a brief time had his capital near modern Pretoria.

The Voortrekkers* founded four separate republics, based in Potchefstroom (from 1838, the largest white settlement north of the Vaal), Utrecht, Lydenburg and the Soutpansberg. Britain recognized the independence of whites living north of the Vaal by the Sand River Convention in 1852, but only in 1858 were the scattered groups of whites brought under the central authority of the South African Republic (SAR),* as the Transvaal state was called, with its capital at Pretoria. For much of the latter half of the 19th century, the SAR was weak, unstable, poorly administered and bankrupt; whites also struggled to exercise authority over African chiefdoms in the region. Their inability to defeat the Pedi was used by the British, who were investigating the possibility of confederation, to justify the annexation of the SAR in 1877. After the British army defeated both the Zulu and the Pedi, the Anglo-Transvaal War broke out as the Transvaal Afrikaners rose against British rule. The Pretoria Convention of August 1881 returned self-government to the SAR, but Britain, fearing a threat to continued imperial rule in the subcontinent, made sure that the SAR could not form alliances with a foreign power or acquire direct access to the sea.

The discovery of gold on the Witwatersrand in 1886 fundamentally transformed Transvaal history. Britain feared the potential threat to its interests held by the Transvaal's wealth, and political and economic considerations precipitated the South African War* of 1899–1902, during which the SAR lost its independence and became a crown colony. After the war, Sir Alfred Milner* hoped to introduce thousands of new British immigrants to the territory to outnumber the Afrikaners and undermine their culture through a determined anglicization policy, but his plans were foiled by the devastating economic consequences of the war. Fundamental adjustments to formal black–white relations, however, were not considered. The original SAR constitution had declared there would be no equality in church or state; only white males could enjoy the benefits of citizenship. In the Treaty of Vereeniging,* which ended the war in 1902, Britain undertook not to extend the franchise to blacks, and during negotiations for the Union of South Africa in 1908 and 1909 the Transvaal opposed any extension of the non-racial franchise of the Cape.

In 1910 the Transvaal became one of the Union of South Africa's four provinces, and Pretoria became the national administrative capital. During the 20th century, the Transvaal came to play an increasingly dominant political and economic role in the country. Johannesburg, situated on the Witwatersrand, in the centre of the Transvaal's mineral belt, became the commercial, financial and industrial heart of the country. Much economic power lay in the hands of English-speakers throughout the century, though Afrikaner capital gained strength from the 1950s. Afrikaner nationalism, however, was most robust in the Transvaal, in Pretoria and the rich agricultural districts of the province. The increasingly powerful National Party (NP) of the Transvaal largely dictated the pace of the country's political life from the mid-1950s until the 1980s, when Transvaal Afrikanerdom split between those in the NP prepared to entertain some notions of reform and those who moved into more conservative parties to the right.

In the Witwatersrand region, townships housed the labour supply of the mines and industries on which the country's wealth depended. It was here that there began those events which represent the most powerful symbols of black resistance to apartheid and white oppression, the Sharpeville massacre,* the Soweto uprising* and the township revolt.* After the election of 1994, the Transvaal ceased to exist as a province. Four new provinces were created out of it: Gauteng,* North-West Province,* Northern Province,* and Mpumalanga.* [B. Bozzoli, ed., *Labour, Townships and Protest* (Johannesburg, 1979), *Town and Countryside in the Transvaal* (Johannesburg, 1983), *Class, Community and Conflict* (Johannesburg, 1987)]

TRANSVAAL, ANNEXATION OF (1877). To promote the confederation* of South Africa, Lord Carnarvon* appointed Theophilus Shepstone* to proceed to the Transvaal* (South African Republic*) and annex it if its citizens were willing. Using the Transvaal's weak government and its inability to defeat the Pedi* as an excuse, and ignoring clear evidence that the Transvaal Boers did not want to come under British rule, Shepstone raised the Union Jack in April 1878 and became first British administrator of the Transvaal. British rule aroused much resentment among the Boer community, and the Boers rose in revolt in 1880.

TREASON TRIAL (1956–1961). Following the adoption of the Freedom Charter at the Congress of the People held at Kliptown, south of Johannesburg, in 1955, the police arrested 156 of the people involved and charged them with treason, on the grounds that they were working for revolution. The trial dragged on, and the remaining accused, including Nelson Mandela,* were finally acquitted in 1961, the state having failed to establish any revolutionary intent behind their actions. [A. Sampson, *The Treason Cage* (London, 1958)]

TREKBOERS. Dutch term for frontier farmers. White semi-nomadic Dutch-speaking sheep and cattle farmers began to leave the south-western Cape, with its Mediterranean climate, from the end of the 17th century. They moved into the drier interior where extensive pastoralism and hunting were the only possible modes of production. In the first half of the 18th century, there was plentiful land in the interior, and few geographical obstacles to expansion in northerly and easterly directions. Khoisan peoples of the region were variously dispossessed of their land, killed, expelled, or permitted to work as squatters or labourers on the 6000-acre farms which the trekboers allocated to themselves. One main line of advance was eastwards, parallel to the mountain ranges, to the Zuurveld area and the Fish River, where the trekboers met Xhosa stock farmers in the 1770s. Others moved their herds and their ox-wagons around or across the barren Karoo, and beyond the boundaries which the colonial authorities tried periodically to fix. Though trekboer life was largely self-sufficient, they maintained irregular contact with Cape markets to ensure that they were supplied with essential commodities such as firearms and ammunition. Most conducted simple, isolated lives, remote from the control of the Cape authorities. Despite this, they continued to regard themselves as colonial subjects, unlike the Voortrekkers of the 1830s, who deliberately sought to free themselves of colonial control. [P.J. van der Merwe, *The Migrant Farmer in the History of the Cape Colony, 1657–1842* (Athens, 1995)]

TRICAMERAL PARLIAMENT (1984–1994). One of P.W. Botha's most important reforms, it lay at the heart of the new constitution of 1984. Coloureds and Indians were brought into central government in separate houses of parliament: a House of Representatives for Coloureds and a House of Delegates for Indians, though provision was made for the three houses to meet together under certain circumstances. The exclusion of Africans from this new arrangement helped fuel the township revolt,* and the failure of the tricameral parliament to resolve the government's crisis of legitimacy was an important reason for the decision by De Klerk* to negotiate a settlement with the African National Congress and others. These negotiations led to the dissolution of the tricameral parliament in December 1993, prior to the general election of 1994, but only after it had approved the interim constitution of 1993, drafted by the Multi-Party Negotiating Forum,* thus providing legislative continuity. [R. Schrire, *Adapt or Die* (1989)]

TRUTH AND RECONCILIATION COMMISSION (TRC). The idea for such a commission was put forward in a speech by the new Minister of Justice, Dullah Omar, to the first democratic parliament in July 1994. At this time Alex Boraine (1931–), former MP and executive director of the Institute for a Democratic Alternative in South Africa (ISDASA), headed a non-governmental organization, Justice in Transition, which argued that South Africa should follow other countries in creating such a commission. The aim was to find out what had led to gross violations of human rights, and to deal with that past by granting amnesty to those who made full disclosure of what had happened.

The TRC was set up by Act of parliament, and its 17 members, headed by Archbishop Desmond Tutu,* were appointed in December 1995. Its human rights' violations committee investigated gross violations of human rights between 1960 and 1994 (the cut-off date was initially December 1993, but was then extended to the date of Mandela's inauguration). Numerous public hearings were held in many parts of the country in 1996 and 1997, and over 20,000 statements by victims of gross violations of human rights were recorded. The amnesty committee heard applications by over 7000 people for amnesty for offences committed in those years. If the offences were politically motivated, and if full disclosure was made, amnesty was granted. Some of the hearings revealed much about the way certain high-profile murders and assassinations, including the death of Steve Biko,* had been carried out. A third committee advised the government on reparations and rehabilitation for victims of gross human rights' abuses, and proposed that a fund of some R3 billion be established to meet those needs. The TRC's final report was due to be presented in July 1998, but the work of its amnesty committee was likely to extend well beyond that date. [A. Boraine et al., eds., *Dealing with the Past* (Cape Town, 1997); A. Boraine et al., eds., *The Healing of a Nation?* (Cape Town, 1995)]

TSWANA. Western Sotho* people, who between the 15th and the 18th centuries gradually occupied most of the central and western area of the highveld. Various chiefdoms among the Tswana experienced a shifting pattern of segmentation and amalgamation during this period. The availability of land enabled dissatisfied people and their followers to break away from chiefdoms and settle in new areas; at the same time, powerful chiefdoms were able to consolidate authority through the conquest of neighbours and the control of natural resources. By the end of the 18th century, however, strains within Tswana societies became more acute: they had reached the limits of their westerly expansion as they began to press against the Kalahari Desert, and an extended drought between 1790 and 1810 intensified competition for pastoral and arable land, as well as for control of trading routes.

During the period of the Mfecane,* these tensions were exacerbated by the arrival of new peoples, both those with aggressive intentions and many displaced refugees. While some Tswana groups managed to rebuild themselves during the 1830s, the presence of the Griqua and, particularly, white Voortrekkers from the end of that decade prevented many from resuming independent lifestyles. Tswana living in the South African Republic* established by the Voortrekkers were forced to compete for land, and were often subject to tribute and labour demands. After the discovery of diamonds,* many Tswana were caught between conflicting British and Boer requirements, causing enormous strains within chiefdoms over alliances and strategies. This was graphically illustrated in the South African War,* when the Tswana entered the conflict as active participants on both sides.

After 1910, many Tswana shared the experiences of Africans across the country: their economic independence disintegrated through the system of migrant labour and the alienation of their land. In 1977, under the bantustan policy of the apartheid government, the republic of Bophuthatswana* was given 'independence', and it was there that people of Tswana origins were expected to exercise political rights. Like the other 'independent' bantustans, however, Bophuthatswana could not survive without significant financial and military support from the South African government. A crisis there in March 1994 proved an important precursor to the successful democratic elections of April 1994, when Bophuthatswana was reincorporated in South Africa. [I. Schapera, *The Tribal Innovators* (London, 1970); K. Shillington, *The Colonisation of the Southern Tswana* (Johannesburg, 1985); A. Jeffrey, *Conflict at the Crossroads in Bophuthatswana* (Johannesburg, 1993); J. and J. Comaroff, *Of Revelation and Revolution* (Chicago, 1991, 1997)]

TUTU, Desmond Mpilo (1931–). Clergyman and anti-apartheid activist. Ordained in the Anglican Church in 1961, he was employed by the World Council of Churches before becoming Anglican Dean of Johannesburg. He was then briefly Bishop of Lesotho and general secretary of the South African Council of Churches before being chosen Archbishop of Cape Town in 1986. Throughout the 1980s he played an important role in mobilizing international opinion against apartheid, and he was a strong advocate of the imposition of sanctions* against the apartheid regime. He was awarded the Nobel Peace Prize in 1984. Once the liberation movements were unbanned, he deliberately adopted a less overtly political position, but remained an influential figure, promoting the idea of the 'rainbow nation', and commenting on events with wit and humour, as well as profound seriousness. In 1995, on the eve of his retirement as Archbishop of Cape Town, he was appointed head of the Truth and Reconciliation Commission.* [S. du Boulay, *Tutu* (London, 1988); J. Allen, ed., *The Rainbow People of God* (Toronto, 1995)]

u

UITLANDERS. Afrikaans word meaning 'foreigners', which was applied to non-Afrikaner whites in the Transvaal before the South African War.* Thousands settled on the Witwatersrand after the discovery of gold in 1886, but restrictive franchise laws made it difficult for new immigrants to acquire citizenship and the vote. Those associated with the Transvaal government viewed the Uitlanders as brash, materialistic and culturally alien, and feared that if they obtained the franchise they would upset Afrikaner political dominance and even cause the independence of the Transvaal from Britain to be revoked. Such fears were almost certainly exaggerated: few Uitlanders wanted Transvaal citizenship. In the aftermath of the Jameson Raid,* the British government made Uitlander rights a key issue in its relations with the Transvaal. In 1899 President Kruger* was prepared to grant the Uitlanders the vote after they had fulfilled a seven-year residence requirement, but this was unacceptable to Sir Alfred Milner. The franchise issue thus contributed to the outbreak of the South African War. After the war, the franchise was extended to Uitlanders, but despite large Boer losses in the war and further immigration from Britain, Afrikaners remained a clear majority of whites, and an Afrikaner political party, Het Volk, triumphed in the whites-only election of 1907. [I. Smith, *The Origins of the South African War* (London, 1996)]

UMKHONTO weSIZWE (MK). Military wing of the African National Congress, established in 1961 after the banning of the ANC in 1960. It undertook sabotage from 1961 and then, from exile, guerrilla training. Its guerrillas entered Rhodesia in the 1960s but suffered a major defeat there at the hands of South African security forces. After the Soweto uprising* of 1976, its numbers were boosted as thousands of young men and women joined its ranks. Many found themselves in Angola,* and some died there fighting against UNITA. In the late 1970s MK operatives entered South Africa to perform acts of sabotage. The guerrilla ethos captured the imagination of many township youth and helped promote the cause of the ANC. Of some 1500 attacks between 1977 and 1989, among the most spectacular were those on the Sasol oil refinery in June 1880, the rocket attack on the South African Defence Force* headquarters at Voortrekkerhoogte outside Pretoria in August 1981, the planting of bombs at Koeberg nuclear power station in December 1982, and the car-bomb which exploded outside the airforce command centre in downtown Pretoria in May 1983 and killed 19 people.

The escalation in conflict in the 1980s played a major role in leading to the negotiated settlement of the early 1990s. But the New York accords of December 1988, providing for a transition to independence in Namibia,* required MK to leave its Angolan camps, and its cadres found themselves as far from South Africa as Uganda. When the ANC agreed, in the Pretoria Minute* of August 1990, to suspend the armed struggle, it did not disband MK, the size of which grew in the early 1990s. Following the democratic election of 1994, its members were integrated into the new South African National Defence Force, but with the downscaling of that force many soon left it. [H. Barrell, *MK* (London, 1990); R. Kasrils, *Armed and Dangerous* (Oxford, 1993)]

UNION (1910). Several British-led attempts to unite the various South African states were made, and failed, in the 19th century (see CONFEDERATION). After the South African War,* when all four of the states were British, Milner* and members of his Kindergarten* took steps to promote the idea: among the schemes he initiated to promote closer ties between the South African states were the amalgamation of the railway networks, the formation of an Inter-Colonial Council, and the appointment of a South African Native Affairs Commission under Sir Godfrey Lagden in 1903 to draw up a South Africa-wide 'native policy'. A South African Customs Union was also created (1903).

Lord Selborne (1859–1942), Milner's successor as High Commissioner, hoped that a federated South Africa would attract large-scale British immigration. Louis Botha* and Jan Smuts* were attracted to the idea of a united South Africa because they thought it would be less subject to British interference. A discussion paper known as the Selborne Memorandum was issued to the colonial governments in 1907 and then published and widely debated. Written by Lionel Curtis at the High Commissioner's invitation, it argued that unity would bring political stability and promote economic progress. Unification seemed likely to pull the country out of the recession from which it had suffered since 1903 and eliminate the tensions that disagreements on customs and railway tariffs had produced. The confidence of Natal's whites in their ability to control their large African population had been shaken by the Bambatha Rebellion.*

A National Convention,* made up of representatives from the various parliaments, and therefore all white, met in 1908–1909 to draw up a new constitution for the united country. It agreed that the four colonies should unite, and that South Africa should be a unitary state and not a federation. The proposals emanating from the National Convention were approved by the four colonies, then incorporated in a South Africa Bill, which went through the British parliament. The Union of South Africa was inaugurated on 31 May 1910, eight years to the day after the signing of the Treaty of Vereeniging.*

A delegation of white liberals and blacks, led by the former Cape Prime Minister, William Schreiner, travelled to London to protest against the colour bar in the Union constitution, but to no avail. Union was widely hailed as a great achievement. It was clearly to Britain's advantage for South Africa to be one large state, able to defend itself, yet within the Empire, and in which there was hope of English–Afrikaner reconciliation and the prospect that the interests of finance and mining capital would be promoted. Nor were Africans entirely overlooked. The Liberal government in Britain hoped that a strong Union would be in the interests of Africans and that the Cape's non-racial franchise, protected by the 'entrenched clauses' of the constitution, which could be altered only by a vote of two-thirds of both Houses of Parliament sitting together, would in time be extended to the other provinces. It was made clear that the wish of the people of the High Commission territories* should be considered when the question of incorporating them arose.

Though liberal historians have condemned the choice of a unitary rather than a federal constitution for so heterogeneous a society, it was believed at the time that a unitary one would prove easier to work and would provide the necessary strong government. Had South Africa not been a close union, white Southern Rhodesians might have agreed to join it in the 1920s. [L. Thompson, *The Unification of South Africa* (Oxford, 1960); E. Walker, W.P. *Schreiner* (London, 1937); A. Odendaal, *Vukani Bantu!* (Cape Town, 1984); B.Magubane, *The Making of a Racist State* (Trenton, 1996)]

UNIONIST PARTY. A political party drawing on English-speaking support, it was the main opposition in the first Union parliament. It emerged from the Progressive Party of the pre-Union Cape Colony, which took the name Unionist Party shortly before Union came into being. After the formation of the National Party, Louis Botha* became increasingly dependent on Unionist support, and it was eventually absorbed by the South African Party* in 1920. Its lineal successor was the pro-British Dominion Party,* founded in 1934.

UNITED DEMOCRATIC FRONT (UDF). The most important internal anti-apartheid organization in the 1980s, it was established at a meeting at Mitchell's Plain outside Cape Town on 20 August 1983. This followed a call by the Rev. Allan Boesak* for opposition to the tricameral constitution and to proposed legislation for African administration. Standing for a democratic, non-racial order, the UDF was an umbrella body that brought together hundreds of youth, student and civic organizations, in a decentralized structure, which was difficult for the government to suppress. The reformist image the government wished to present at first allowed the UDF space to organize, but it was hard hit during the states of emergency from 1985 onwards. The government believed it had played a major role in the township revolt,* and many of its leading office-bearers suffered imprisonment and other forms of harassment. Twenty-two leading activists, including Patrick Lekota and Popo Molefe, were tried on charges of treason and terrorism in the small town of Delmas from 1985; the trial dragged on for years and the accused were found guilty and imprisoned but were set free when the case went on appeal.

Along with other organizations, the UDF was restricted in February 1988. In showing the strength of internal opposition, it played an important role in the process leading to the negotiated settlement of the 1990s. Once the liberation movements had been unbanned, however, it lost its reason for existence, and was disbanded in August 1991 on its eighth anniversary. Many of its leaders played important roles in ANC politics thereafter: Allan Boesak became ANC leader in the Western Cape for a time; Lekota became the first premier of the Free State and then chair of the National Council of Provinces; and Molefe became premier of the North-West Province. [T. Lodge and B. Nasson, *All, Here, and Now* (Cape Town, 1991)]

UNITED NATIONS (UN). The South African Prime Minister Jan Smuts* was the main author of the preamble to the UN Charter, and South Africa was a founder member of the world body, yet it was soon the most criticized country of all in that forum. At the inaugural session in 1946, the Indian delegation brought South

Africa's treatment of its Indian minority before the General Assembly, which also rejected South Africa's plea for the incorporation of South West Africa. From 1952 the whole apartheid system came under regular attack, despite South African objections that it was a domestic matter and fell under article 2(7) of the UN Charter, which had been designed to protect members from interference by others in matters of domestic jurisdiction. After the Sharpeville massacre,* criticism became much more strident, with a UN Special Committee Against Apartheid being appointed in 1962. In that year the General Assembly recommended that member states break all ties with South Africa, including trade links. The following year the Security Council imposed a non-mandatory arms embargo. Gradually South Africa left the various UN agencies: UNESCO in 1956, the International Labour Organization in 1961, the World Health Organization in 1965.

In October 1966 the General Assembly voted to terminate South Africa's mandate over South West Africa. Thereafter, South Africa's continued occupation of Namibia,* and its refusal to acknowledge UN supervision of the territory, became a matter to which the UN devoted much attention. In 1974 the General Assembly rejected the credentials of the South African delegation, preventing them from speaking, but South Africa remained a member of the world body, speaking in the Security Council and having regular discussions with the Secretary General on the Namibian issue in particular.

Calls for mandatory economic sanctions against South Africa came before the Security Council on a number of occasions, but were vetoed by the Western members – the United States, Britain and France. In 1977, however, after the murder of Steve Biko* and the banning of Black Consciousness* organizations, the Security Council did impose a mandatory arms embargo against South Africa. But this was as far as UN sanctions went: in the Cold War era, the United States in particular did not want the Soviet Union to have any decisive say in the removal of sanctions, and so vetoed further sanctions proposed in the Security Council.

South African government suspicions of the UN began to dissipate when the UN played a relatively even-handed role in the transition to independence in Namibia in 1989. UN observers filled a minor role in monitoring the transition to democracy in South Africa in the early 1990s. After the election of a democratic government in April 1994, South Africa resumed its full role in the UN, and again began paying its membership dues. In 1997 the Mandela* government began lobbying hard to secure a permanent seat on an enlarged Security Council. [United Nations, *The United Nations Against Apartheid 1948–1994* (New York, 1994)]

UNITED PARTY (UP) (1934–1977). Governing party until 1948 and thereafter the official opposition to the National Party (NP). The United South African National Party emerged from the fusion of Hertzog's NP and the South African Party* of General Smuts.* Its first major crisis came in September 1939, when Hertzog and his supporters left it over South Africa's entry into World War II.* It lost power in 1948, despite winning a majority of votes, because of the urban concentration of its supporters, the weighting of rural constituencies, and the way delimitation of the constituencies had been applied. This shock defeat, followed in short succession by the deaths of Jan Hofmeyr (1894–1948), Smuts's deputy, and then of Smuts himself in

1950, left the party in great disarray. It continued to outpoll the NP until the 1961 election but, as it lost seats in successive elections to the NP, it lost confidence in its ability ever to return to power. Committed to white supremacy, it offered only the pre-1948 pattern of race relations, the possibility of a few whites representing Africans in parliament, and 'white leadership with justice'. It became, increasingly, a mainly English-speaking party.

In an attempt to make itself more acceptable to the white electorate, the UP moved closer to the NP, and even began to attack that party from the right. In response to the 'separate development' vision of Prime Minister Verwoerd* in 1959, the right-wing in the UP saw an opportunity to brand him a negrophile and urged the party congress to oppose the grant of more land for Africans if such land was to be appended to potentially independent bantustans. Eleven of the more liberal-minded members of the party, who included many of its ablest debaters and intellectuals, could take its conservative drift no longer, and broke away to form the Progressive Party. The UP then enjoyed greater internal unanimity for a time, but the mediocre leadership of Sir De Villiers Graaff and its ambivalent policies continued to alienate those on both its left and its right. Another break-away to the left took place in February 1975. The following year six right-wing members of parliament split off to form a South African Party, while six others formed a Committee for a United Opposition, which soon merged with the Progressive Party. The remaining UP members formed a New Republic Party to the right of the Progressive Party, to which De Villiers Graaff gave his support. This finally brought about the demise of the UP. Its central contradiction was its refusal to abandon white supremacy while opposing a government committed to upholding white supremacy in an extreme form. [D. Graaff, *Div Looks Back* (Cape Town, 1993)]

UNIVERSITIES. The origins of the University of Cape Town lie in the South African College, a private venture begun in 1829 to provide education at a wide range of levels. In 1873 a non-teaching University of the Cape of Good Hope was set up to offer examinations for university degrees; by 1910 it administered eight constituent colleges in the four colonies. Cape Town and Stellenbosch were the first of these to receive independent charters (in 1916 and 1918 respectively). The University of the Cape of Good Hope was transformed into the University of South Africa (Unisa), with headquarters in Pretoria. As the colleges gained independence as full universities, Unisa became a teaching university, but offered degrees through correspondence only.

The older Afrikaans-medium universities emerged out of what had been English-medium colleges: Stellenbosch, near Cape Town; Pretoria, founded after the South African War; and Orange Free State, at Bloemfontein. The Potchefstroom University for Christian Higher Education played an important role in the development of Afrikaner nationalism after 1919. In the mid-1960s a dual medium English–Afrikaans university was founded at Port Elizabeth, and the Rand Afrikaans University was established for Afrikaners in Johannesburg.

The four English-speaking universities – Cape Town, Witwatersrand (in Johannesburg), Rhodes (in Grahamstown) and Natal, with its campuses in Durban and Pietermaritzburg – suffered from an emigration of many of their leading staff for political reasons after 1960 and, given South Africa's increasing isolation, from their inability to attract academics from other countries. They remained, together with the English-speaking churches and the English-language press, the main voice of white liberal opposition to the apartheid regime.

Prior to 1960 the universities of Cape Town and the Witwatersrand and the University of Natal Medical School admitted black students on merit. The numbers were never large. In 1959 legislation, which the 'open universities' strongly opposed, provided that blacks could henceforth attend such universities only by permit. Four new ethnic universities were established: the University of the North, for Sotho-, Tsonga- and Venda-speakers; the University College of Zululand for Zulu-speakers; the University College of the Western Cape, for Coloureds; and the University of Durban-Westville (as it became), for Indians. At the same time, Fort Hare* was taken over by the government as a university for Xhosa-speakers. The non-residential University of South Africa admitted all races as students, but examinations were given and degrees awarded on a segregated basis. With the 'independence' of the bantustans of Transkei, Bophuthatswana and Venda, new universities were established in those territories; though nominally non-racial, they had very few non-African students. In 1981 a new university, called Vista, was founded for Africans in urban areas, and it opened campuses in Mamelodi township outside Pretoria, Soweto outside Johannesburg, Port Elizabeth and elsewhere. Meanwhile, the African 'tribal' or 'bush' universities, despite the repressive atmosphere on their campuses, became centres of dissidence in the late 1960s and 1970s, with Black Consciousness* finding wide support among their students.

In the late 1970s it became somewhat easier for blacks to obtain permits to attend the universities of Cape Town and the Witwatersrand, and a few blacks were admitted for graduate work at some of the Afrikaans-medium universities. In the 1980s, after the University of Cape Town opened its residences to all, the number of African students began to increase significantly, and the permit system fell away. An attempt by the government to introduce a quota system came to nothing, and the universities regained the right to admit whom they wished. From the mid-1990s much attention began to be given to transforming the staff composition of universities, at a time when government funding was being cut back.

URBAN FOUNDATION. Following the Soweto uprising in 1976, big business interests in South Africa decided to become actively involved in improving the quality of life for the country's urban African population. The Urban Foundation was then established, with its first director being ex-judge Jan Steyn. Chiefly occupied with improving black housing, it invested nearly half a billion rands in development and housing loans between 1978 and 1988, and launched over 800 housing projects in African townships. Another major area of activity was the upgrading of educational and recreational facilities in African areas. In the early 1990s more money became available for such projects through the Independent Development Trust, set up with government money allocated to social development purposes, and the Urban Foundation was disbanded.

URBANIZATION. The first major urban settlement in South Africa was Mapungubwe, on the Limpopo River, a city-state which flourished in the 13th century. Perhaps ten thousand people lived there then. Centuries later, perhaps tens of thousands lived in the largest Tswana* settlement, Dithakong, first visited by literate whites in 1801. The Dutch settlement on Table Bay soon developed into a relatively large town, later known as Cape Town. As white settlement spread into the interior, small market centres developed, each with a Dutch Reformed church. In the trekker republics, towns served security as well as administrative functions. Large towns developed at the new centres of mining activity, above all Kimberley* in the early 1870s and Johannesburg* after 1886.

Settlement in such urban centres was for whites: by custom, rather than law, Africans had to live on the outskirts. In Grahamstown in the eastern Cape, a separate Fingo (Mfengu*) location was demarcated in the 1840s, while separate Indian areas were set out in Durban and Johannesburg so as to restrict Indian commercial competition. African locations were provided in Cape Town in 1901, and in Johannesburg and other large cities a few years later. From the 1920s Afrikaner migration from rural areas increased, in the face of agricultural collapse. African migration to the cities became much more significant in World War II,* pushed by rural impoverishment and pulled by the prospect of jobs at relatively high wages in the cities. Large squatter settlements developed on the outskirts of the major centres. In response the National Party government helped build townships like Soweto outside Johannesburg. At the same time, Group Areas* legislation further divided cities and towns, and stricter influx control sought to reverse African urbanization, leading to overcrowding in most townships by the 1970s. By 1991, 89% of whites and 50% of Africans were urbanized, and urban growth rates were over 3% per year.

The Natives (Urban Areas) Act of 1923 provided that municipalities could fund locations from profits from the sale of beer in municipal beerhalls, but conditions in the townships remained poor, with no electricity and often inadequate sanitation. Transport costs were high, and life insecure. Gradually municipal autonomy was weakened; and in 1972 the central government took over administration of all African urban locations. Finally, in the 1980s the attempt to reverse the flow of Africans to the cities was abandoned, and African urbanization took place at a greater rate than ever. After the township revolt of the 1980s the culture of non-payment for services became so deeply entrenched in many townships, however, that even when services were provided they were not paid for. When the townships were merged with the adjacent towns in new local authority structures after 1994, great fiscal and collection problems remained to be solved. [A. Lemon, ed., *Homes Apart* (Bloomington, 1991); M. Swilling et al., eds., *Apartheid City in Transition* (Cape Town, 1991); D. Smith, ed., *The Apartheid City and Beyond* (Johannesburg, 1992)]

VAN DER KEMP, Johannes Theodorus (1747–1811). Missionary of the London Missionary Society.* One of the first missionaries at the Cape, where he arrived in 1799, he lived initially among the Xhosa* on the eastern frontier, but then worked among the Khoikhoi at the Bethelsdorp mission, which he established near Algoa Bay in 1803. His severe criticism of the way the colonists treated their Khoikhoi servants and labourers in the eastern districts of the Cape alienated both the authorities and local colonists. [I. Enklaar, *Life and Work of Dr. J. Th. van der Kemp* (Cape Town, 1988)]

VAN DER STEL, Simon (1639–1712). Merchant, army officer and Commander and Governor of the Cape between 1679 and 1699. He oversaw the expansion of white settlement into the Stellenbosch and Drakenstein districts after the subjugation of the Khoikhoi there, and he travelled widely beyond the colonial boundaries in search of mineral wealth. He has generally been considered a reformer, particularly for his fiscal discipline, his improvements to the Cape's defences and his success in developing the wine industry. He also enriched himself, and farmed his prosperous estate Constantia, outside Cape Town, in his retirement. His son Willem Adriaan (1664–1733), who succeeded him as Governor of the Cape in 1699, acquired extensive arable land, cattle and slaves. Complaints from colonists concerning what they regarded as corruption eventually led to his removal from office in 1707. [R. Elphick and H. Giliomee, eds., *The Shaping of South African Society* (Cape Town, 1989)]

VAN RIEBEECK, Jan Anthonisz (1619–1677). Ship's surgeon, merchant and official of the Dutch East India Company,* who in 1652 established the refreshment station at the Cape of Good Hope to supply ships of the Company trading between Holland and the East. He served as first Commander of the Cape from 1652 until 1662, and many whites have regarded him as the 'founding father' of South Africa. During his rule, agricultural farming among white officials of the Company was promoted, the first slaves were imported, a war was fought against the Khoikhoi pastoralists, and a fort was built – the origins of the Castle, which stands in Cape Town today. A large Van Riebeeck festival was held in Cape Town in 1952 to commemorate his arrival. [R. Elphick, *Khoikhoi and the Founding of White South Africa* (Johannesburg, 1985)]

VEGKOP, Battle of (1836). The first significant battle to be fought between Africans and the Voortrekkers* in the South African interior. A Voortrekker force under Hendrik Potgieter successfully defeated the army of the Ndebele* king, and so opened the way for trekker advance northwards.

VENDA. Bantu-speaking people living in the far northern region of South Africa, north of the Soutpansberg range, who spoke a distinct language closely connected to

Shona, the majority language of Zimbabwe,* as well as to Sotho.* Venda settlement of this region dates back to the 17th century, when the royal lineage recognized today probably moved south across the Limpopo River.* Noted as ironworkers and miners of copper, the Venda maintained close relations with people north of the Limpopo. Because of their remote area of settlement, they maintained their independence during the period of the Mfecane.* For much of the 19th century, under their leaders Makhado (d. 1895) and Mphephu (c.1868–1924), they offered resistance to white encroachment, particularly after they had obtained large supplies of guns in exchange for ivory. When the Transvaal finally suppressed this resistance in 1898, Mphephu withdrew across the Limpopo River into Zimbabwe with about 10,000 followers, but returned after the British took control of the Transvaal in 1900.

In the apartheid era, the bantustan of Venda was led to self-government and then 'independence' in September 1979 under Patrick Mphephu, who installed himself first as paramount and then as president. Though an opposition Venda Independence Party won a majority of the elected seats in the legislature in the 1973 and 1978 elections, Mphephu retained power thanks to support from nominated members and by using emergency powers to imprison opponents. In the 1980s both corruption and oppression increased, and eventually a military ruler took over. Venda was reincorporated into South Africa with the introduction of the interim constitution of April 1994, as part of the Northern Province.

VEREENIGING, Treaty of (1902). Treaty signed in Pretoria on 31 May 1902 to end the South African War.* Its terms were initially approved by Boer and British negotiators at Vereeniging, then a small town on the Vaal River. The treaty terminated the independence of the two defeated Boer states, the South African Republic and the Orange Free State. Britain in turn made some important concessions: no war indemnity was to be levied on the Boers; £3 million was to be paid for war damage; and the former republics were promised that the question of giving the vote to blacks would not be decided until self-government was granted, which meant in effect that blacks would not obtain the vote in those territories.

VERWOERD, Hendrik Frensch (1901–1966). Apartheid ideologue and National Party Prime Minister (1958–1966). Born in the Netherlands and brought to South Africa at an early age, he became founding editor of the Nationalist newspaper *Die Transvaler*, then entered parliament in 1948 and was appointed Minister of Native Affairs by Prime Minister Malan* in 1950. This often charming man revealed himself to be a zealot in the application of apartheid in its most extreme and logically consistent form. He realized that to 'sell' this notion abroad, he had to repackage apartheid as 'separate development', and therefore decided that the bantustans should be led to self-government and 'independence'. When appointed Prime Minister, he pledged himself to establish a republic,* and because of opposition to apartheid from other members of the Commonwealth,* he withdrew South Africa's membership, shortly before the inauguration of the Republic on 31 May 1961. He survived an assassination attempt in 1960, in the aftermath of Sharpeville, but a second one was successful. Dimitri Tsafendas, the parliamentary messenger who stabbed him to death on the floor of the House of Assembly, insisted that a snake in his intestines had led him to do the deed. Tsafendas was not tried, but confined to mental institutions. As South Africa became democratic and rejected apartheid, Verwoerd's name was removed from public places. [H. Kenney, *Architect of Apartheid* (Johannesburg, 1980); D. O'Meara, *Forty Lost Years* (Johannesburg, 1996)]

VILJOEN, Constand (1933–). Having joined the South African army at the age of 18, he rose to become its chief in 1976, and was Chief of the South African Defence Force* from 1980 to 1985. He emerged from retirement in 1993 to become leader of the Afrikaner Volksfront.* Present in June 1993 when the Afrikaner Resistance Movement (AWB)* sacked the World Trade Centre where the new constitution was being negotiated, he won the support of those on the far right who rejected AWB thuggery, and benefited when the AWB was forced out of Bophuthatswana* in March 1994. After the Volksfront rejected participation in the democratic election, he registered a new party, the Freedom Front, for this purpose, and when the Constitutional Principles* were changed to permit self-determination, he agreed to join the new politics. From May 1994 he served as the leader of the Freedom Front in parliament, and continued to advocate the establishment of an Afrikaner *volkstaat*. [P. Waldmeir, *Anatomy of a Miracle* (London, 1997)]

VOORTREKKERS (Dutch, 'those who travel ahead'; 'pioneers'). Frontier farmers who rebelled against British rule at the Cape between 1834 and 1840, by participating in the migration later called the Great Trek*; unlike the earlier trekboers,* they wished to establish new states in the interior where they could be free of British domination. Some 15,000 Voortrekkers left the Cape during the latter half of the 1830s.

VORSTER, Balthazar Johannes (John) (1915–1983). National Party Prime Minister from 1966 to 1978. Interned during World War II for his pro-Nazi sympathies, the grim-faced Vorster became Verwoerd's Minister of Justice in 1962 and introduced detention without trial to deal with political opposition after the Sharpeville massacre.* As Prime Minister he was more pragmatic than Verwoerd, welcomed diplomats from Malawi and pursued an 'outward' policy which involved talking to black African heads of state on condition that apartheid was not discussed. He allowed P.W. Botha* to persuade him to sanction the invasion of Angola,* but was prepared to put pressure on the Rhodesian regime to accept the principle of majority rule, and agreed to a Western plan for Namibia* which involved a United Nations-supervised transition to independence. He fell from office as a result of the Information scandal. (O. Geyser, ed., *B.J. Vorster* (Bloemfontein, 1977); D. O'Meara, *Forty Lost Years* (Johannesburg, 1996)]

W

WALVIS BAY ('Whale Bay'). The only large natural harbour on the coast of Namibia,*
it was visited by the Portuguese explorer Bartolomeu Dias* in 1486, but not
exploited for a long time because of the lack of fresh water inland. From the late
17th century, whales were hunted off the coast of what became known as South
West Africa, and from the 1830s traders, missionaries and collectors of guano
increasingly used Walvis Bay. In the 1860s, Britain proclaimed sovereignty over
twelve offshore islands, which were annexed to the Cape in 1874. By that time,
traders and missionaries at Walvis Bay had requested British protection, and in
1875 the Cape parliament sent a commissioner, who recommended the annexation
of the entire coast. Britain would authorize the annexation only of Walvis Bay itself,
which occurred in 1878. Walvis Bay was in turn incorporated into the Cape Colony
in 1884. Three weeks later, Germany proclaimed a protectorate over the remainder
of the coast of South West Africa. The boundary between Walvis Bay and the
German territory was much disputed, and the issue was only resolved in 1911, after
Walvis Bay was included in the new Union of South Africa in 1910. For reasons of
administrative convenience, however, Walvis Bay was administered as part of South
West Africa from 1922, when it reverted to South African control, until 1977. The
Western negotiators (the 'Contact Group'), who from 1977 tried to secure the independence of Namibia, agreed to leave Walvis Bay out of the discussions, knowing
that the South African government was adamant that it should remain South
African territory. In the 1970s Walvis Bay's fishing industry was devastated by over-
fishing mainly by South African companies.

After Namibia gained independence in 1990, its government sought to gain control of the port, through which most of its trade passed. In 1992 an agreement with
the South African government was secured whereby Walvis Bay was to be administered jointly. In 1993 negotiators drawing up South Africa's interim constitution
agreed to cede control of Walvis Bay to Namibia. Namibia formally took over the
enclave from South Africa at the end of February 1994. [L. Berat, *Walvis Bay* (New
Haven, 1990)]

WATERBOER FAMILY. Andries Waterboer (c.1790–1853), who was of Khoisan origin,
was from 1820 leader of the main body of Griqua* in what became known as
Griqualand West. He strove to end divisions between competing Griqua clans,
fought off Sotho* and Tswana attacks, and concluded treaties with the Ndebele*
and the British. In 1853 he was succeeded by his son Nicholaas Waterboer
(1819–1896), who is mainly remembered for his claim to the diamond fields in the
Kimberley region after 1867. The British annexed Griqualand West in 1871, and
Nicholaas, expelled from his territory in 1878, died in Griqualand East in 1896.

WESTERN CAPE. New province created in April 1994 out of the former Cape
Province. The provincial capital is Cape Town.* With the arrival of a democratic
order, the majority of Coloureds, having long sought to distinguish themselves

from Africans, gave their allegiance to the National Party (NP) rather than the African National Congress, in spite of their suffering under apartheid. The result was that the NP won a majority in the new province in the April 1994 election, and Hernus Kriel of the NP became the province's first premier. The provincial legislature approved a constitution for the province in 1997, which took effect in early 1998.

WHEAT INDUSTRY. Wheat was first planted by the Dutch in the south-western Cape in the 1650s, and wheat farming became one of the main economic activities of whites during the 17th and 18th centuries. Considerable quantities of the crop were exported to the East Indian colonial possessions of the Dutch. In the 19th century, the mineral discoveries in the interior stimulated wheat production. Although the country was forced to import wheat for some decades thereafter, the crop became a significant export item in the late 20th century.

WHITES. The term used in place of 'European' by the Mining Regulations Commission (1910) on the ground that Coloureds might be 'of European extraction'. At the beginning of the apartheid era, segregated amenities were labelled for 'Europeans' and 'Non-Europeans'. From the 1960s, however, as the Afrikaner leadership wished to assert its claim to belong to Africa, the term 'white' replaced 'European'.

WIEHAHN COMMISSION. A government commission under Professor Nic Wiehahn was appointed in 1977 to investigate the country's labour legislation. Its appointment came as a response to the labour unrest beginning in 1973 and to pressure for change from abroad, mediated in part through the multinational companies active in South Africa, in the wake of the Soweto uprising.* The first report of the commission, issued in 1979, recommended that the registration of African trade unions* be permitted, as a way of controlling the new militant African labour movement. It also recommended the abolition of the principle of statutory work reservation, though it suggested that existing work reservation determinations should remain in force until they could be phased out in consultation with relevant white unions. By an amendment to the Industrial Conciliation Act, this major reform was enacted into law.

WIND OF CHANGE speech (3 February 1960). Speaking to a joint sitting of both Houses of Parliament in Cape Town, the visiting British Prime Minister, Harold Macmillan, spoke of the growth of African nationalism, and of how he was convinced that an irresistible 'wind of change' was blowing throughout the continent. South Africa, he said, could not remain isolated from it, and therefore political power should be extended to all on the basis of individual merit. Prime Minister Verwoerd* immediately rejected this analysis, telling Macmillan that South Africa was different, that whites would remain in charge, and that ethnic nationalism among Africans could find outlets in the bantustans.

WINE INDUSTRY. Dutch East India Company* officials planted the first vines close to the new settlement on Table Bay in 1655. Though the wine industry grew gradually thereafter, until the 19th century little was exported because of the inferior quality of most Cape wines. In 1813, however, the British reduced tariffs, which led to an immediate boom in exports; by 1822 the value of wine exported from the Cape exceeded all other exports put together. But the withdrawal of preferential tariffs by the British in 1825 and 1831 proved a major blow to the Cape industry. It was again hard hit in the 1880s when the vines were attacked by a pest, phylloxera.

In 1927 the Ko-operatiewe Wijnbouwers Vereeniging (KWV) was established to supervise and direct the industry's fortunes. In the apartheid era, there was a widespread international boycott of South African wine. With the collapse of apartheid, and the removal of sanctions in the early 1990s, South African wines were once again exported in large quantities.

WITWATERSRAND. Word derived from Afrikaans, meaning 'ridge of white waters'. Also known as 'Egoli ('place of gold'), the Reef or merely the Rand, this hilly ridge north of the Vaal River has produced more gold than any other place on earth. The gold-bearing rock extends for 62 miles, and in some places is 23 miles wide. Johannesburg,* which became South Africa's largest city, grew at the centre of the Witwatersrand.

WODEHOUSE, Sir Philip Edmond (1811–1887). Cape Governor and High Commissioner from 1862 to 1870. Though these were years of economic recession, Wodehouse expanded British influence in southern Africa, most notably by annexing Basutoland* in 1868. He resisted pressure to grant responsible government to the Cape, believing the colony was not ready for it.

WOMEN. Historical writing on women and gender relations in South Africa expanded rapidly from the mid-1980s and became a major historiographical concern as historians sought to recover the history of women and develop insights into the role of women in the past. Despite sometimes deeply contested theoretical and conceptual debates among historians, and the recognition that women of different classes, races and backgrounds had widely varying experiences, women's history developed into a significant and semi-autonomous branch of research.

In precolonial Bantu-speaking societies, which were based on precapitalist agricultural farming, women's reproductive and productive labour, which represented wealth, was controlled by men. Great social value was placed on fertility, and women also played an important role in the cultivation of crops and the production of food; women therefore enjoyed a recognized, though defined, social status. Early settler society in the 18th and 19th centuries, both Boer and British, was similarly patriarchal, although arguably women enjoyed less recognition for their function as workers and in the home. Colonial society offered limited social mobility to some women, in that working-class and lower-middle-class immigrants were able to establish themselves as part of the colonial elite, and delegate some domestic responsibilities to servants. Public questioning of the colonial social order was rare, a notable exception being the feminist writer Olive Schreiner* at the end of the 19th century.

After the discovery of gold on the Witwatersrand and the development of industry in emerging urban centres from the end of the 19th century, gender relations were reshaped to fit the demands of the new economy. Increasing numbers of women were drawn into work outside the home, although the great majority worked in positions which carried limited status and remuneration, such as clerical positions, nursing and teaching. During the 1920s and 1930s, white women entered the garment and food industries in particular, but began to be replaced by black women in the 1940s as whites moved into new positions in the service sector of the economy. Considerable tensions, exacerbated by official segregationist policies, existed between black and white workers. Urbanization among black women occurred slowly in the early 20th century, for the migrant labour system, which drew men to the mines, depended on women to remain in the rural areas to maintain agricultural productivity and traditional homesteads. Increasing numbers of women were obliged to act as heads of households, which in turn led to considerable social tension within rural African society.

White women obtained the vote in 1930 after a campaign by a white suffrage movement; this in turn paved the way for women's involvement in public life. Black women only began to play a prominent role in national public life from the 1950s, although glimpses of their potential political involvement had been witnessed as early as 1913 in organized protest against the pass laws.* Demonstrations against the extension of the pass laws proved a focal point for women's protest during the 1950s, co-ordinated by the Women's League of the African National Congress and the non-racial Federation of South African Women. Pass laws were extended to include African women in 1963, effectively undermining their right to live and work in urban areas. Women played a prominent role in campaigns leading to the abolition of pass laws in 1986. African women were able to exercise the franchise for the first time in 1994, winning it at the same time as African men.

In the 1990s women's issues enjoyed greater prominence than before, with more women in leadership positions in the economy and in politics and with gender equality written into the 1996 constitution.* [C. Walker, ed. *Women and Gender in Southern Africa* (Cape Town, 1990); C. Walker, *Women and Resistance in South Africa* (Cape Town, 1991); I. Berger, *Threads of Solidarity* (Bloomington, 1992)]

WOOL INDUSTRY. Indigenous fat-tailed sheep are associated with early Khoikhoi settlement in South Africa. Merino sheep were first introduced in 1789 and became the basis of the wool industry, which expanded rapidly, so that by the 1840s wool had become the Cape's most important export. In the 1870s wool was overtaken by diamonds* as the colony's main export, but remained one of the country's most important agricultural exports.

WORLD WAR I (1914–1918). On 4 August 1914 South Africa automatically found itself, as part of the British Empire, at war with Germany. Louis Botha,* the Prime Minister, and Jan Smuts* both supported the war wholeheartedly. The government's decision to accede to a British request to invade German South West Africa led to an Afrikaner rebellion* by whites opposed to South Africa's involvement in the war. The rebellion was soon suppressed and by mid-1915 South African forces had occupied South West Africa. Smuts then took command of the East African campaign against German forces in what is now Tanzania. Over 20,000 South Africans fought in this campaign, and over 1500 died.

A South African brigade fought in the battles on the Somme in 1916 and suffered heavy casualties in the Battle of Delville Wood. A South African Native Labour Contingent, of over 20,000 blacks, who were not allowed to bear arms, worked for the Allied armies in France. In February 1917, 615 of these men were drowned at sea when the troopship carrying them, the *Mendi*, sank in the English Channel. Altogether 12,452 South Africans died on active service in the war as a whole. During the war Smuts was invited to join the Imperial war cabinet, and played an important role in Allied deliberations on how to bring the war to an end. [A. Grundlingh, *Fighting Their Own War* (Johannesburg, 1987); N. Clothier, *Black Valour* (Pietermaritzburg, 1987)]

WORLD WAR II (1939–1945). When Britain declared war on Germany on 3 September 1939, the South African cabinet divided on whether or not South Africa should participate. Hertzog* and other former National Party* members who had entered fusion* with him believed that South Africa should assert its independence of Britain. As parliament was sitting, the issue was put to the House of Assembly, which voted (on 4 September 1939) 80 to 67 in favour of South Africa entering the war. Hertzog then asked Sir Patrick Duncan, the Governor-General, to dissolve the Assembly and call a general election. Duncan refused, and Smuts* became Prime Minister for the second time, and at once declared war on Germany (6 September). To many Afrikaner supporters of the United Party* this seemed to run counter to the 'South Africa first' principle of fusion, and they withdrew their support, making virtually inevitable Smuts's defeat at the polls in 1948. In its first years, however, the war brought enormous dissension within Afrikaner ranks, with some Afrikaners prepared to undertake illegal acts, including sabotage, to oppose it. As late as 1944, many Afrikaner nationalists expected the Germans to win the war, and hoped that this would provide the opportunity for the establishment of an Afrikaner republic.

During the war some 390,000 men and women volunteers served in the armed forces, far more than in World War I. Union forces first took part in the Ethiopian campaign, which led to the capture of Addis Ababa from Italian forces. They also seized Madagascar and participated in the North African campaign. Ten thousand South African troops were trapped by General Rommel at Tobruk. South African forces then took part in the invasion of Italy, and fought their way up the Italian peninsula with the Allied forces. South African pilots played an important role in bombing raids on Poland. During the war 123,000 blacks served in non-combatant roles. Almost 9000 South Africans died in hostilities.

A great number of Allied ships passed the Cape during the war, and tens of thousands of Allied troops had shore leave at South African ports. The war boosted the South African economy; consequently large numbers of Africans poured into the towns in search of work. [N. Orpen, *South African Forces in World War Two* (Cape Town, 1968–1979); M. Roberts and A. Trollip, *The South African Opposition* (London, 1947); A. Seegers, *The Military in the Making of Modern South Africa* (London, 1996)]

XHOSA. Originally, the Xhosa (the name is thought to derive from a Khoikhoi term meaning 'angry men') were those who recognized the authority of the Tshawe royal clan, which had established a chiefdom in the northern Transkei* during the 16th century. Over the next two centuries, this chiefdom expanded over a wide area through conquest and incorporation of a variety of people, including Khoikhoi willing to accept Tshawe authority. During the time of Phalo (1715–1775), two main groups emerged, the one under the senior 'great house' of the Gcaleka in the east, the other under the 'right-hand house' of the Rharhabe in the west.

It was the latter who first encountered whites moving eastwards towards the end of the 18th century, and in 1779 the first in a series of frontier clashes took place, clashes which were to continue sporadically for a century and lead to Xhosa defeat. Over 20,000 Rharhabe were expelled from the Zuurveld in 1811–1812. They divided between the followers of Ngqika,* who was prepared to co-operate with the colonial authorities, and Ndlambe, who was determined to oppose them. Settler pressure continued. The Xhosa, already suffering severely, were greatly weakened by the cattle-killing* of 1857. In 1878 the Gcaleka living in the Transkei were also defeated and brought under colonial rule.

In time all Nguni people who lived in the eastern Cape and Transkei came to be called Xhosa, whether they were Thembu, Mpondo, Mpondomise, Bhaca or Mfengu, and their common language became known as Xhosa. That Xhosa people were exposed to Christianity, Western ideas and education earlier than other Africans helps explain why so many of them took leading roles in proto-nationalist and nationalist organizations in the 20th century. [J. Peires, *The House of Phalo* (Johannesburg, 1981); L. Switzer, *Power and Resistance* (Madison, 1993)]

XUMA, Alfred Bitini (*c.*1898–1962). After studying in the United States and Europe, Xuma returned to practise as a physician in Johannesburg in 1928. His obvious abilities led to his election first as vice-president of the All-African Convention in 1935, and then in 1940 president-general of the African National Congress (ANC). The ANC was in a sad state of disorganization when he took it over, but under his leadership it became a more efficient, more centralized organization, which began to attract a wider following. He forged an alliance with Indian anti-segregationists in 1946, and in that year lobbied successfully at the United Nations* against South Africa's plans to incorporate South West Africa.* Essentially conservative, Xuma did not welcome pressure from the ANC Youth League* for more militant action, and he was ousted as president in 1949.

YUSSUF (also Tjoessop), Sheikh (1626–1699). Exiled by the Dutch East India Company* from Java, he arrived at Cape Town in 1694 and settled outside the city. Though he spent only the last five years of his life at the Cape, he had a great influence as a religious leader and teacher. A memorial to his name stands at Faure, on the Cape Flats, and he is now venerated by Muslims as the man who brought Islam to the Cape. The tercentenary of his arrival was marked by festivities and celebrations in Cape Town, immediately prior to the first democratic election in April 1994.

....

ZIMBABWE (formerly Southern Rhodesia; from the Shona, meaning 'place of stones'). Links between South Africa and the land north of the Limpopo River were strong in the precolonial past. In the late 1830s, the Ndebele* crossed from the Transvaal into south-western Zimbabwe, where they settled. White hunters, traders and missionaries soon began to follow them in increasing numbers. In 1890 the British South Africa Company* occupied part of 'southern Zambesia', and renamed it after Cecil Rhodes.* Many of the whites who settled in Zimbabwe came from the Cape; as late as 1970, more than 20% of settlers were South African-born. When the BSA Company administration came to an end, the settlers voted in a referendum (1922) not to join the Union of South Africa as a fifth province, despite pressure from Jan Smuts* and mining interests for incorporation. After the collapse of the Central African Federation in 1963, the Southern Rhodesian government forged closer ties with South Africa, particularly in the field of military co-operation, and the race policies of Rhodesia also came more closely to approximate those of South Africa than they had previously.

After Southern Rhodesia's unilateral declaration of independence in November 1965, South Africa refused to join the rest of the international community in imposing economic sanctions. The continued supply of petroleum, fuel and military hardware from South Africa was crucial to the country's survival. From August 1967, South African paramilitary police were deployed within Rhodesia to assist the Rhodesians so as to prevent guerrilla incursions aimed at South Africa; in 1967 and 1968 Umkhonto weSizwe (MK)* detachments moved into Rhodesia en route to South Africa, but were defeated before they reached their goal. From the mid-1970s, as Angola and Mozambique moved to independence, and the Rhodesian bush war increased in intensity, the South African government began to pressure the Rhodesian Prime Minister, Ian Smith, to forge a settlement with moderate black leaders. When this was done it failed to win international recognition or end the war. In the election of early 1980 under the Lancaster House agreement, the South African government supported Bishop Muzorewa; Robert Mugabe's victory came as a considerable shock to Pretoria.

Although post-independence Zimbabwe was heavily dependent on close economic ties with South Africa (the bulk of the country's imports and exports were transported by South African railways through South African ports), the political paths of the two countries diverged sharply in the 1980s. Zimbabwe gave diplomatic recognition to the African National Congress, but was unable to impose sanctions on South Africa or permit MK guerrilla bases to operate from Zimbabwean soil. Most whites who left Zimbabwe during the 1980s settled in South Africa. After the 1994 election in South Africa, close official ties between the two countries were forged for the first time, but Zimbabwe remained concerned about the way South Africa might use its vastly greater economic power.

ZULU KINGDOM. In the late 18th century, the Zulu clan was but one of a number of small groups among the northern Nguni. By the 1820s, a powerful Zulu state, one of the most dominant polities in southern Africa, had emerged under the control of Shaka. Historians continue to debate the reasons for the rise of a militarized and authoritarian Zulu state. It is possible that the expansion of international trade, in ivory, cattle and possibly slaves, from Delagoa Bay after the 1760s sparked competition for resources and trade routes and promoted political centralization among the various northern Nguni chiefdoms. Other reasons advanced by historians to explain the rise of the Zulu state include population growth, following the introduction of maize in the 18th century, which put pressure on scarce resources; severe drought and ecological crisis in about 1806; and such innovations as the short stabbing spear, new formations in battle, and the use of the *amabutho* system for military purposes.

It would seem that Shaka* took advantage of the conflict between the Ndwandwe and the Mthethwa to consolidate his power between the Thukela and White Mfolozi rivers before 1818, through his skilful use of the *amabutho*. He then extended his domination northwards to the Mkhuze River after defeating the Ndwandwe. He built a militarized, centralized state in this region, a core state surrounded by vassal communities in varying degrees of subordination, who paid him tribute. His armies raided as far north as the Pongola River area, and to the Mpondo territory in the south. In 1828 he was assassinated by two of his half-brothers, one of whom, Dingane,* succeeded him.

The Zulu state remained vulnerable to internal strains between chiefs, and these were intensified by growing external pressures, in the form of British traders and missionaries, as well as Boer trekkers. Dingane viewed the trekkers as a threat, and had a group under the leadership of Piet Retief* murdered in 1838. His army was then defeated by the trekkers at the Battle of Blood River,* and he was driven from his kingdom by Mpande (c.1798–1872), one of his disaffected half-brothers, who was in league with the trekkers. Mpande took control of the region north of the Thukela, while the trekkers laid claim to the land to the south. With the arrival of the British in 1843, and their annexation of the region to the south of the Thukela as the colony of Natal, Mpande won from the new colony recognition of the independence of the area north of the Thukela.

By the 1850s, Mpande's authority had weakened, and a dispute over the succession to the kingship resulted in civil war in 1856. Mpande favoured his son Mbuyazi as his successor, but another son, Cetshwayo,* emerged victorious. Though he only assumed full power on Mpande's death, he had by then consolidated his control. At that time perhaps 150,000 people between the Thukela and Pongola rivers saw themselves as Zulu, and Cetshwayo was able to put an army of 40,000 men into the field. Despite such resources at his disposal, Cetshwayo was threatened on two flanks: British and colonial officials in Natal feared his military might and wanted to challenge his independence, while at the same time Boer farmers in the Transvaal wanted to move onto Zulu land. The British High Commissioner, Sir Bartle Frere,* finally decided to move against the Zulu kingdom at the end of 1878, resulting in the outbreak of the Anglo-Zulu War* in January 1879.

The war and the subsequent settlement imposed by the British exacerbated tensions between various chiefs and the Zulu royal house, tensions which led to civil war in 1883. Cetshwayo, who had been sent into exile by the British, was permitted to return to govern part of his former kingdom, but his capital was sacked in July 1883 and he soon died under mysterious circumstances. His successor, Dinuzulu,* granted land to a group of Boers from the Transvaal in return for help against his main rival, Zibhebhu (c.1841–1904). This helped persuade the British, in 1887, to annex what remained of the Zulu kingdom. Dinuzulu then went into rebellion, was arrested and tried for high treason, and sent into exile on the Atlantic Ocean island of St Helena. After his return in 1898, he sought to gain recognition as Zulu king, but unsuccessfully, and his ambivalent role in the Bambatha Rebellion, taken by whites as evidence of treason, brought him a four-year sentence of imprisonment.

Once the Zulu kingdom had effectively been destroyed as a political unit during the 1880s, Zulu men were increasingly forced into wage labour outside the kingdom's borders. Though the royal family ceased to exert the control it had enjoyed for much of the 19th century, the role of the king and his *inkosi* nevertheless remained very important in 20th-century KwaZulu. [J. Guy, *The Destruction of the Zulu Kingdom* (London, 1979); J. Laband, *Rope of Sand* (Johannesburg, 1995)]

ZUURVELD (also Suurveld). The land between the Fish and Bushmans rivers in the eastern Cape. White trekboers first came into substantial contact with the Xhosa* in this region. The Zuurveld was ideal for summer grazing, and small Xhosa groups, escaping the domination of those further east, had lived and farmed there for several generations before regular contact with white settlers began in the 1770s. The first armed clash erupted in 1779, but neither then nor in subsequent wars in the late 18th century were the whites able to dislodge the Xhosa. While the Zuurveld was officially part of the Cape Colony from 1780, large numbers of Xhosa remained within it until 1812, when Boer commandos,* aided by British troops, expelled 20,000 of them. A line of military forts was then built, the chief of which became the city of Grahamstown.* In 1820 some 5000 British immigrants were settled in the Zuurveld to prevent Xhosa from returning to the area. The Zuurveld was then renamed Albany. [N. Mostert, *Frontiers* (London, 1992)]

ZWIDE (c.1790–1825). Little is known for certain about the life of this ruler of a relatively powerful northern Nguni chiefdom. It is thought he ruled from c.1805. Through military shrewdness and perhaps use of the *amabutho*,* he was able to defeat the armies of the Swazi and of the Mthethwa under Dingiswayo in about 1818, making possible the rise of the Zulu under Shaka.* Shaka then inflicted a heavy defeat on him at the Battle of Gqokoli Hill, thought to have taken place in 1819. Zwide then fled north from what is now KwaZulu with his remaining troops. [A. Duminy and B. Guest, ed., *Natal and Zululand from the Earliest Times to 1910* (Pietermaritzburg, 1989)]